4-13-04

To NOEL,

Best Wishes,

LOST BLACK SHEEP
The Search for World War II Ace Chris Magee

Robert T. Reed

edited by
Constance C. Dickinson

Hellgate Press/ PSI Research
Central Point, Oregon

Lost Black Sheep: The Search for World War II Ace Chris Magee
© 2001 by Robert T. Reed
Published by Hellgate Press

HELLGATE PRESS
a division of PSI Research, Inc.
P.O. Box 3727
Central Point, OR 97502
(541) 245-6502
info@psi-research.com e-mail

Managing editor: Constance C. Dickinson
Editorial assistants: Jan Olsson, Harley Patrick, and Gina Froelich
Book designer & compositor: Constance C. Dickinson
Cover and map designer: J. C. Young

Library of Congress Cataloging-in-Publication Data

Reed, Robert T., 1945–
    Lost black sheep : the search for World War II ace Chris Magee / Robert T. Reed ; edited by Constance C. Dickinson.
        p. cm.
    ISBN 1-55571-549-4
    1. Magee, Chris. 2. Air pilots, Military—United States—Biography. 3. United States. Marine Corps—Officers—Biography. 4. United States. Marine Fighter Squadron, 214th—History. I. Dickinson, Constance C. II. Title.

VE25.M343 R44 2001
940.54'4973'092—dc21
[B]   2001016822

Hellgate Press is an imprint of Publishing Services, Inc., an Oregon corporation doing business as PSI Research.

Printed in the United States of America
First edition 10 9 8 7 6 5 4 3 2 1

 Printed on recycled paper when available.

To my parents, Mary and the late Elmer "Bill" Reed
For being the greatest role models a growing kid could ever hope to have,

and

To the Black Sheep Family
For showing an old sailor that the Marine Corps motto
is much more than just a catch phrase. Semper Fi!

There's a race of men that don't fit in,
  A race that can't stay still;
So they break the hearts of kith and kin,
  And they roam the world at will.

They range the field and they rove the flood,
  And they climb the mountain's crest.
Theirs is the curse of the gypsy blood,
  And they don't know how to rest.

If they just went straight, they might go far;
  They are strong and brave and true;
But they're always tired of the things that are,
  And they want the strange and new . . .

Robert W. Service
"The Men That Don't Fit In"

Contents

Acknowledgments

⌒

With little to go on when I began this text, I consider myself most fortunate to have found so many kind and knowledgeable individuals willing to assist me with valuable information and suggestions.

First, I owe a huge debt of gratitude to three gentlemen who held extensive interviews with Chris Magee, and were kind enough to allow me to use some of the information they'd gathered: Neal Gendler of the *Minneapolis Star-Tribune*; Bruce Gamble, formerly of the U.S. Naval Aviation Museum; and Chris Steel, Magee family historian.

There is no way this book could exist without the enthusiastic help of the men of the original Black Sheep Squadron, especially Bruce Matheson, who graciously volunteered to edit the original manuscript both for facts and for my occasional grammatical miscues; and my good friends Jim Hill and Fred Losch, who not only provided some great reminiscences but were also kind enough to offer me the hospitality of their homes on numerous occasions. Thanks also to their wonderful wives, Muriel Hill and the late Jean Losch for many kindnesses. Other Black Sheep I would like to single out for their contributions to the book are John Bolt, Denmark Groover, Bill Heier, Bob McClurg, Ed Olander, and the late Dr. Jim Reames.

From Israel's first fighter squadron, the 101, I want to thank Mitchell Flint, Gideon Lichtman, the late Rudy Augarten, and particularly Aaron Finkel and Leon Frankel. My gratitude also to another veteran of the 1948

War for Independence, transport pilot Julian Swing, whose insightful manuscript "God's Little Air Force" provided valuable background material.

Family and friends of Chris from the Chicago area were also very cooperative in providing information and opinions that added greatly to the story. My sincere thanks go out to Zona Musser and her children, especially Betty Samelson, as well as Helen Magee, Joan Allen, and Norm Pritchard. Perhaps my greatest source of inspiration has been Ed Smart. Every conversation I've had with this fascinating gentleman has motivated me to write.

I would also like to thank Anne and Tom McNeil, Mary Reed, Anne Yorke and John Engh for their input; and Bob and Connie Cleary, who have encouraged me to write about Chris since 1988.

A nod of appreciation for an entirely different reason goes to Angie Kropko of Data Logic for resurrecting some thirty lost pages from the graveyard of my Mac's hard drive.

An extension of my appreciation also to Emmett Ramey for publishing Chris's odyssey as one of Hellgate Press's stories of special people doing extraordinary things for their country; and to editor and designer, C. C. Dickinson for bringing my words and images to life.

Finally, and perhaps most important of all, I offer my undying thanks to the late, great Frank Walton, who was not only a key member of the Black Sheep but also the Good Shepherd who kept them together and sought out the strays. Were it not for this Renaissance man's desire to "set the record straight" about his squadron, this book would never have been written, and I would have missed out on some of the most memorable experiences of my life.

The Book and *The Hook*

＿

Frank Walton was fighting mad. And, even in his late sixties, Frank was not a man to be provoked. The big redhead's rangy physique was still lean and muscular, the product of a fitness regimen that included long daily swims in the Pacific, conveniently located just steps from the Oahu condominium he shared with his wife Carol. Equally formidable was his intellect; it was this aspect of Walton's character he would call upon to quell the beast within.

The object of Walton's anger was a popular, seemingly innocuous weekly television series called *Baa Baa Black Sheep* (later retitled *Black Sheep Squadron*) which was among the new shows of that fall season of 1976. It was purported to be the "fact-based" adventures of famed U.S. Marine fighter pilot Gregory "Pappy" Boyington and the "gang of misfits" he recruited then trained to become one of America's greatest fighting units during World War II. Boyington himself was technical advisor for the show and even made the claim that the stories were "about ninety percent accurate." Walton saw things differently. He served as intelligence officer for the real Black Sheep Squadron (VMF 214) and considered the series a travesty—an insult to the men he'd served with. He later described it as "a hoked-up, phony, typical Hollywood-type production depicting the Black Sheep as a bunch of brawling bums who were fugitives from courts-martial." He also accused the show of having "a detrimental effect on the professional careers of a number of the former Black Sheep," and on "the widows, mothers, fathers, and children of those Black Sheep who had given their lives in the service of their country."

Walton decided it was time to "set the record straight," so he sat down at his typewriter and wrote the "real" story in the form of a magazine article. As a former Deputy Chief of the Los Angeles Police Department (LAPD) and high ranking U.S. State Department official, he had the prestige necessary to get his article published in a forum that the greatest possible number of television viewers would have the opportunity to read—*TV Guide.*

Not surprisingly, many of Walton's former squadron mates were delighted to read his article (Boyington being a notable exception) and wrote letters of thanks and congratulations. The Black Sheep were a proud bunch. Even though "Pappy's Boys" served as a unit for just a few months (July 1943 to January 1944), the experience was the high point of each man's life and many—including Walton—lived very full lives. Earlier in 1976, Frank arranged a hugely successful reunion of the squadron. In all, seventeen of the thirty-four survivors from the fifty-one original Black Sheep met in Hawaii for the memorable get together. It was their first gathering since September 1945, when they celebrated Boyington's homecoming following his release from a Japanese prison camp. For that momentous occasion, the Corps flew several West Coast-based members of the squadron to a much-publicized shindig at San Francisco's St. Francis Hotel.

Another reunion followed in 1978, and in 1980 the Black Sheep were invited to the National Air and Space Museum of the Smithsonian Institution to participate in an "induction" ceremony for the F4U Corsair, the fighter plane they helped make famous. Eighteen members of the squadron, including Walton and Boyington, attended the event. It was there that Walton decided to write a book that would tell the whole, true story of the Black Sheep Squadron. His book would be much more than a reminiscence about young warriors in combat, however. It would also tell of the men they became and the lives they led in the four decades that followed the war.

The writing of Walton's epic proved to be a daunting task, one that would demand much of his time for the next six years. Fortunately, he'd kept extensive war diaries and concise flight records in his role as air combat intelligence officer. He was also gifted with a remarkable memory. And, of course, he had the support and cooperation of the other Black Sheep. In the process of writing his book, which he titled *Once They Were Eagles*, Walton traveled extensively throughout the country to engage in one-to-one, in-person interviews with most of his former squadron mates, although in a few cases the conversations took place via telephone. One of the pilots, however, seemed to have dropped off the face of the earth. His name was Chris Magee.

Magee was the Thoreau of the Black Sheep. Soft-spoken and well-liked with an intellectual capacity that was the awe of all who knew him, he was the sort of guy who marched to a different drumbeat. A blue bandanna—either covering his hair or around his neck—was almost always part of Magee's attire in the South Pacific. He could often be found off by himself in a coconut grove lifting weights or reading books on subject matter that could best be described as esoteric. He was anything but an effete book-worm, though. Walton would later write:

> *Chris "Wildman" Magee was perhaps the ultimate combat fighter pilot. Utterly fearless and totally aggressive, he had the knack of knowing where the action was, plus complete mastery of the airplane; he could make it do things no other pilot could. His record of nine Zeros was exceeded in our squadron only by Boyington's total.*

In his efforts to locate Magee prior to the 1976 reunion, Walton had to go so far as to enlist the help of contacts he made in his years with the LAPD, and even the FBI. Relatives and friends lost track of Chris years before. Finally, an address in Chicago was found, and Walton quickly fired off a letter that provided data about the proposed reunion, and included a request for biographical information and an update on Magee's postwar activities.

Weeks passed with no reply, so he sent another letter. Walton feared that his old squadron mate may have moved or not received the correspondence for some other reason. Then, one day, he found a rather thick envelope in his mailbox. It was postmarked "Chicago, IL." One can only imagine the emotions Frank must have felt as he began reading the extraordinary, neatly handwritten letter it contained.

> *Greetings, Frank,*
>
> *Strange how a few words can do more to reveal something of the nature of time than all the equations a team of Einsteins could formulate in a life-time of blackboard gymnastics. It isn't so much that words throw a bridge across a considerable gulf between "now" and "then" events as it is that they*

collapse all intervening activities below consciousness, and unite the "now" with the "then" as if by some alchemical implosion, some magic infusion.

Such, somehow dramatized, was the effect of your letters, which I picked up recently when I dropped by my former pad in Chicago South Side to check the possibility that mail may have strayed that way.

I've been to Florida a couple times this year, roving the Gulf Coast, into the Everglades, and down through the Keys. And Westward Ho! too. Colorado, etc. A change of pace after six years as editor/writer/reporter for a Chicago community newspaper of approximately 30,000 circulation.

Aside from two days and nights of intense involvement every week, I was free to set my own pace, so there was some compensation in terms of freedom, which I needed.

There was further compensation in the form of a discipline imposed by the ever-present demand of the next deadline. But once a week for six years is a bit too much of that kind of compensation for me.

The paper was sold and the new owner brought in his own editor, so I'm free of the printer's ink mold, and have spent a number of months recuperating from a bad case of brainlock, induced by overexposure to journalese.

Before that job, I edited another community newspaper for a couple of years.

Previous to these forays into the legitimate, I was a house guest of J. Edgar Hoover at his resorts in Atlanta and Leavenworth, where due to SNAFU bureaucratic behavior in the manner of record keeping, teamed with a paranoid penchant for secrecy, my durance vile went considerably beyond what had evidently been intended.

During my sojourn, I taught a wide variety of high school classes, picked up some 80 college credits via extension courses, and became editor of Leavenworth's quarterly magazine, "New Era," a slick, fifty-plus-page organ with pretensions to literary excellence. In fact, it was included in a survey and index of literary "Little Magazines." We also had close and friendly ties with Engel's famed Writers' Workshop at the State University of Iowa.

Some of my work was reprinted in other publications around the world that are oriented to more esoteric fare. For instance, the Sai Aurobino Ashram in Pondicherry, India. I was deep into the psycho-spiritual thing long before the recent boom began. And I don't mean the Tim Leary, Baba Ram Das, Allen Ginsberg, Holy Man circuit bit, or any of this swooning over Eastern mysticism. The West has its own tradition, only touched upon by C. G. Jung.

*Anyway, retreating further yet, timewise, I was active in the Caribbean area in the mid-1950s, and before that was working with construction crews in Greenland, above the Arctic Circle, setting up the air warning network. Earlier, in 1949, I was in Aspen, Colorado, tape recording highlights of the Goethe Bicentennial Celebration, the event that kicked off Aspen's ascent to an off-the-beaten-path cultural center. Albert Schweitzer (*Reverence for Life*) was guest of honor; his first absence from Africa in twenty-five years.*

In 1948, I was flying ME-109Gs for the Hagannah in Israel (while Herr Hitler did snap rolls in his Nazi hell. Must have been a blowtorch on the bollocks to hear about Jews in Messerschmitts!) But that wasn't until I went through a cloak and dagger smuggling operation in New York and Europe.

So, that's a fair abbreviation of my post-Black Sheep days. Although there are those who would say, cynically, of course, that for me they never ended, that they in fact became more than an upside down euphemism, more than a play-name adopted by a bunch of great guys whom it would be almost miraculous to reminisce with over a vat of milk punch.

Well, Frank, it was a high, hearing from you. I'd enjoy being on the receiving end of any other information you seine from the stream of years.

Walton finished reading Magee's long letter, and discovered that the envelope contained an additional sheet of paper. It was a copy of one of Chris's published poems. Entitled "Postscript from One Who, Like His Age, Died Young," the verse was prefaced by an introductory paragraph.

Several years after World War II, the wreck of a U.S. Marine Corps fighter plane was discovered in the interior jungle of New Ireland, in the Solomons, by a former Royal Australian Navy Coast Watcher. A jungle kit was recovered from the cockpit of the Corsair; among its items of survival gear was a wax-sealed, fungus-resistant plastic folder containing a box of ammunition for a .45 automatic and a sheet of paper with these lines.

I have skimmed the ragged edge of lightning death
And torn from bloody flesh of sky a thunder song.
Across the nakedness of virgin space
I've blistered my frozen hand in feathered ice
And dared angelic wrath to smash
The snarling will of my demon steed.

Far above sun-glint on winded spume,
High executor of laws no man has made,
I've welded Samurai knights into fiery tombs
And hurled them down like the plumed Minoan
Far down the searing heights to punch
Their livid crates in the sea.

'Enemies,' you say. They were not mine.
More than blood brothers, I swear,
With tawny skin and warrior eye.
Bushido-bred for hell-strife joy.
Much closer my kin, my race than those
Who cud-chew their lives can ever be.

'War-lover,' you say, 'sadist, psychotic'—
That sick cycle of canned cliches masking
Your lust for eternity fettered to time.
Go, epigonic pygmies, make peace with hell,
Drag the myths of our ancient might
Through the miserable muck of a cringer's dream.

What could you know
Who have never heard
The soaring sound of the Valkyries,
Felt thunder-gods jousting with livid peaks:
You who have never dared to walk the razor
Across the zenith of your peevish soul?

Walton re-read the pages. What a letter! What a life! The news of his contact with Magee spread quickly among the surviving Black Sheep. It was universally agreed that a way would be found for him to attend the upcoming reunion.

No one was more excited about the possibility of seeing Chris again than Fred Losch. Now a highly successful businessman in the Los Angeles area, Losch had maintained a close friendship with Magee even after the Black Sheep Squadron disbanded. They had, in fact, served together in two other squadrons, VMF 211 and VMF 911, from the spring of 1944 until the end of the war. Fred was best man at Chris's wedding in the fall of '44. Losch was very fond of both Chris and Molly, the pretty, idealistic Navy nurse he had married. Did the union last? He doubted it. A free spirit like Magee wouldn't be comfortable for long as a married man, and Molly seemed a very traditional sort. Plus, the letter to Frank mentioned nothing about wife or family. Fred last heard from his buddy in the summer of 1946, when Chris telephoned him at his apartment near the UCLA campus where he was completing his bachelor's degree. The topic of conversation was an opportunity Chris heard about in Central America to fly as mercenary fighter pilots in a revolution. The pay was rumored to be quite lucrative: $1,000 per month plus large bonuses for shooting down the other side's aircraft. Fred had to beg off, as he was already enrolled for his final semester. He never found out if Chris accepted the offer.

Chris did not attend the '76 reunion, and although Walton, Losch, and others later sent letters to his last known address, none were answered. What had happened to their missing comrade became a subject of considerable speculation among the surviving squadron members. To a man, they all wanted to see their unconventional buddy again. One of the pilots, fellow Chicagoan Jim Hill, made several inquiries into Magee's whereabouts without success. During a business trip to Chicago, Losch asked a friend who resided there if it would be possible to check out Magee's last mailing address, a seedy bar on Chicago's South Side. Losch's friend described the bar's locale as a place he "wouldn't go at high noon, much less at night."

Years passed without a word from Chris. With his publisher's deadline fast approaching, and the postwar biographies of all the Black Sheep, save Magee, completed, Frank made a crucial decision: he would let Chris tell his own story. The letter and accompanying poem would be printed verbatim, with Walton providing only an introduction and a closing paragraph speculating on his old squadron mate's whereabouts.

When *Once They Were Eagles* arrived on the nation's bookshelves in 1986, Frank held out a ray of hope that either Chris or someone who knew him would read the book, and, perhaps, the lost Black Sheep would find his way back to the flock.

∞

The Mercedes 220D sedan sped along the tree-lined country road that snaked through the Massachusetts countryside. The driver expertly downshifted and turned left onto an intersecting avenue, then quickly accelerated beyond the posted speed limit. At the side of the road remnants of a recent snowfall still clung to life against the bright afternoon sunshine as the Mercedes entered a sparkling, modern residential neighborhood. The fine, though not extravagant, two story homes all sat on lots of an acre or more. Only the brown lawns and the leafless trees despoiled the overall effect of a suburban paradise.

Three turns and six shifts later, the pilot guided the diesel-powered craft up a wide driveway into its hangar, shut off the engine, unfastened the seat belt, opened the car door and stepped out.

"Come on, girls, help me with the groceries," she softly told the two small heads exiting the rear seat as she walked back to open the trunk.

The female A. J. Foyt was Anne McNeil, a pretty five foot, three inch bundle of energy with flawless skin, pearly teeth, and thick, curly brown tresses that gave her the appearance of one a decade younger than her forty years. True, Anne would have preferred to be five pounds slimmer, but then who wouldn't?

The two pre-schoolers who tumbled out of the back door represented the younger half of Anne's four children. They were as different as night and day. Julie, age three, was Day. Her cornsilk hair, bright blue eyes, and sunny, outgoing disposition were a delight to everybody who came in contact with her. Emily, four-and-a-half, was Night. With lush, wavy chestnut locks that would someday be the envy of her peers and intelligent, but unfathomable blue-green eyes, Emily could be shy or playful, moody or mysterious, but never dull.

Anne's older children—Tommy, eleven and Megan, eight—were in school. Tommy, though a bit on the small side, was showing signs of becoming a fine athlete. Dark-haired and handsome like his father, Tommy was soft-spoken and intelligent although he tended to neglect his studies for other activities. Megan was the all-American girl. Pretty, athletic and very popular with her schoolmates, she also managed to be an "A" student.

A half hour later, with the groceries put away and Emily and Julie taking their afternoon naps, Anne finally got the chance to sit down on the living room sofa and relax. Soon, she would have to take Megan to piano lessons and Tommy to hockey practice, but now she was ready to enjoy half an hour by herself. Anne was a registered nurse, and had worked part-time at the local blood bank prior to the birth of Emily. Since then, though, she concentrated on being a full-time mom, and really enjoyed it. Her husband Tom, a Boston native, ran a successful business and was a devoted family man. The McNeils were Catholic, although Anne was raised in the Methodist Church and converted a few years after her marriage to Tom.

Anne sifted through the pile of mail on her coffee table, finding little of importance: advertisements, a couple of business letters for Tom, a magazine also for Tom. She glanced at the magazine: it was the winter 1986–87 edition of *The Hook*, a slick, quarterly publication that went out to U.S. Navy and Marine Corps carrier-qualified pilots, past, and present. Tom, a Lieutenant Colonel in the Marine Air Reserve and Commanding Officer of his unit, had received the magazine for years, but his wife didn't read it. Anne started to put *The Hook* down, then stopped. She felt a strange, inexplicable desire to browse through this magazine that had never previously held any interest for her. Slowly, she began turning the pages, passing by articles on the latest in military aircraft technology and wartime reminiscences. When she reached the book review section she stopped. Several titles were listed, but one immediately caught her eye—*Once They Were Eagles: The Men of the Black Sheep Squadron* by Frank E. Walton. Anne's heart suddenly began to beat faster. Her attention was now focused as she began to read.

The reviewer, in his glowing appraisal of the book, explained that the author—who had been the legendary squadron's Air Intelligence Officer—decided to write the story in order "to set the record straight" about the Black Sheep. Walton, the review continued, was angered by the way the popular television show of the late-seventies had depicted Pappy Boyington's pilots as a group of misfits and troublemakers. The critic went on to say that the author not only painted fascinating personality sketches of the squadron's flyers during the war, but also included recent interviews of all the living Black Sheep. A sentence near the end nearly knocked Anne off the sofa:

> *Especially illuminating were the comments about combat fighter piloting by Chris "Wildman" Magee and John Bolt, two of the squadron's aces.*

That night, after the kids were put to bed, Anne showed Tom what she had read. His mouth dropped open as he read the last paragraph.

"My God," he said, "this is incredible! Do you think he's still alive?"

"I don't know," she answered, "but we've got to get that book."

"Definitely."

And the next day, they did.

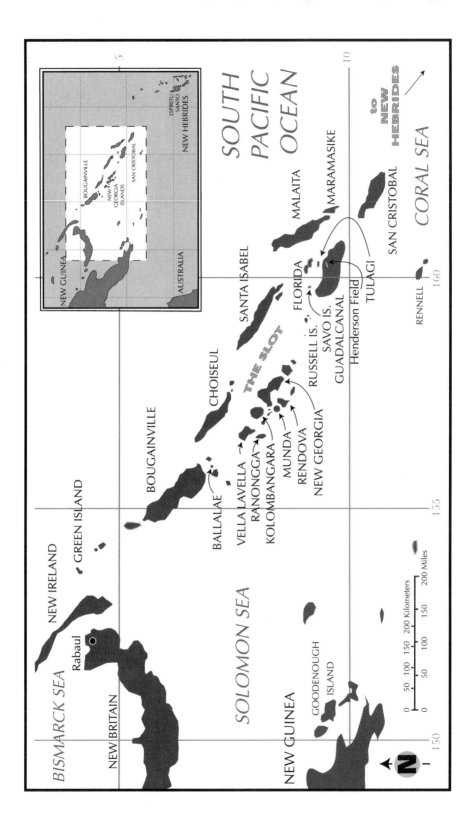

Part I

The Hero

Chapter 1

South Side Hijinks

A mixture of awe and apprehension was evident on the face of the red-haired boy as he watched his buddy—a lean, athletic youngster with dark, wavy locks—confidently shinny his way up the free-standing flagpole that stood a few feet in front of the Shakespeare public school. The pole swayed slightly in the South Side Chicago breeze as other kids stopped what they were doing and moved in for a better look at the daredevilry of the climber, who appeared to be about thirteen or fourteen. Summer vacation had begun, so with no teachers around to demand an end to the activity the youth continued all the way to the top of the pole without any verbal opposition.

Ed Smart, the slightly younger fellow on the ground, breathed a sigh of relief when his friend "C.L." reached the top. Climbing the Shakespeare school flagpole was hardly an unusual feat; he'd seen several other kids do it before. In fact, for many of his friends from St. Ambrose—the Catholic school up the street attended by both boys—it was practically a rite of passage during the late 1920s and early thirties. What C.L. did next, however, may have been unprecedented.

With his legs wrapped securely around the staff, the boy began rocking back and forth. Soon, with the aid of the wind, he had the pole swinging like a metronome. The number of spectators looking up from terra firma had now increased to three or four dozen, all wondering the same thing: "What is that crazy kid trying to do?"

They didn't have to wait long. Timing his flight perfectly as the pole swung in the direction of the two-story school building, C.L. let go and was catapulted toward the roof. As the onlookers watched in horrified amazement, he landed on the parapet, then rolled over onto the roof proper. A second or two later, he emerged, grinning sheepishly to the applause of the admiring youngsters on the ground.

Ed smiled with relief, but he wasn't really surprised by the actions of his friend. C.L. Magee was undoubtedly the brightest guy he knew, but was also the least predictable and most daring. The feat just performed was not done to impress the onlookers, but rather to test his own agility and courage. C.L. wasn't one to boast of his accomplishments to others, nor did he find it necessary to curry anyone's favor. Still, he was an affable sort, and Ed liked him a lot, as did most of the kids in the neighborhood.

The two boys had known each other since the early 1920s when their mothers would take them and their siblings to the swimming pool at the University of Chicago. Ed resided with his parents and brothers Tom and John in exclusive Hyde Park while C.L.—almost two years his senior—lived with his family in a spacious apartment in Kenwood, an adjoining neighborhood populated largely by upper middle class residents. The duo were part of a large, predominantly Irish Catholic group of boys from St. Ambrose who played sports together or went swimming in nearby Lake Michigan during the warm months. C.L.'s reputation for fearlessness was well-established. He enjoyed playing with friends on the slanted roofs of South Side churches—a potentially lethal activity if one should slip or a rain gutter happened to break off—and loved to dive from the top of fifteen-foot-high rocks over wood pilings into the lake.

C.L.'s parents, Fred and Marie Magee moved to Chicago from Omaha, Nebraska in 1918 when C.L. was just a year old. Omaha was but a brief stopover for the Magees, however, as both had been born and raised in Pittsburgh, Pennsylvania, where Fred's family wielded considerable political clout. He had, in fact, named his firstborn after his uncle, Christopher Lyman Magee, a popular and powerful former city "boss" who rose to prominence not only in Pittsburgh, but in the national Republican Party during the last quarter of the nineteenth century. This elder C.L. Magee had no children of his own, so his nephews were the fortunate recipients of his power brokering. After their beloved uncle's death from colon cancer in 1901 at age 53, Fred and three of his five brothers—Will, Chris, and Charles—all became leading citizens of the city, especially Will, the eldest, who was twice elected mayor. Charles entered politics as well, and was elected state senator before his untimely death at age thirty-four. The other two Magee brothers, Ed Jr. and Thomas also died before reaching forty. As a young man, Fred joined the staff of the *Pittsburgh Times*, a major daily newspaper his Uncle Chris had purchased, and eventually rose to the post of editor-in-chief. His journalism career was cut short, however, because of failing eyesight, something he blamed on the close-up editing work he'd had to do over the years. He then accepted a position in Washington, D.C. as an aide to a Pennsylvania congressman.

Fred moved with his new bride, the former Mary Ellen Considine—who was better known as "Marie"—to Omaha in 1916, and joined the commodities exchange there. He was forty at the time, and his wife, a daughter of immigrants from Counties Clare and Mayo in western Ireland, was fifteen years younger. Fred was actually fifth generation Irish on his father's side, the original Magees having been the "lace curtain" Protestant variety from County Derry in Ulster. His mother, however, was a strict Catholic whose parents emigrated from the Alsace-Lorraine region that borders France and Germany, and Fred and his siblings were raised in that religion.

In Chicago—where Fred joined the grain market exchange—the family increased by two: Zona Marie, born early in 1919 and Frederick McNickle Magee, Jr., who arrived in 1921. The elder son was called C.L. by his family from the beginning, while Fred Jr. also acquired a nickname, "Buddy." Zona, who had been named for Zona Gale—a popular author at the turn of the century—was always called by her proper name. Fred Sr., an affable, laid back sort, was in his fifties by the time all of his children reached school age. Between his rather advanced years and the job at the exchange, he had neither the time nor the energy to be much of a disciplinarian, so Marie ruled the roost at home. She was a small, but formidable woman who tried to keep the children under her thumb while insisting that her household be as neat as a pin, with everything in its proper place. It must be assumed that she either wasn't aware of C.L.'s often dangerous activities, or simply turned a blind eye to what was going on.

The practice of wearing blinders was commonplace during the twenties and thirties in Chicago where corruption ran rampant in all levels of city government and the police force, and most of the citizens either had dealings with Al Capone or knew someone who did. That so many—probably out of fear more than anything else—held the notorious gangster in respectful awe says a lot about the moral climate of the city. Youngsters, of course, became increasingly aware as they grew into adolescence of the dichotomy between what they were taught in church and school, and what was happening in the very real world where they lived. The city's decadence continued even after Capone's imprisonment for income tax evasion, and the moral confusion of the youth was not helped by the media's insistence on romanticizing the exploits of Depression-era bank robbers like Bonnie and Clyde, Pretty Boy Floyd, and John Dillinger.

Beginning in the mid-1920s, and for the next several years, the three Magee children spent the better part of every summer in Pittsburgh. Their parents took them to the train station, then placed them in the care of a porter for the long rail trip. When they arrived in the Steel City, Marie's parents—the Considines—would pick the trio up and take them to their home. Later, the children always spent a few weeks with their Magee grandparents and with their Uncle Chris and his family. At some time during their stay, they usually called on bachelor Uncle Will Magee—the former mayor—as well. Those summers were times of great fun for the youngsters, whether they were listening to their tiny Grandmother Considine's dramatic storytelling—which featured tales of Celtic heroes and supernatural creatures like banshees—or enjoying the company of cousins while exploring the Magee family's ancestral city and its sights.

Fred prospered in his position at the exchange, but lost it when the Depression came along. Unlike many others, however, he was fortunate enough to find new employment right away—an office job with the electric company. It was a big comedown, incomewise, but the family managed to make ends meet throughout the thirties.

If the Depression meant lowered expectations for adults in the neighborhood, it provided new opportunities as far as C.L. and his adventure-seeking friends were concerned. In addition to throwing the boys on their own resources for play, it provided them with bricks and boards from buildings left unfinished; materials for which they found many uses, especially for constructing hideouts in hidden recesses of these buildings. Another popular, though dangerous, practice of the kids in the South Side neighborhood was hitching rides on the rear bumpers of cars or the backs of buses and trucks. On one memorable occasion, C.L. and three friends hopped on the rear of a truck and didn't get off until it reached Kankakee, almost sixty miles south of Chicago. When he finally got back home late that evening, C.L. was able to convince his worried, irate mother that the foursome had been kidnapped, then let go when the abductors learned they were not the rich kids they'd intended to snatch. That this farfetched story had any credence was probably due to the still-fresh memory of the notorious Leopold and Loeb murder-kidnapping that happened just blocks from the Magee residence a few years before.

Like most growing boys C.L. took a great interest in sports, participating in almost every athletic endeavor available to him at St. Ambrose and later at Mount Carmel High, also a parochial school. He was on the slender side, but his exceptional balance and coordination helped him excel on any team he joined. If there was one activity that occupied him more than any other, though, it was reading. C.L. had an unquenchable thirst for knowledge, and read almost every book he got his hands on. Among his favorites were stories about real-life World War I aviators like "Red Baron" Manfred von Richthofen and Eddie Rickenbacker and the heroes of Arthurian Legend. The Knights of the Round Table became his role models, and the great air aces were, to him, the modern equivalents of Arthur, Lancelot, and Galahad. Merlin was a source of fascination to the boy as well, and the tales he read about that legendary sorcerer doubtlessly contributed to what would be a lifelong interest in magic and the occult.

After C.L. graduated from Mount Carmel in 1935, he kicked around for awhile until Fred Magee helped him obtain a job delivering light bills for fifteen dollars a week. That the young man did not enter college right away was perhaps due to the family's financial situation, which was sufficient to cover the costs of food, clothing and shelter, but little else during the Depression. In the middle and late thirties, C.L. and his friends sought recreation at church-sponsored dances—the best place to meet girls—and in various athletic activities. He and Ed Smart both dabbled in Golden Gloves boxing, and managed to sneak into most University of Chicago home football games to watch the great Jay Berwanger showcase his considerable talent. Other less savory activities his crowd enjoyed were visits to one of the bookmaking parlors which proliferated in Chicago and occasional trips to Calumet City (aka: "Calamity City") near the Indiana State Line where the guys could rent the services of thinly-clad taxi dancers for a dime a dance.

When C.L. was nineteen, he came to the aid of a friend who had somehow gained possession of a weight lifting set. The young man's parents wouldn't allow him to work out in their house for fear of the damage the heavy barbell equipment might do to the floor, so C.L. volunteered a place. It wasn't his parents' home, of course. Easy going Fred Magee probably did not mind, but Marie—who could charitably have been described as "tidy"— would have gone through the roof at such a suggestion. There was no opposition, however, to using the largely vacant basement of the Magee's apartment building as a weight training center.

It should be mentioned that at the time most coaches and fitness "experts" were opposed to the concept of athletes working out with heavy weights, preferring instead a program largely based on calisthenics. The theory was that while regular use of barbells would "bulk up" the individual, it was also likely to cause a loss of flexibility, creating a condition referred to as "muscle bound." C.L. was aware of the current wisdom, so he decided to visit one of his favorite places, the library, and bring home several books on the subject. From these volumes he determined that by combining certain flexibility exercises with the weight training he could maintain his natural athleticism. Soon, C.L. and his friend were working out

Twenty-year-old Chris (in background) and brother Bud, age sixteen (far right), with friends from their South Side neighborhood (L to R) Godfrey Stake, Paul McDevitt, Johnny McDevitt (1937)   *Chris Magee Collection*

together almost every day, and with results that can be described as impressive, to say the least. After only five months, the once slender Magee had added some thirty-five pounds of solid muscle to his five-foot, ten-inch frame, jumping from about 145 pounds all the way up to 180 pounds.

In 1938, C.L. enrolled at the University of Chicago. With his innate athletic talent and recently developed musculature he easily succeeded in making the freshman football team, where he played end. He would box and run track as well during the academic year. The now twenty-one-year-old wasn't all that dedicated to his studies, although his voracious appetite for reading continued. His taste in literature was starting to change, though. While he still enjoyed the occasional adventure yarn, he was showing increased interest in the classics and more esoteric subjects like philosophy and the occult.

Money was often hard for a young man to come by in the late 1930s, but resourceful guys like Magee and Smart could be very creative when they needed a few bucks. One scam that worked on occasion involved C.L., Ed, and Ed's older brother, Tom. Ed would enter Sportsman's Park, a popular horse racing facility, and find a seat at the very top of the grandstand where he had a clear view of both the race track and the city street that paralleled it. Tom, meanwhile, posted himself in a phone booth next to the street with a pair of binoculars. Immediately before a race was scheduled to go off, he would call C.L., who was waiting in another phone booth several blocks away and across the street from a bookie joint. Ed watched the race, and if—during the stretch run—one horse seemed to be pulling away to an easy victory, he would raise one or both hands high above his head with his extended fingers indicating the winner's number. Tom, peering through the binoculars at his brother, passed on the information to C.L., who would immediately hang up his phone and cross the street to lay down a bet on the winning horse. Not all races had such clear-cut victors, of course, so Ed had to be selective. Most bookies refused to take any action after the scheduled post time, but occasionally clocks were a minute or two slow, or the bet taker wasn't paying close attention to the time. In any event, the game the trio was playing was a safe one: they had nothing to lose if they were shut out at the betting window and plenty to gain if they weren't.

Bud Magee turned eighteen in 1939. He'd been hanging around with his brother and the older crowd for some time, so it was no surprise that he now started turning up at their favorite watering holes. C.L. was very protective of Bud, so one evening when a table full of newspaper haulers began to hassle his scrawny, bespectacled younger brother he quickly moved to the rescue. Feeling a certain safety in numbers (there were about six of them), the truckers turned their attention and insults to C.L.—not a very smart idea. The older Magee then invited the entire table to step outside. His antagonists complied, but no doubt lost some of their confidence when Ed Smart and a couple of other friends joined the brothers. The big melee never really materialized. Smart managed to get in one good lick before the police suddenly appeared and everyone scattered. The bartender had seen the donnybrook coming, and called the local authorities while the participants were still in the bar.

C.L. would complete just one full year at the university. Any interest he may have had in academic matters was about to be put aside because of events happening in another hemisphere.

Chapter 2

The Would Be Warrior

E ngland and most of Europe weren't prepared for war when Hitler invaded Poland in September of 1939, but C.L. Magee was ready, willing, and eager to join the fray as soon as he heard the news. What he lacked in military training, he more than made up for in attitude. As far as C.L. was concerned, everything he'd done up to that time—the sports, the games of derring do, the body building, even the books about knights and warriors he enjoyed so much—contributed to his physical and mental preparation for war. His somewhat ambitious goals were to get to Europe, learn to fly, then challenge the Nazis for air supremacy.

To carry out the first part of his plan, C.L. and two friends hitchhiked to New Orleans in January 1940, hoping to find work on a ship that would take them to Europe. The latter-day Lafayette Escadrille hopefuls immediately found obstacles in their path to glory, however. First it was the weather. The trio was looking forward to the tropical climate of the Mississippi Delta, but the winter of 1940 turned out to be the coldest of the century in New Orleans. The home heating systems were not adequate to handle the freak weather conditions, and the outdoor water pipes—located too close to the surface of the ground—simply froze.

Undaunted and unfazed by the cold—they were, after all, from Chicago—C.L. and his companions walked the docks every day, inquiring about shipboard employment. After a month or so of frustration, they were finally directed to the back room of a store on Canal Street where C.L. and one of his friends—the third member of the Chicago threesome found a girlfriend and lost interest in going to Europe—met with the skipper of a cargo vessel. The seaman seemed very receptive to hiring on the sturdy young men and probably would have done so had C.L.'s buddy not blurted out the truthful, but wrong, answer to his question, "What nationality are you?" They were informed by the man that they were out of luck because the Neutrality Law in effect at that time prohibited Americans from entering the war zone.

With their dreams of fighting on hold, the two friends hitchhiked back to Chicago, leaving their love-struck buddy behind. C.L. wasn't home long when he decided to join the Royal Canadian Air Force, which was already sending men and planes across the Atlantic to aid the British cause. He and Smart talked another friend, Johnny McKibben—one of the few young men in the neighborhood who actually owned a car—into driving to Windsor, Ontario with them so that all three could enlist. They learned soon after arriving, however, that none had enough college credits to qualify for pilot training, so they returned home.

Chris at Spartan School of Aeronautics (1941)   *Chris Magee Collection*

Having failed twice to get into the war as an aviator, C.L. decided to pursue his final option, the U.S. Army's flying cadet program. He considered this the least desirable choice because America was not at war, and what he wanted was real action right away. The program had a two-year college requirement at the time, but this would be waived if the applicant passed an equivalency test. The twenty-three-year-old was thus forced—perhaps for the first time in his life—to really "hit the books" (textbooks, that is). His motivation was different this time, however, and after four months intense study of elementary and advanced algebra, plane and solid geometry, physics, chemistry, and trigonometry, he passed the written exam and the physical. Early in January 1941, he was assigned to a cadet class that would begin March 22.

C.L. was unhappy about having to wait nearly three months, however, so he went back to Canada to find out if the requirements had changed. They had, but not enough. Two years of college was now the minimum for pilot candidates. In April 1941, shortly after entering the U.S. Army's Spartan School of Aeronautics in Tulsa, Oklahoma, C.L. found out there was another way of getting into the RCAF: through the Clayton-Knight Committee. However, to merit consideration by the committee the candidate was required to have logged at least thirty-five hours flying time.

With this information, C.L. concocted and carried out a simple, yet effective plan. Since aerial combat was at the heart of his desire to learn to fly and he couldn't see his getting into war anytime soon in the USAAF, he decided to get the flying time needed to qualify him for the RCAF then "wash out." Since many pilot trainees suffered this fate, he foresaw no problem in failing the program after completing thirty-five hours, and there was none. In fact, C.L. was a "natural" pilot. Flying came easily to him, even though he'd never driven a car in his life. It was perhaps due to his command of the Ryan trainer the cadets flew that he could so convincingly exhibit the inept landing techniques that resulted in his washing out. Afterwards, he politely turned down the Army's suggestion that he take up training as a navigator or bombardier.

On May 20, 1941, C.L. Magee left the U.S. Army Air Force's flying cadet program, having completed twenty-five hours, twenty-eight minutes of dual control flying and nine hours, fifty-nine minutes solo.

During the six weeks prior to his departure for Canada he decided to put all his affairs in order. One of these was the disposition of library books which were accumulating in his room. C.L. never had much patience for the rather slow procedure of checking books in and out from the Chicago Public Library branch in his neighborhood, so he learned to avoid the process by selecting the reading matter in which he was interested, then slipping out a seldom used exit. Rather than risk losing his library privileges should he be caught returning the unchecked-out volumes, he simply hung on to them. One day that June after he and Ed Smart had filled several cardboard boxes with literally hundreds of the books, he called the library to report that a "tenant" moved out of his building after telling the Magee family he wanted to "donate" his book collection to the good people of Chicago. C.L. and Ed helped the library's driver load the cartons onto his truck. Fortunately the man never bothered to examine any of the books, for they all had Dewey Decimal codes clearly visible on the outside of the bindings.

On July 5, C.L. hitchhiked to Windsor with young Blackie Lucas, a hulking, unpolished high school dropout who shared his interest in boxing. Magee had competed at the college level, while the teenager had shown promise as an amateur heavyweight. Blackie's father had once been New York's state welterweight champion. His godfather was none other than Al Capone. The youngster "borrowed" the identity of a better-educated lad from the neighborhood to help him meet RCAF standards, but this couldn't keep him from failing his induction physical because of a deviated septum. Undaunted, the duo decided to try again, riding the rails to Toronto stowed away behind the coal car. They arrived at the Toronto recruiting center filthy with coal dust and very hungry. The RCAF provided them with a shower and complimentary breakfast in the basement cafeteria. Lucas devoured a dozen eggs. The doctor administering the physical in Toronto found no reason to disqualify Blackie because of his nasal condition. Oral examinations were also required of new cadet recruits. Since Blackie's educational shortcomings and lack of social graces were a cause for concern, Chris volunteered to take the exam for him. Soon, both were on their way to St. Hubert Field near Montreal for basic training.

The RCAF enlistees were a mixed bag, some joining for idealistic reasons, others—like the two Chicagoans—for the adventure, while a significant number were either on the lam or simply considered undesirable in civilian society. Off-base fighting in bars and on dance floors was commonplace, both among the airmen and between the RCAF and the local citizenry. The French Canadians seemed to hate anyone who spoke English, regardless of whether the individual was Canadian or American.

Official RCAF photo of Flying Cadet C.L. Magee (c.1941)   *Courtesy of Zona Musser*

On the morning after a large-scale melee involving C.L., Blackie, and some of their friends with another group of airmen, a hearing officer told C.L. his actions were going to cost him several weeks confinement to his barracks. Later that same day the officer had a complete change of heart after he learned more about the fight. It seems that Magee's opponents from the night before were a group of known troublemakers that the brass had been trying to get rid of. Instead of administrative punishment, C.L. and his friends were given weekend passes.

If the men in C.L.'s class expected to go directly into flight instruction after their six weeks of basic training were complete, they were in for a big disappointment. Instead, all were sent to guard a supply depot for twelve long weeks. Some were so bored they contemplated going home, but not Magee. Three months with little to do except get into trouble tried his patience, but he was confident that sooner or later he'd live out his dream of flying in combat. When his orders for ground training school finally came through, he was sent to Victoriaville, a French-speaking town of about 10,000, located seventy-five miles southwest of the city of Quebec.

Once again, the RCAF cadets were treated with hostility by the residents. Those who attended the local Catholic church and could understand French reported that the priests constantly bemoaned the presence of the airmen, sternly warning the villagers to keep their daughters away from them.

Elementary flight training began at the Miramichi facility in Chatham, New Brunswick, on December 20, 1941, less than two weeks after Pearl Harbor. Although his country was now

RCAF Cadet Magee waits for skies to clear enough for his scheduled training flight at Chatham, New Brunswick (January 1942)
Chris Magee Collection

officially at war, it was Magee's belief that he would get into action sooner as a member of the RCAF than he would with any of the U.S. Armed Services. He found the ski-equipped, open cockpit Fleet Finch bi-plane trainers easy to fly, but sometimes difficult to land due to the tricky winter visibility conditions. Because of the gray skies and snow-covered land surfaces, ground and sky tend to blend together, causing the horizon to virtually disappear. After a while, some ingenious member of the brass ordered

RCAF Cadet Chris Magee at Summerside, Prince Edward Island (March 1942)
Chris Magee Collection

that shrubs be planted in a long line paralleling the runway so a pilot could better judge his altitude before landing. The navigation-aiding flora arrived too late, however, for Blackie and several others who washed out because of unsatisfactory landings.

Having successfully finished elementary training, Magee was sent to Summerside on Prince Edward Island for service flight training, the final schooling RCAF airmen had to complete before receiving their wings. The rinky-dink Finches they had been flying were replaced by something that actually resembled a true fighter aircraft. The Harvard II was identical to the U.S. Navy's SNJ and the Army's AT-6 Texan, and boasted closed cock-pits, retractable landing gear, and full instrumentation.

Around this time, the twenty-four-year-old finally shed the "C.L." tag that had been his since birth. With his Chicago friend gone, the remaining pilot trainees simply assumed he preferred to be called Chris, and, in fact, he did. Family members and friends from the old neighborhood would, however, continue to refer to him by his initials or by one of the many nicknames he'd acquired over the years. Among these were Spiderman, earned because of his climbing ability, and Zark, short for Flash Gordon's nemesis, Zarkoff—a cartoonish serial villain he could imitate quite well.

Graduation from service flight training was just a few weeks away in early May of 1942, when a group of officers representing the various U.S.

Armed Services arrived via train at Summerside. The purpose of the visit was to recruit Americans serving in the RCAF, if they wanted to return. Chris enjoyed his Canadian experience but was always a patriot at heart. He was willing to consider what the U.S. Army, Navy, or Marine Corps had to offer, but laid out three conditions: he would fly fighters; he would not be given instructor duty; and he would be sent overseas to a combat zone. Only the major in charge of Marine recruitment was willing to make these guarantees. Still, Chris felt he owed the RCAF an opportunity to match the offer. When his commanding officer told him he lacked the power to do that, his mind was made up.

On May 9, 1942, Chris was discharged from the Royal Canadian Air Force, having served 309 days. Along with about ninety other Americans from the RCAF who opted to transfer into the U.S. Navy or Marine Corps, he reported to the Naval Air Station in Atlanta, Georgia early in July. Despite the 180 hours flight time he'd accumulated between the U.S. Army and the RCAF, he was officially designated a U.S. Naval Aviation Cadet. He soon found himself at the stick of a craft he was quite familiar with, only it was now called an SNJ-3 instead of a Harvard II.

A surprising number of cadets were killed in crashes during the early weeks of the training. Chris blamed this on a lack of night and instrument flying, things the RCAF taught pilots in the elementary phase of its program. Otherwise, the training was not dissimilar to what he'd already been through; only the non-flying apparel was different. For the next four months he wore the uniform of the U.S. Navy, finally exchanging it for a Marine Corps officer's set on November 14, just before he was awarded his Navy wings-of-gold. By then Second Lieutenant Magee was learning the more sophisticated aspects of being a

Chris during Navy flight training at Lee Field, Jacksonville, Florida (October 1942)
Chris Magee Collection

Naval Aviator—formation flying, aerobatics, gunnery, etc.—at NAS Lee Field, Jacksonville, Florida.

Fighter training began at Jacksonville's Cecil Field on January 23, 1943. Chris finally found himself in proven combat aircraft, the Grumman F4F-3 and F4F-4 Wildcats (the chief difference between the two planes being that while the F4F-3 had only lap seat belts, the newer model F4F-4 was equipped with a much safer system of shoulder restraints). The Wildcat was the workhorse fighter of the Pacific Fleet, but its days were numbered. The stubby-nosed little craft was simply overmatched by the faster, nimbler Mitsubishi fighters—called Zeros—used by the Japanese. Unfortunately, its replacement, Grumman's bigger, more powerful F6F Hellcat, was still a few months away from large scale deployment. There was also talk of another fighter—a sleek, if rather strange looking bird called a Corsair being produced by Chance Vought Aircraft in Connecticut. Data was sketchy on the plane, but rumor was it could outperform anything in the Pacific Theater.

The Wildcat had more than its share of idiosyncrasies, beginning with the takeoff technique. The landing gear had to be cranked up and down by hand, meaning that while the pilot tried to control the stick with his left hand, the right was busy with the gear lever. Learning to coordinate the process and produce a smooth climb took a lot of practice. From ground level it was easy to spot a beginner by the way his craft would appear to "porpoise" on takeoff. Another problem occasionally encountered by pilots was that the Wildcat's electric prop had a tendency to unexpectedly slip from one pitch into another, a condition that could prove deadly if it occurred during takeoff. Chris faced that situation one day while performing simulated carrier landings at Cecil Field. Just as he left the ground, his prop suddenly jumped from full low (maximum takeoff power) into full high pitch (maximum cruise) causing the engine to cut out. Chris brought the plane down immediately, but found himself taxiing toward the end of the runway at flying speed with no safe way to stop his progress. The field beyond had recently been cleared of trees, but not the stumps. Only a rut running across the end of the landing circle stood between Chris's plane and those sawed-off sentinels. Years later, he would write about his narrow escape from the Grim Reaper:

Meanwhile . . . I'm hoping friction will overcome inertia before the stumps do. About two instants later I'm out of runway and heading for the stumps, which are waiting . . . with kind of a malevolent ecstasy as if they were about to even things with me for all the toothpicks I had shattered, or for the time I chomped down on a tongue depressor when it tried to gag me.

But it was not to be. This was not the day of the stumps. It was Mother Earth to the rescue. Or, rather it was a rut in her that denied the stumps their victory. The rut, until that day unregarded and without hope or fame, perhaps merely the careless gesture of a lax bulldozer jockey who had gone off to another rutless field without even a backward glance; that rut, that Good Samaritan of ruts, was to be immortalized among my memories. I should have among my sacred souvenirs a jar of that hallowed ground. Too much? Well, maybe a small vial, a teaspoonful, a speck? To think I once had a mouthful of it and had thoughtlessly spit it out, not realizing the import it should have occupied . . . .

Blake once saw the world in a grain of sand. I saw the world saved, preserved in an unsung rut of earth. Many a rut is born to serve unseen. How could I ever see a rut again without seeing that rut?

Stumps think only of themselves, standing erect in the landscape, the image of rampant egos.

But ruts, they live secret lives, passively.

The wheels of the plane hit the rut at high speed, causing the craft to turn around, flip over and stop upside down, tail first before reaching the stumps. Chris escaped with a slight bump on the head and the aforementioned mouthful of dirt. Others weren't so lucky. In one letter to a friend he reported that no less than twelve pilots had been killed during the previous week. His roommate, a Wisconsin native who also trained in the RCAF, died in the crash of a Lockheed Hudson the day after he was awarded his wings.

Chris completed fighter training in late March and was sent to NAS Glenview, Illinois, for five days of actual carrier landing practice on USS *Wolverine* in Lake Michigan—that there were no Marine squadrons stationed aboard aircraft carriers at the time was irrelevant. The ability to land on aircraft carrier flight decks was (and is) a requirement of all U.S. Naval Aviation fighter pilots.

With the necessary eight successful arrested landings under his belt, Chris was given two weeks leave prior to his departure for California and, finally, the war in the Pacific. Glenview was just a short distance from home, and there was plenty going on in the old neighborhood, especially in the Magee household, to keep him occupied. Brother Bud was finally drafted into the Army after countless attempts to enlist and was away in training. The acute nearsightedness and astigmatism that caused recruiters to turn him down apparently didn't bother the local draft board.

While pleased to have their eldest son home, Fred and Marie Magee's attention was nevertheless centered on daughter Zona, who was about to get married. Her husband-to-be was a local boy, Gustav "Gus" Musser, a tall, dark, and husky fellow about two years Chris's senior. Gus was also a Naval Aviator, and had recently completed seaplane school. He, too, had orders to the West Coast and was planning to bring his new bride along with him.

Chris with sister Zona (L) and parents Fred and Marie Magee shortly before Zona's wedding to Gus Musser (spring 1943)

Chris Magee Collection

The wedding took place halfway through Chris's leave. Almost all of Chris's old pals were already overseas, and Zona's friends who attended were either married or brought dates. The sole unescorted young woman at the reception was Bud's latest girlfriend, a beautiful eighteen-year-old brunette named Jean Scott. Chris had known Jean for years. She had, after all, grown up in his neighborhood. Much time had passed since he'd last seen her, however, and the little girl he remembered had bloomed into the fairest of maidens.

Jean Scott (c. 1943) *Courtesy of Jean Scott*

It wasn't surprising that the only two members of the wedding party who weren't attached to anyone else present were drawn together. There was clearly a mutual attraction between the handsome Marine officer and the striking young lady, but Chris faced a real dilemma. Jean, after all, was seven years younger than he and, of course, was his brother's girl. Still, she was as delightfully personable as she was lovely, and he saw no harm in a little platonic socializing. So, the two of them spent the rest of Chris's leave enjoying movies, dances, and other innocent, fun-filled activities together. That the future held at least the possibility of a more serious relationship must have occurred to both of them, but this was not the time to think of such things. Chris, after all, would soon be going to war, and so would Bud, the man Jean fully expected to marry—until his brother came along to inadvertently confuse the issue.

When his leave ended, Chris travelled by train to San Diego, where he reported to Miramar Naval Air Station to prepare for duty in the South Pacific. On April 30, 1943, he typed Jean a letter describing his life in Southern California.

Dearest Jean:

Finally the gods and the Marine Corps have given me a chance to write to you. They have been running us wild around here for the last few days—gathering equipment for overseas, etc. They even threw in a few route marches and a bit of crawling around on our hands and knees to keep us in shape. Crawling on my stomach through an especially tough bit of undergrowth, I came face to face with a six foot snake. No doubt he thought I was the prodigal son of his tribe, for putting a friendly rattle about my shoulder he says, "Brother, you look kind of dirty and hungry; how about coming up to the house for supper?" Now, never having had much to do with snakes socially—or any other way for that matter—and not being much inclined to change our relationship I politely declined his kind offer. At first I thought he was going to use physical violence to back up his proffer of hospitality but when he spotted my knife and steel helmet I guess he figured that was too much to swallow, so he soothed his injured pride by sticking his tongue out at me as he retreated into the brush. Come to think of it he never did say what he intended to have for supper—or should I say whom. Oh well, those snakes are a slippery outfit at best.

I had quite a ride down here on the train, ran into a few people connected with the movies—Rita Johnson, Irene Manning, and Slim Summerville; also some guy studying Japanese who tried to give me a few pointers on the subject. He might as well have tried to plant geraniums in the Sahara Desert because my mind absorbed about as much of what he was talking about as a camera fiend snapping away without any film in his devil box . . . . Then I met another brainstorm who had a case of whiskey in his berth. Said he'd brought it along because he had heard that the southwest part of the U.S. was dry country. After that I decided to make up for some of the sleep I'd missed on my leave.

We're not doing any flying at all while we are here and don't expect to until we get to the South Pacific. We are supposed to get some of the newer fighter planes then. If we do maybe we can do the Jap morale a little real harm. A few blockbuster calling cards at the palace of that son of — the sun in Tokyo might change their ideas about shooting captured American fliers to keep them from blasting Japan off the map. I think the best cure tho would be to call a no quarter war and fight them at their own game. Let the Japanese papers carry the stories about American atrocities for awhile. I don't know where they got the idea that war could be more humane anyway. It only makes it last the longer.

I was in Los Angeles Saturday and Sunday with a few of the boys, and we had quite a time. We went up to Hollywood and looked the place over. Seems pretty interesting to me—all kinds of joints and other things to see. One in particular I remember called the Jade. It was all laid out with Chinese arts, statues of Buddha and other gods, paintings and tapestries, and all kinds of ornaments. Wish you could have seen it—quite an atmosphere. The fellow that owns the place seems to have spent quite a bit of time in China, and these are part of the things he has collected while over there.

The next morning we went to sunrise services at the Hollywood Bowl. They were at 5:30—never mind looking so surprised—I didn't get up that early, I just didn't bother going to bed at all! There were about 70,000 other people there, too, and a good many of them had been waiting there for hours, but we got there at the last minute and got seats right down in front. After all, what's 70,000 people compared to the old all star game technique. I still can't see what people waste hours sitting in the damp and cold for—when at best the services lasted only 45 minutes . . . and we have the ungodly crust to go to the zoo and laugh at our brother monkeys.

Did you get the Worry Bird I sent you from Albuquerque, N.M.? He's a special kind of fellow so hang onto him—that is, if he's still in one piece after his travels. He's very particular about the kind of company he keeps and the best is none too good for him, so watch your Ps and Qs or he'll back right out of your window one of these days and whirl himself off into oblivion. Don't feed him too much either or he'll have to fly forwards instead of backwards, and begin to worry so much about where he's going that he won't be able to do your worrying for you. A very temperamental fellow this Worry Bird. Take good care of him, and he will bring you only the best of luck.

Did you make up for your lost sleep yet? Every time I look at that picture I get a kick out of it. You look so darn much like a sleepy stiffie and so contentedly tired as tho you had just taken a tight pair of shoes and kicked them under the table. Yep, really a cute kid. Arf! I had a hell of a good time in Chicago on this leave, so much better than any before that it would be a sacrilege to even try to compare them. My only regret is that we didn't start the first day of my leave instead of when it was almost half over. Only trouble there is that I'd probably have had to take a few extra days off to see that you had a decent burial, you know—line your rough box with empty ale bottles and hang a worn out pair of shoes at either end, then bury you to the tune of a volley of corks bursting in air—very military . . . .

Well, my sweet, I guess it's about time for me to sign off. I wish Uncle Sam would give me another leave or else hurry up and get this G— D— war over with. Look at all the time I'm wasting. So long, cutie, just remember that too much ale and too much sitting do not combine to build the classical figure—in other words don't over exercise your elbow if you want to keep a classie chassis.

Love,

Zark

If Chris was expecting to be shipped off to the war right away he was in for a disappointment. The old U.S. Armed Forces refrain of "hurry up and wait" was being played again. He was cheered up considerably, though, by a phone call from Ed Smart, who was stationed at an airfield in Lomita, a suburb of Los Angeles.

Ed joined the Army a month or so after Pearl Harbor and entered an enlisted pilot program. Now, as a staff sergeant flying P-38s, he was preparing for imminent departure to England as part of the 55th Squadron of the 20th Fighter Group. With Chris on temporary duty at Marine Corps Air Station, El Toro, just an hour away, the two old friends managed to get together for a night on the town in Hollywood and an opportunity to compare notes on

Ed Smart (1942)
Courtesy of Jean Scott

the doings in their old neighborhood. Chris wasn't surprised to learn that his red-haired buddy had a crush on Jean Scott. Smart and Magee were often attracted to the same girls.

Ed was stationed in the Los Angeles area for awhile and not only was friendly with several movie stars but also was familiar with the rich and famous crowd's favorite watering holes—places where a couple of fighter pilots were never allowed to pay for their own drinks.

With no planes available at either Miramar or El Toro, Chris and about ten other pilots took a bus to the El Centro air station, about 150 miles inland, to get the necessary flying hours to qualify for their April and May flight pay. In a letter to Jean, he described El Centro as being "out in the desert where our only playmates will be an ungainly lot of Gila monsters who are disgusted with their lot. They still can't figure out why they are condemned to live in such a place as that where the temperature is always (close to) the degree of boiling." The Marine pilots' assignment at the desert facility: fly SNJ-4s as instructors for rear seat air gunners.

On June 5, 1943, in San Diego Harbor, Chris and several hundred other servicemen boarded *Rochambeau*, an old French ocean liner that had been converted to a troop ship. Their destination: the southwest Pacific. Chris was finally going where the action was.

Chapter 3

Preparing for Combat

—

With one of its engines not operating, *Rochambeau* could have been likened to the proverbial "slow boat to China" were its eventual destination not to more southern climes. Because its snail-like pace made it highly vulnerable to any Japanese submarines that may have been patrolling the area, the old liner was escorted by U.S. Navy destroyers during the last part of the voyage. Chris was assigned to an officer's bunkroom with three other pilots for what turned out to be a journey of almost three weeks duration. Two of them, Bob "Alex" Alexander and Don Moore, would later serve with him in the Solomons. Alex was a handsome, muscular blond from Iowa who excelled in track, wrestling, and gymnastics at Iowa State before joining the Marines near the end of his junior year. Moore, who Chris knew from Miramar, was a native of Amarillo, Texas, and, like Chris, received flight training in the RCAF before transferring to the Corps. Both young men had serious girlfriends back in the States whom they were planning to marry.

To facilitate the passage of time during the seemingly interminable cruise, the passengers found a variety of activities to amuse themselves. Moore spent a good number of hours practicing on the big silver trombone he'd brought with him. Chris filled his sea locker with books to stimulate his mind and a barbell and two pairs of forty-pound adjustable weights to keep his physique toned.

The ship finally docked in New Caledonia on June 23, and shortly thereafter Chris was sent to Espiritu Santo in the New Hebrides. It was there on July 2 that he was introduced to the Chance Vought F4U-1 Corsair. It was love at first flight. The Corsair outperformed the Wildcats he'd flown in every category. It was faster—capable of speeds in excess of 400 knots—bigger, and more powerful. It climbed and dived better and was easier to maneuver. The "ugly duckling" with the inverted gull wings had superior range thanks to a 332-gallon fuel capacity. Its 2,000 horsepower Pratt and Whitney "Double Wasp" air-cooled radial engine was more reliable than the in-line type, which would seize up if its ethylene glycol coolant system was ruptured. If the Corsair had one shortcoming it was that the visibility from the cockpit—set well back toward the rear of the plane to accommodate a large internal fuel tank behind the prop—left something to be desired, especially when landing. It was for this reason that the Navy at first rejected the F4Us as carrier-based fighters and turned them over to the Marines.

Chris brought Jean up to date on his current activities—at least as much as the Marine Intelligence censors would allow—and mused about his recent voyage in a letter typed on July 5.

Dear Jean:

I am writing this from somewhere in the South Pacific. Uncle Sam says hush hush on just where, but it shouldn't be hard to come pretty close with a half way decent guess. We've been here long enough to be pretty well used to jungles and all those other sights that are at first so strange to the eyes of one from north of the equator.

We had a nice trip across and none of our outfit was seasick at all. You can't believe how much water there is in this old world of ours. Honest, it's all over the place. After being on it as long as I was you can't help but think that the scientists are grossly underestimating the immense quantity of liquid that you see stretched out before you. They will say that it is only 3/4 of the earth's surface but soon you begin to believe that there is nothing else in this old world but water. Sometimes when your mind begins to wander you may think of the vast depths beneath you and realize for the first time that there are thousands of feet, even miles of water between you and the ocean floor. Then you may begin to remember the story that Jules Verne wrote so many years ago, "Twenty Thousand Leagues Under the Sea."

What is it like down there? What type of creatures live down there where the light never penetrates? The deepest a man has ever gone is about 3,000 feet and the ocean is known to be over 30,000 feet in spots. Even at that depth Professor Beebe saw myriads of strange creatures ... and many of them had head lights so that they could find their way around in the stygian darkness of those unbelievable depths.

Thus your imagination has plenty to feast upon when you begin to think about the ocean and its unsolved mysteries.

I suppose you've seen by the papers that things are finally starting to move out here. Maybe now those little Jappies will begin to get what every American has been hoping for them to get ever since Pearl Harbor.

We get a movie every night out here and they are pretty up to date, but as a rule are a bit on the propaganda side. Artie Shaw was out here last night. He's a chief in the Navy now and has an all Navy band that is the pick of the men in the service. They were really swingaroos, but they didn't have any hepcats to keep in the groove so they left early. Really felt like putting that jive to a little practical use, but as yet I haven't caught on to the type of rug cutters they've got out here, although those bushy headed natives look as tho they would be able to get wild over the right music. I want to see them in action before I start picking up any of their stuff. Where were you? Maybe we could have showed those natives a new angle on an old technique.

Well so long, cutie, I'll see you in the newspapers. Give my love to the gang and tell them to write if they can spare a few minutes from their troubles. Above all don't you forget to write—and plenty soon. Maybe I'll send you a kangaroo from Sydney, Australia, if I get down that way.

Love,
Zark

On July 25, Chris was assigned to Marine Fighting Squadron (VMF) 124. It was the outfit that produced the first Corsair "ace" (a pilot who shot down at least five enemy planes), Ken Walsh, then in his third and final combat tour with the unit. Chris spent the rest of July and all of August reading informational materials about the Corsair and familiarizing himself with its capabilities through training flights and gunnery practice. By the end of August he had over 68 hours in the cockpit of an F4U, and was more than ready to take on the enemy's Mitsubishi-built fighters—officially called Zeros but also dubbed "Zekes" or "Meatballs" by American pilots.

VMF 124 was disbanded early in September, and the pilots who had completed three, six-week combat tours were, in accordance with Marine

Corps policy, shipped back to the States. Chris, whose service in the Pacific thus far had amounted to training only, was put in a "pilots pool" along with other newcomers and flyers from recently disbanded squadrons with less than the required three tours. These men were, in a sense, orphans, all hoping to find an adoptive family as quickly as possible.

Chris soon learned that a new fighter squadron was being formed under a leader who had a reputation for aggressiveness in the air and the record to prove it: he'd served in China with the famed American Volunteer Group—best known as the "Flying Tigers"—and claimed six kills. The fledgling unit was designated VMF 214, a number formerly owned by a squadron nicknamed "The Swashbucklers." That outfit had been disbanded not long after its commanding officer, Major Bill Pace, was killed in action. The new leader was Major Gregory Boyington, a short, solidly-built native of Idaho who, at thirty, was considered old by fighter pilot standards. Boyington had previously served as executive officer of VMF 122 in April on Guadalcanal but saw no action during that period. In fact, he had been out of action altogether for nearly four months—the result of a broken leg that occurred during a barroom brawl shortly after the tour ended. That the controversial, hard drinking Boyington was put in charge of a squadron at all was due in no small part to Major General James Moore. The general certainly must have had some reservations about Boyington but since the man was combat proven, the right rank, and, of course, available, he decided to give him a shot at leadership.

Since there was an abundance of men in the pilot pool trying to get into the new squadron, Boyington had the luxury of being selective. Automatically making his team were men like John Begert, Hank Bourgeois, Bill Case, Bob Ewing and five others who had shot down enemy planes in earlier tours. Boyington accompanied those without actual combat experience on familiarization flights, and quickly ascertained that a number of the newcomers, including Chris, Don Fisher, and John Bolt were "born pilots," while others had the skills necessary to quickly become top notch flyers, as well. A few just didn't meet his standards, however, and were sent back to the pool. And then there was Bob McClurg.

McClurg, a slight, talkative resident of New Castle, Pennsylvania, really wanted to fly fighters in combat but, despite his best efforts, just couldn't seem to figure out the intricacies of the Corsair. He likely would have been left behind on Espiritu Santo had Boyington not noticed some intangible factor in his character makeup that told him the irrepressible young man had potential. When VMF 214 departed for Guadalcanal early on the morning of September 12, 1943, its twenty-eight pilots included Chris, his *Rochambeau* roommates Bob Alexander and Don Moore, and a very happy (and relieved) Bob McClurg.

The men in Chris's unit represented every geographical area of the United States, and everybody seemed to get along quite well. Among the first he would form a close friendship with were two fellow Chicagoans, Jim Hill and Bruce Matheson. Jim, sometimes called "J.J.," was a quiet sort, tall and slender with jet black hair. That he was a "North Sider" meant he had to take an occasional ribbing from Chris and Bruce, both of whom had been raised on the South Side of town—or as Matheson always called it, "the good side." Matheson—or "Mat," as he was better known—was twenty-two, a year younger than Hill. He was tall like Jim, but more physically imposing, and had dark, matinee idol good looks. He also had a great sense of humor, and his vocal talent was always welcome when 214 had one of their frequent singalongs. Usually quiet George Ashmun from New Jersey was the leader of the choral group, which also included Pennsylvanians Sandy Sims and Paul "Moon" Mullen. Other songbirds were big, likeable Don "Mo" Fisher, a former pre-med student at the University of Florida, and ex-NAS Jacksonville flight instructor Ed "Oli" Olander, an erudite, slightly plump Amherst graduate who was also known as "Big Old Fat Old Ed."

Several of the pilots came from south of the Mason-Dixon line, and these were designated "Yamheads" by the northerners. It was a title that would be worn with pride by the likes of Fisher and fellow Floridian John Bolt (aka: Ol' John Blot), Hank Bourgeois of New Orleans, Burney Tucker from Tennessee, and Denmark Groover Jr., a native of Quitman, Georgia, whose hair stuck out from his scalp in a way that reminded the others of a porcupine, thereby earning him the nickname "Quill."

Major Stanley Bailey, the squadron's executive officer, was a muscular but short, spit-and-polish type who sometimes even carried a swagger stick—the very antithesis of Boyington. A competition equestrian in his native Vermont, he was no slouch as a fighter pilot either, having shot down two Japanese aircraft during a like number of combat tours. Captain Bob Ewing, the flight officer, was a familiar face to Chris. Ewing served in a similar capacity with VMF 124 and was credited with three "kills," one less than two-tour veteran Hank McCartney, a graduate of Houghton College in New York.

Other pilots included Bill Case, an Oregonian entering his third combat tour with one Zero to his credit; Kansas City native Bill "Junior" Heier, who, like Chris and Don Moore, had transferred from the RCAF; Ed "Harpo" Harper, a studious sort who'd left the University of Idaho to join the Corps; Warren T. "Long Tom" Emrich of Wichita, Kansas, whose thick, dark locks made him quite the ladies' man; Bob "Meathead" Bragdon, a Princeton graduate and all-around athlete; Walter "Red" Harris, a good-natured former zoology major from the University of Nebraska: and Rolland "Rollie" Rinabarger, who like Case had completed two years at Oregon State University before joining up.

Two key members of the squadron would not be flying into combat. Navy Lieutenant "Diamond" Jim Reames, the flight surgeon, was a southerner with an accent as thick and smooth as honey. A graduate of the University of Tennessee's medical school, he served on hospital planes evacuating wounded Marines from Guadalcanal prior to joining Boyington's squadron. Because of his rank and advanced age (twenty-six), the good doctor was awarded the title "King of the Yamheads." The pilots would soon discover—many to their chagrin—that he was also a master poker player. Air Intelligence Officer Frank Walton was, at thirty-four, the elder statesman of VMF 214. The big, muscular redhead was a world-class swimmer—he won the national backstroke championship in 1929—and was a sergeant with the Los Angeles Police Department when he joined the Marines in mid-1942. He was sent to the South Pacific and assigned to the First Marine Air Wing Intelligence Office in mid-August 1943. After two weeks of intelligence training Walton was told he was being transferred to a newly formed fighter squadron whose commander had a reputation for getting drunk, then becoming highly belligerent. Walton's actual intelligence duties were a little fuzzy; however, it was made clear to him that because of his size and police background, one of his most important responsibilities would be to keep Greg Boyington out of trouble.

VMF 214's designated role in the Pacific war was to support bomber operations and take on the Japanese Zeros as U.S. Forces drove northward from Guadalcanal up through the Solomon Islands and eventually to Japan itself. Blocking the route in the Solomons were two formidable obstacles—Bougainville and the heavily fortified Japanese base at Rabaul, New Britain. While there were no plans to take Rabaul, it still had to be neutralized and the only way to accomplish that was to conquer Bougainville—a large island protected not only by thousands of enemy troops with hundreds of anti-aircraft gun emplacements but also by no less than five airfields.

Because VMF 214 was formed at Espiritu Santo and not stateside like most squadrons, it was assigned no aircraft or ancillary personnel. The twenty Corsairs the men flew to Guadalcanal to begin their unit's first combat tour were borrowed planes, many of them in less than satisfactory condition mechanically. The remaining eight pilots, along with Reames and Walton made the trip via an R4D transport plane. Individual gear was stored with the group quartermaster, as each man was allowed to bring just a single handbag of personal items for the entire six-week combat tour. For Chris this meant no barbells and books, just essentials like socks, underwear, trousers, and toilet articles.

As the planes approached Henderson Field, the pilots could easily see that Guadalcanal had recently been the scene of a great, bloody battle. Wrecked Japanese ships and troop barges dotted its shores and surrounding reefs, and parts of the interior jungle had been laid waste by bombs and exploding naval and artillery shells. Most of the men of VMF 214 would remain only a few hours before flying their Corsairs on to the Russell Islands, just a half hour away. The short distance may as well have been a thousand miles, for the Russells were a tropical paradise with coconut palms and pristine white sand beaches surrounded by clear blue water.

The next morning, September 13, the squadron was assigned "Scramble Alert" duty, so Boyington took advantage of having everyone together to give his men a pep talk. He also used the time to make a few suggestions about how to engage enemy fighters while avoiding dogfights, where the Zeros had an advantage because of their superior maneuverability. That evening everyone gathered at the hut shared by Boyington, Walton, and Doc Reames for a little fellowship and singing. By now a casual familiarity was emerging between the squadron commander and his pilots, who called him either by his first name or by "Skipper," "Gramps," or "Grandpappy." It was at this impromptu get-together that the men decided they needed a nickname. Several suggestions were made and rejected, until someone came up with "Boyington's Bastards." The moniker met with near unanimous approval. All the pilots were orphans in the sense that they weren't connected to any other existing squadron when they got together. They hadn't exactly been treated like members of the Marine Corps family either, possessing few reliable planes and no mechanics they could call their own.

Despite the overwhelming popularity of the name, "Boyington's Bastards" were not to be. When Walton presented the pilots' choice at Island Group Headquarters the next day, Captain Jack DeChant, the Marine

Corps public information officer, shook his head and told him it was unacceptable. Civilian newspapers, he logically reasoned, would never print the word "bastard." DeChant then suggested that the squadron might consider using an expression that meant essentially the same thing: "Black Sheep." The change was enthusiastically accepted by the men. Bill Case and some of his fellow pilots were responsible for designing the squadron emblem, a shield containing a rather pathetic-looking, flop-eared black sheep in a circle of stars, crossed by a bar-sinister denoting illegitimacy, topped by a head-on outline of a Corsair. Thus was born the Black Sheep Squadron: a name that would soon became a part of the American collective consciousness due to the extraordinary feats of its pilots and in no small part to the news and publicity efforts of Frank Walton.

The Black Sheep flew their first combat mission on September 14, borrowing four more planes in order to reach their complement of twenty-four. The assignment: escort Army Air Force B-24s on a bombing run targeting the Kahili Air Base at the south end of Bougainville. Anticipation of some real action was running rampant among the pilots as they approached their objective, but it turned out there was little anti-aircraft fire and they were not engaged by any Japanese aircraft. To make matters even worse, most of the bombs dropped by the B-24s missed the air strip altogether, landing in the ocean. A similar escort mission on another target the next day again resulted in no contact with enemy fighters.

The disappointment Chris and his mates must have felt would be short lived, however.

Chapter 4

Wildman

—

For nearly four years—ever since Hitler's troops invaded Poland in the fall of 1939—Chris Magee dreamed of engaging the Axis Powers in aerial combat. His journey to achieve that goal carried him to New Orleans, Canada, Oklahoma, back to Canada, then to Georgia, Florida, Illinois, California, and across the Pacific Ocean to Espiritu Santo, Guadalcanal, and the Russell Islands. On September 16, 1943, he saw his dream come true.

Led by Boyington, the twenty-four Black Sheep Corsairs were assigned the task of flying high cover for Marine SBD Dauntless dive bombers and TBF Avenger torpedo planes in a strike on Ballalae (spelled Ballale by our troops), a well-fortified island in a bay south of Bougainville. The bombers would fly at 13,000 feet, protected by three levels of fighters including New Zealand P-40 Warhawks at 16,000 feet, U.S. Navy Hellcats at 19,000 feet, and the Corsairs maintaining an altitude of 21,000 feet. The rendezvous took place on schedule—early in the afternoon—over New Georgia, and the Allied force moved northward toward Ballalae. As the bombers closed in on their target, the sky was suddenly filled with another kind of aircraft—Zeros—which were attacking from above. The Black Sheep found themselves outnumbered by nearly two-to-one. For the next half hour, a deadly battle raged over some 200 square miles of air space.

Chris would describe his initial combat experience a half century later to Bruce Gamble of the Naval Aviation Museum: "All I could do was keep spinning my neck and looking. You're more or less trying to see what's coming at you rather than what you can get because everything was happening so fast. I think getting through the first combat mission ... helps you to stay alive because things slow down; they don't happen for you at the same speed anymore."

A vivid memory of that day was his first sight of an enemy fighter taking a hit. "Just as I glanced over, it was ... like a fist came down right into the middle of the cockpit of that Zero," he told a Chicago civic group in 1990. "The wings went up, the tail and nose went up and a ball of fire came out of it. And, along with the ball of fire comes a Japanese pilot. Here he is at twelve thousand feet, and he pulls the ripcord right away. He's hanging there is this brown rice-colored suit. This all happens in one instant, then you're gone. When your conceptual activities kick in you realize that somebody had shot him. Then, all of a sudden you're in a tremendous melee—planes going in all directions. You've been trained as a fighter pilot, but you haven't been trained for this kind of speed and action. Your senses are not prepared for this." During the course of the battle Chris was able to attack a Zero and set it afire. He was too busy to see whether it actually crashed, however, so he had to claim a "probable" rather than a "confirmed" kill.

That evening after returning to their Russell Island base, Chris learned that his squadron tallied eleven confirmed and nine probables in the course of the afternoon's action. Of the kills, Begert and Fisher accounted for two apiece while Alexander and McClurg each were credited with one. The big scorer that day—to no one's surprise—was Boyington, who shot down an astounding five enemy aircraft. The Black Sheeps' excitement about their impressive debut performance was tempered considerably, however, when they realized that not everyone had come back. The missing face was that of Flight Officer Bob Ewing, one of the more experienced pilots in the unit. No one had actually seen Ewing go down, and any number of things could have happened to him. All that was certain was that he was officially "missing in action."

The next morning, September 17, after a futile search for Ewing, the Black Sheep planes flew 130 miles northwest to Munda, just off the south coast of northern New Georgia, their new "permanent" base. If the Russells were a tropical paradise, Munda was on the other end of the scale—a real dump. The ground Marines had only recently conquered the island, and Navy Seabees were still putting the final touches on the coral air strip. A few jagged stumps were all that was left of a large coconut grove that had been leveled by bombs and naval guns. Wrecked aircraft were bulldozed away from the runway by the Seabees—out of the way of their construction work. Boyington, Bailey, Reames, and Walton were assigned a sixteen-foot square tent, while all the other pilots were quartered in one hut with very little space between the mosquito netting-equipped bunks. The showers were tin cans with holes punched in them, hung beneath fifty-gallon oil drums filled with rain water. And, there was no shortage of water. Warm rain fell frequently day and night, creating perpetually muddy grounds. Munda was hot, muggy, and full of flies, and there was a smell of death in the air—not all the Japanese bodies were buried yet.

While the men attempted to get some sleep that first steamy night, they were awakened at about 0100 by air raid warning sirens and the loud drone of unsynchronized airplane engines. It was a specially-altered Japanese bomber that had been dubbed "Washing Machine Charlie" because of the sound it made. Charlie usually dropped a few small bombs during his nightly "raids," but these seldom did much damage. His main purpose was not to destroy but to annoy, and he was quite successful that night as all the Marines scrambled for the muddy foxholes until the sound of the noisy engines and their own anti-aircraft fire faded away. An hour and a half later, while most of the Black Sheep were again sleeping in their bunks, Charlie returned and produced the same reaction as before. The men became less fearful of this nightly mischief as the days went by, though, and some—including Chris—even learned to sleep through the warning sirens, then scramble quickly if the bombs started exploding close by.

Despite the disturbances of their first night in Munda, the pilots of VMF 214 rose early on the morning of September 18 to provide air cover for a Navy task force bringing men and supplies for the Marines' beachhead at Barakoma, Vella Lavella. Chris took off with the others but soon noticed that his plane had an oil leak. He returned to base and quickly found another, then got airborne in pursuit of his squadron mates. As he reached Vella Lavella he saw some Corsairs above a cluster of clouds, and moved in to join up. No sooner did he get into the formation when the clouds parted to reveal a large group of Japanese "Val" dive bombers moving toward the American task force unloading supplies off the beach below.

Flying at about ten thousand feet, the Corsairs immediately sprang into action. The bombers were preparing to dive when the fighters caught up to them. Chris got on the tail of one, which quickly pulled up and tried to get away. Even though the Val was unusually quick for a dive bomber it was no match for a Corsair. Chris fired a quick burst into his foe and saw flames spring from the cockpit. He didn't wait around to see if it went into the drink, though. There were at least fifteen more Vals in the group, and all were about to drop their deadly loads on the American ships.

Passing around a large cumulonimbus cloud, he confronted an even larger group of Vals, which were starting to draw anti-aircraft fire from the task force. Chris was now alone, but he attacked with six .50-caliber machine guns blazing. The enemy pilots apparently reasoned that other Corsairs were about to appear through the clouds, because they turned from their intended target and dove away from him. Chris utilized his fighter's superior speed to catch up with the Vals. Levelling off just a few hundred feet above the surface of the ocean, he began to fly "beam" runs, attacking the fleeing planes first from one side then the other, making his Corsair a difficult target for their tail gunners. During the pursuit he noticed several large splashes in the water which he later concluded were bombs being jettisoned by the Vals. How much carnage actually ensued is uncertain, as Chris didn't have time to count his victims. He clearly saw two of the bombers crash into the ocean, though, and was willing to concede that the first one he'd attacked and set afire was a "probable."

Turning for another sweep on the Vals, Chris suddenly heard what he described as "a sound like a hailstorm on a tin roof." He looked up and saw he was being attacked by at least five Zeros, one of which had just fired several machine gun bullets into the rear of his plane. Normally, the smartest thing for a Corsair pilot to do in this situation would be to use his plane's superior power to dive away from the trouble. Chris was practically at sea level, however, so he pointed his Corsair in the direction of the friendly ships and began to "skid and slip around," a defensive maneuver that made it extremely difficult for an enemy to stay on his tail. He didn't get hit again, and the Zeros soon gave up the chase rather than risk getting shot down by the heavy anti-aircraft fire coming from the American vessels.

With the enemy gone, Chris climbed back to 10,000 feet in hopes of joining up with his squadron mates. None were in the area, however, so he chose to fly solo cover above the task force until someone else showed up. Finally, some U.S. Army P-38 Lightnings did come along, and he headed back to Munda, where he gingerly brought his damaged aircraft in for a safe landing despite a flat tire. Afterwards, Chris counted thirty jagged holes from enemy bullets in the tail, fuselage, and wings. Referring to the incident during the interview with Bruce Gamble, he quipped, "They missed all the vital parts, and the most vital of all—me."

News of Chris's derring do spread quickly among the other Black Sheep. The man they called "Maggie" or "Fox" soon acquired still another nickname:"Wildman." Frank Walton—whose air intelligence officer duties included going over official combat reports, studying gun camera films, and debriefing each participating VMF 214 pilot after a mission—was so impressed he decided the heroics merited special recognition.

With Boyington's enthusiastic approval he officially recommended Chris for the Navy Cross, an award second only in prestige to the Congressional Medal of Honor. That Chris had shot down at least two enemy aircraft was noteworthy, but it was because his daring solo attack had caused a large group of bombers to abort their mission—thereby saving countless American lives and preventing costly damage to ships and equipment—that convinced Walton to write up the recommendation. By the time Chris was presented the medal on February 14, 1944, he'd scored nine kills, which among the Black Sheep was second only to his skipper.

Awards ceremony, Espititu Santo, February 14, 1944: Chris (L) with the Navy Cross, Denmark Groover with a Purple Heart
Chris Magee Collection

Chris solidified his Wildman reputation a few days after the run-in with the Vals. He procured a rusty hand grenade from ground Marines based on Vella Lavella and brought it along on a routine patrol over Choiseul. When the assigned mission was over he, Boyington, and the others dropped altitude and went hunting. After using up most of his ammunition on other targets, he spotted a boatload of enemy soldiers crossing a channel and joined with Pappy on a strafing run.

The gunfire didn't stop the boat's progress, so Chris came around again. He was out of bullets, but he still had the grenade. Holding it in his right hand as he moved into position, he gripped the control stick with his left hand and attempted to pull the ringed pin with his teeth, "just like in the movies." Unfortunately, this was real life and he nearly broke a couple of teeth trying to remove the pin from the rusty grenade. Chris was undaunted though, so holding the stick steady between his knees he used both hands to yank the ring free as he approached the vessel from an altitude of less than 100 feet.

When Chris reached his hand out of the cockpit to throw the grenade, the slipstream hit his arm and pushed it backwards, but, as he said later, "It was one of those lucky shots." The "pineapple" exploded where it would do the most damage, a few feet above the deck. The air burst was mistaken for anti-aircraft fire by the nearby Boyington, who shouted over his radio, "They're firing at us." Chris just chuckled, then announced, "Forget it, that was a grenade."

Chris looked forward to getting into the air every day, even though many of the missions he flew were uneventful. Any time spent in the cockpit of a Corsair was preferable to the Black Sheeps' existence on Munda, where rain fell daily and the men fought ongoing battles with pestilence, dysentery, malaria, mildew, mud, and assorted reptiles. They had

Pursuit flier outguesses Japs in Solomons battle

by I. A. McKillop

First Lieutenant Christopher L. Magee, formerly of Revenue Accounts and son of Fred Magee, Fisk Station, has been doing a phenomenal job of fighting Japanese planes in his Corsair pursuit plane.

C. L. Magee

Recently while traveling alone to join his squadron in protecting a naval task force, he encountered 15 Jap dive-bombers, shot down two of them and probably destroyed another before being forced to evade Jap Zeros who were protecting the bombers. Successfully eluding the Zeros, he continued his patrol and finally landed with one flat tire and 30 holes shot in his plane.

On another mission he machine-gunned a barge full of Jap soldiers, then swooped down and with a typical baseball pitch, blew the Japs to pieces with a hand grenade.

Magee's younger brother, Fred, Jr., now stationed with the Fifth Army in Italy, was drafted after 18 unsuccessful attempts to enlist. The boys' brother-in-law, Ensign Gustave Musser, is a naval bomber pilot in the South Pacific.

to survive on a continuous diet of Spam, beans, dehydrated potatoes, and similar delicacies. The nocturnal visits of Washing Machine Charlie did nothing to enhance morale, either.

Chris described his life on Munda in a letter written to Jean Scott at the end of the Black Sheeps' first tour. Jean had only recently moved with her parents to San Francisco.

My Dear Jean:

Strange that I should receive a letter from you today ... I heard from home that you moved to the West Coast, so since I didn't have your new address I was torn between whether to wait until I could get it from home or go ahead and write anyway and depend upon the U.S. mail to see that you got it eventually. You arrived in the nick of time to rescue me from my dilemma. Thanks a lot for the redhead's address. I heard he was in Europe but didn't have the necessary information that would have enabled me to write him ....

I still don't get it. What are you doing in California? Do you want to wake up some morning and find yourself disgustingly healthy? What do you think of "Frisco" (don't let any of the natives see that) as a whole, or should I say hole? Have you seen any of those ancient landmarks the town is famous for? Maybe you're too tired for that stuff .... When we're up at the front we arise at anywhere between the hours of three thirty and four A.M. and don't get back 'til seven that night. After that our time's our own ... so we go to bed. Sometimes the little yellow boys from up the road come down to pay us a visit while we are sleeping and bring a few of their tokens of esteem with them. Then we have one of those friendly little battles with about fifty guys with one thought in their collective minds—who'll get to the foxhole first? About four or five of these episodes in a night, and we get up the next morning (3:30) refreshed and eager to go. Singing like larks we slop thru mud anywhere from six inches to a foot deep, depending or not on whether it rained during the night, and arrive lightheartedly (and a bit light headed) at the mess hall where we partake of a delightful breakfast of powdered eggs, dehydrated potatoes and a choice between powdered milk and water. For some reason that I've never been quite able to understand most of the fellows prefer water, drowning their eggs in copious amounts of the liquid. Oh yes, I forgot to mention that most wonderful treat of all, Spam, the ham that was. If ever there was a dish concocted by man to delight his appetite at an early hour in the morning, SPAM is it. In fact we live only for the ecstatic moment when that prince of foods is laid before us. So great is our joy in meeting that I have seen strong men break down and weep when a plate of dehydrated eggs and Spam was laid before them. The most wonderful thing of all is that we never need to fear running out of the delicacy, for the government has enough of it stored up out here to last a hundred years. On top of that we have no fear of the natives stealing it. Once we found a case of Spam missing, and in the course of hunting the entire island over for our pride and joy we came upon a native village where there was not a soul still alive. In the center of the compound we found the empty box, and strewn in all directions were the empty tins, and beside each was the body of a native. I suppose that when the full realization of their dastardly deed came upon them, they were so filled with remorse that they all took some potion, known only to themselves, and thus paid for their crime against the white brother. The few dogs running around the place seem to ignore the Spam we tempt them with from time to time preferring, it seems, to forage for themselves in the rubbish heaps. But then I never have approved of a dog's sense of what is good to eat and what isn't . . . . To go on with my story, however. After the meal is over we call the cook in and congratulate him on his finesse with pot and pan and award him the medal for proficiency in the culinary arts. After we carry him back to his bunk and put a stake over his eye, we leave for a rendezvous with our waiting aircraft greatly refreshed from our meal and the bit of exercise that the cook had led us in as a finale.

These air raids are something you should see . . . . More casualties are suffered in the mad midnight dashes for the fox holes than ever were from the bombs themselves . . . . The first night we were up at the front everyone was sound asleep in his bunk when the siren blew three times, signifying a red alert, and indicating that Tojo had sent a few of his boys down to look things over and maybe lay a few Japanese firecrackers where they'd do us the least good. Everyone got up and ran, not walked, to the nearest exit. However, all arrived safe and sound at the shelter. No casualties—this time. After standing around for about a half hour waiting for the fun to begin, we were relieved of our anxiety by the all clear signal indicating that the raid had been a false alarm and we could all go back to bed—which we did. It couldn't have been more than a half an hour before the siren wailed its warning again, but this time only a few of the fellows headed dutifully to the fox hole. The rest of us stayed in bed. Tojo wasn't going to fool us again; besides, we needed the sleep if we were to fly the next morning. Just about that time our AA guns began to raise hell nearby. We heard engines high above us, then came the whisper of bombs hurtling down on us. Swiss, swiss, swiss and then pandemonium broke loose in our hut. About fifty guys came tumbling out of their bunks, some wide awake, some half awake, and others still asleep but moving just as fast as anyone else. Awake or asleep, one thought and only one filled their collective minds: get to the fox hole and get there right now!

There were two major battles fought that night: one outside where the AA boomed and the white fingers of the searchlights hunted the skies for the invaders; the other inside our hut where all hell had boiled over, and terror walked thru the darkness as the whispers in the sky grew louder and louder.

That was a night to remember, not only as a lesson in mob psychology but for the little incidents that were later to appear so comical. One of the fellows was christened the "Mole" after that night's trials. When the first wave was almost to the door the leader stumbled over some object on the floor and went down. There was suddenly a big pile up as the mob behind surged forward and in turn tripped and fell over those ahead, but regardless of what position they were in everyone still had only one thought in mind, "Get to the fox hole!" You could never believe unless you actually saw it—the number of positions that people can be in and still be moving. Sideways, backwards, forwards, on their stomachs or on their backs, it made no difference how they were handicapped; everyone was still moving. Later we discovered that the cause of it all was a fellow in an end bunk who only half awake had tumbled out of his bed onto the floor and had been crawling on his hands and knees for the nearest exit when the human tidal wave had overtaken him in the darkness. This was our friend, the future "Mr. Mole." Next morning he was treated for splinters and abrasions, as were several others on the casualty list of the "Battle of the Fox Hole." These were not the only wounded warriors of the midnight scuffle. Others who had their beds too close together also suffered . . . . In such close quarters as we had, this can mean plenty of trouble, and how! Heads smashed together, feet were walked on, and figures flew out of the door with their mosquito netting still draped over their heads and looking for all the world like a band of ghosts fleeing from judgement day. No one groaned, moaned, or even took time out to say such as they were sustaining these injuries. They suffered in stolid silence, true spirit of the fighting man.

The bombs had already hit a safe distance away; long before anyone got near shelter. A great lesson was to be learned from the next morning's box score of the night's casualties: Victims of the night's bombing raid—zero; Victims of the Battle of the Fox Hole—ten.

There is another interesting side to these night bombings. It is the constant feud between the "Christians" and the "non-Christians." Christians are those fox-hole hounds that at the first sound of a siren crawl out of their bunks and make for the shelter where they stand dutifully 'til the all clear has sounded, a fine example of fortitude and patience. An example which is loudly derided by their braver, or is it lazier comrades, the non-Christians who lie in their beds and "sweat out" the raids, that is wait until the AA batteries open up before they seek the refuge of the fox hole. Since most of the alerts are false alarms, the non-Christians get many more hours of sleep or at least rest that their more unfortunate friends go without. But you should hear the howls that come up from the Christians when the Japs do come over and unload their eggs and the non-Christians come tumbling out of their bunks into the fox holes. The patience boys chortle in fiendish glee over the way the tables have turned. Favorite expression at such a time seems to be "Oh, ho, so you've got religion now, eh?" This is the same as "I told you so," and produces the desired effect of quieting the braggadocio of the non-Christians for a few days or at least until the next false alarm when the Christians come trooping sadly back to their beloved sacks.

Well, Jean, my sweet that's about all that this typewriter of mine can take for awhile. Already the keys are smoking dangerously, a warning not to be taken lightly. Right now after the tough job behind him he's in the mood for demanding a letter from you—but quick. As for me, if you don't know, I've been in plenty of fights with the Rah, Rah boys from Tokyo; although that's not quite the way I describe them to my male correspondents. Write soon and give me all the dope you have on hand, if any. Until then, gorgeous, I'll say Adieu, mon cherie. Ah L'Amour, L'Amour, the mother of life and the mistress of the gods. Cupid where is thy fatal sting. Each month, each week, each day, each hour, each minute, each second, each moment have found me waiting, waiting, waiting, waiting, waiting, waiting (gets monotonous, doesn't it!) waiting for that happy moment when I can hold— your neck in my grasp and demand the reason that you waited only five months to drop me a line; and I do mean drop! Ah those nights, those days of loneliness, waiting, waiting—AH NUTS!

> *Best regards and all my love except*
> *my papa, my mama, etc. etc.*
> *Zark*

One of the biggest problems faced by the pilots was the condition of the aircraft. To a man they loved their Corsairs, but the mechanical skills of those who maintained them were—to put it charitably—dubious, at best. There were certainly some competent individuals among the ground crew, but most had simply been recruited from unrelated civilian fields and assigned airplane maintenance duty with little or no training. Chris therefore took it upon himself to learn as much as he could not only about the performance capabilities but also the inner workings of the Corsair. He read every piece of available literature, asked questions of the few mechanics he trusted and, when possible, carefully tested and checked out each plane assigned him before rolling down the runway to take off.

Although Chris got along well with all his squadron mates, he was looked upon by the others as a bit of a free spirit. It was on Munda that he took to wearing a blue and white bandanna around his head. He wore the kerchief to keep the coral dust kicked up by planes on the runway out of his hair, but it soon became his trademark. When the pilots were away from the air strip in their camp he would roll up the bandanna and tie it loosely around his neck. His footwear wasn't exactly government issue either. Chris had "appropriated" a pair of bowling shoes in Espiritu Santo from the personal effects of a pilot killed in action. The set proved far more comfortable and durable than the Marine pilots' standard leather flying boots, which had a tendency to rot quickly in the wet climate of the tropics.

Chris (center) at Munda with two Black Sheep who didn't come home, Bob Alexander (L) and Don Moore (September 1943)   *Chris Magee Collection*

The missions Chris flew during the ten days after his encounter with the bombers over Vella Lavella were mostly routine patrols, and he had no contact with enemy aircraft. He had, however, attacked and set afire the Japanese cargo ship near the coast of Choiseul on September 21 and strafed the Gizo Airfield three days later, as previously mentioned. Some of his comrades encountered Zeros, though, and by September 26 the Black Sheep increased their total score to twenty-three with thirteen probables. The victories were not achieved without cost, however. On a strafing run at the big Kahili Airdrome, Junior Heier—flying farthest inland of a four plane division—tried to avoid a ground explosion and plowed through a palm tree. He managed to keep his plane going as far as Vella Lavella before the engine seized up, and he was forced to bail out into the ocean. Fortunately, he was soon picked up by a group of Seabees in a garbage scow.

"Quill" Groover and Rollie Rinabarger weren't quite so lucky. On September 23, Groover took several hits from attacking Zeros, losing his right aileron and elevator, radio, and several instruments. There were two large holes in his left wing. Worst of all, a shell smashed through the cockpit, breaking his right arm and ankle, leaving that entire side of his body numb. Somehow he managed to shake off the enemy fighters and head home, eventually landing safely on Munda. Doc Reames bandaged him up, and put him on a plane to the U.S. Naval Hospital on Guadalcanal.

Rinabarger was attacked from the rear while flying high cover over a bomber strike on Kahili, Sunday, September 26, and he took a bullet in his left hip. He nursed his damaged Corsair back to Munda, but oil on the windshield blocked his vision causing him to misjudge the runway. His right wing crashed into a parked grader, and the plane spun and rolled over. Because of the seriousness of his wounds, Rollie was evacuated to New Zealand to recover.

Least fortunate of all, though, was Red Harris, lost in action September 27 during an air battle pitting Bill Case and himself against some forty Zeros who were attacking American bombers. The two had become separated from a group of ten Black Sheep off southern Bougainville after a scrambling encounter with enemy planes and a fifteen minute storm. Harris was a newlywed, and his bride had watched him sail away from San Diego just three months before.

On September 29, Chris was called into the ready tent along with Bruce Matheson and Jim Hill. There they were introduced by Walton to a civilian named George Weller, a war correspondent from a Chicago newspaper. He had been en route to Australia, but he was forced to land at Munda due to inclement weather. During a conversation with Walton—the Black Sheeps' unofficial public information officer—he learned that three of the pilots were from Chicago, and asked to meet them. Weller interviewed all three, taking pages of notes, then decided to chat with several of their comrades as well. Later, he wrote a series of syndicated articles about the Black Sheep that appeared in newspapers across the country. He also filed several stories about the Chicago residents for his own paper, which resulted in close friendships forming between Fred and Marie Magee and the parents of Matheson and Hill.

The Black Sheep received orders that evening to return to the Russell Islands the following afternoon, a cause for celebration. A strange and sobering occurrence, that final September morning of 1943, took the air out of their party balloons, however. Stan Bailey, Burney Tucker, and Bob Alexander were returning from a routine dawn patrol when they spotted four boats off the tiny island

Windy City warriors (L to R) Bruce Matheson, Jim Hill, and Chris in a photo that appeared frequently in Chicago area newspapers from fall 1943 through spring 1944   *Chris Magee Collection*

of Sosoruana, near Kolombangara, and moved in for a closer look. Flight leader Bailey told the others over the radio to wait for his word before attacking. As the trio of Corsairs came in on a low level approach, he recognized the craft as being American PT boats and quickly advised Tucker and Alexander. Bailey and Tucker then pulled up, but Alexander kept going. Whether he didn't receive the message for some reason or accidentally triggered his guns will always remain a mystery. What is known is that Alex opened fire on the nearest boat, killing three crewmen, and the PTs shot back. The handsome and popular young Iowan's plane was hit, then crashed onto a Kolombangara beach and slid into the dense jungle. Chris took the loss of Alex philosophically. The two became friends on *Rochambeau* and remained close, but war leaves little opportunity for mourning.

Two months later, after Kolombangara was secured, Tucker led a group of Black Sheep that included Boyington, Walton, and three others to the site where Alexander's plane had disappeared into the jungle. Ironically, a PT boat from Vella Lavella carried them to the location. Despite a tropical downpour, Tucker knew exactly where to look. Once ashore it took the men just a few minutes to hack their way with machetes through the dense jungle growth to the remains of the plane and of Alex. They buried him in a shallow grave between a circle of white rocks brought up from the beach, making certain his head was pointed toward Tokyo—the ultimate destination of American forces. Then, in a simple but poignant ceremony, Boyington lined up his troops at attention on either side of the makeshift grave and led them in a farewell salute. "So long, Alex," was all he could say.

The Black Sheep would stay in the Russells for just one week, but it was a welcome reprieve from Munda. There was plenty of good food and clean clothing, and six bags of mail—the first they had seen since leaving Espiritu Santo nearly three weeks before. At night, the men could watch movies in an outdoor theater or get together for singalongs.

Chris flew just one mission during his stay in the Russells, a "fighter sweep" over Kahili. Boyington was, perhaps, the first Marine squadron commander to employ this tactic in the South Pacific. The fighter sweep was not an original concept; in fact, it was common practice in World War I.

Prays for Fighting Sons

Mrs. Marie Magee, 919 E. 50th st., prays for safety of her sons who are in action half-way around globe from each other. In pictures are her boys, Marine Lieut. Pilot Chris (left), in the South Pacific, and Fred Jr., with the Fifth Army in Italy.

Boyington's idea was to reduce the number of fighter aircraft the Japanese would have available to send up against American bombers by having his Corsairs goad them into battle. It was aerial combat in the purest sense, with no bombers to get in the way. On the October 4th fighter sweep, some thirty Zeros took off from Kahili to meet the challenge. Boyington, leading a Black Sheep sextet, attacked and shot down three Zeros in the space of thirty seconds, an amazing feat of airmanship. The remaining Japanese planes quickly turned tail and headed back to their base.

On October 7, the Black Sheep returned to Munda. Chris had no real opportunities to engage enemy fighters during the first week back, but others were more fortunate. Ed Olander got his first confirmed kill—he already had three probables—on October 10. Bill Case got his third with the Sheep and fourth overall a day later.

The squadron was reduced by one on October 13. Virgil Ray took off on what can only be called a "milk run," an errand to Guadalcanal and the Russells. He left the Russells late that afternoon for the forty-five-minute hop to Munda, but never got there. A storm developed during the flight, and likely contributed to his loss. An extensive sea and land search was carried out by all available planes the next day, but Ray was never found. During the search, Bill Case and Tom Emrich were scrambled to intercept Japanese aircraft north of Vella Lavella. Both would engage the enemy, with Emrich scoring a probable and Case getting his fifth confirmed kill—making him the Black Sheeps' second ace.

Nearly a month had passed since his heroics over Vella Lavella when, on October 17, Chris finally was presented with an opportunity to increase his score. By now he had been given the responsibility of "division leader," and headed up a contingent of four planes. The trio of pilots that made up the rest of his group usually consisted of Jim Hill, Bob McClurg, and Junior Heier. Chris was one of fourteen Black Sheep who joined with seven pilots from another Marine squadron for a fighter sweep that day. Boyington had come up with a clever strategy: send four Corsairs in at a low level to attract the Zeros while seventeen more followed unseen, high in the clouds. As it turned out, no less than fifty-five enemy planes rose to the bait, and Pappy and his boys pounced on them with a vengeance.

The Marines scored twenty confirmed kills and a number of probables during the forty-minute fray—the action was too fast and furious to keep track of the probables. Boyington, as usual, was top gun with three kills, but Chris, Heier, and Burney Tucker each knocked down two. John Bolt, Bruce Matheson, and Ed Olander got one apiece. All twenty-one American planes returned to base, although the ones belonging to Matheson, Ed Harper, and Don Moore were damaged by enemy gunfire. Harper, who along with Matheson had received minor injuries, was forced to make a belly landing when his landing gear wouldn't come down.

The afternoon of next day, October 18, when Boyington waged a war of words over Kahili with an unknown English-speaking enemy on the ground, is one none of the eleven Black Sheep or eight VMF 221 pilots who were there could forget. Chris certainly didn't. Knowing that the Japanese listened in on the American radio frequencies, Pappy challenged them to "come up and fight." When his foe countered with "why don't you come down, Major Boyington?" he did as asked, swooping down solo over the airfield and spraying it with .50-caliber bullets while anti-aircraft fire erupted all around him. Pappy climbed back up to join his fellow pilots, then goaded his foes again: "Now come up and fight, you dirty yellow bastards!" It was too much for the commanders of the Japanese

CHICAGOAN BAGS 3 JAP FIGHTERS IN 3 MINUTES

U. S. HDQ. IN SOUTH PACIFIC Oct. 22 (AP).—Two marine fighters with a net bag of four Japanese planes in as many minutes, became aces during an attack by 19 American planes on Kahili airdrome, Bougainville Island, Monday.

Lt. Christopher Magee of Chicago shot down three Zeros in 3 minutes to bring his score to seven. He was flying upside down when he got his first plane. Lt. Paul Mullen of Pittsburgh blasted his fifth Jap plane into the sea off Bougainville.

Magee and Mullen are members of Maj. Gregory Boyington's "Black Sheep" squadron. Boyington in the same raid raised his total to 20, highest among flyers now active in the South Pacific.

Lt. James J. Hill of 6214 North Richmond avenue, Chicago, shot down his first enemy plane in the Bougainville sweep.

fighter squadrons to accept lying down. To refuse to engage the Americans would have meant a loss of face their code of honor wouldn't permit.

The American pilots circled patiently above the clouds as one by one the Zeros took off and began to climb toward them. When there were about forty of the "meatballs" in the air, Boyington gave the order to unleash the dogs of war. Chris got his first Zero of the day on his initial pass across a climbing Japanese formation. As he turned for a second run, he spotted another enemy diving away from a tangle of planes. Chris dove after the Zero, followed it until it started to pull up, then destroyed it with a quick, deadly burst of machine gun fire. He climbed back into the fray, which was turning into a mad scramble, and soon found himself behind another "Zeke" (Zero). The Japanese pilot was apparently unaware there was a Corsair on his tail, because he made no effort to use his fighter's legendary agility to evade the attack. Chris pressed his firing button, sending the adversary spinning down in flames, and tallied his third score of the afternoon. Following a fifteen minute pounding that saw them lose eighteen of their number, the remaining Japanese aircraft scattered to the four winds. One pilot from VMF 221 was missing in action, but all eleven

Black Sheep returned safely. Several of them scored kills, including Boyington—his twentieth—and Jim Hill, who got his first.

Bill Case racked up his seventh victory of the tour and eighth overall—second only to Boyington in the squadron—but he would remember the day for another reason. Because of his diminutive stature, "Casey" usually raised his seat to the maximum level for better vision. However, with his third and final Pacific tour about to conclude he decided at the last moment to "play it safe." Prior to taxiing down the runway for takeoff, he tried to lower the seat a few notches to give himself added protection from the immovable armored seat back. As luck would have it, the seat got stuck about halfway between where he was and where he wanted to be.

During the pitched battle over Kahili, Case was looking for his second kill when a Zero slipped behind him and opened fire. One of the bullets passed through the rear of the cockpit and grazed the top of his helmet before shattering the front windshield. The force of the bullet knocked his head forward. "I would have been killed if I were sitting just a half inch higher," he later said. "And, if the bullet had missed me completely, my head would have stayed up and the glass would have come back into my eyes."

It would be Casey's last combat sortie. There was only one day left in his tour, and Boyington reasoned the young pilot had used up all the luck allotted to him. Case saw his narrow escape as more than mere luck. In the years to come he told anyone who would listen that only divine intervention could have caused his seat to jam in the position it did.

That evening, the men of VMF 214 learned that their relief squadron had arrived. Doc Reames broke out his supply of "medicinal" brandy, and the Black Sheep celebrated. The party took place in a large Quonset hut, a modern convenience that the Seabees had recently erected. The pilots rehashed the day's action, sang a few of their favorite songs, and mostly talked about Sydney, Australia, where all would soon be going for a well-deserved week of R&R. It was two o'clock in the morning before the last of the partygoers straggled to their bunks.

Tent mates Boyington, Walton, and Reames were rudely awakened by an operations officer from Group Headquarters at 0345. He informed them that four pilots were needed to strafe the airdromes at Kahili and Kara, where a reconnaissance report said bombers were massing for an early morning raid. Walton angrily suggested that there was, after all, a relief squadron available, but the officer cited the new unit's lack of familiarity with the area. Boyington didn't argue; he simply woke up his pilots and had them all muster in front of his tent, then asked for volunteers. The groggy men had difficulty understanding the skipper's request, and there was no response at first. Then Pappy grumbled, "I guess I'll have to do this alone." He never would have asked any of his men to do something he was not willing to do himself.

"You're not going without me, Greg," Chris said as he stepped forward, and Bob McClurg quickly followed. Several other sleepy pilots raised their hands as well, and Pappy selected George Ashmun as the fourth man. Chris and Don Moore had often discussed the efficacy of night raids and even presented their ideas to the skipper. Boyington was enthusiastic about the tactic, but his bosses had always vetoed the plans—until now.

The four Corsairs took off from Munda at 0450 and immediately encountered a severe tropical storm. They switched on their wing lights in an attempt to maintain visual contact, but the poor night visibility and high winds caused Ashmun to become separated from the others. When his efforts to relocate his three comrades proved futile, George decided to make a strafing run on the Ballalae fighter airdrome for lack of anything better to do. Despite having to maintain radio silence in order not to alert the Japanese, the remaining three were able to stay together all the way to Bougainville. There Boyington signaled the others with a wave of his wings, turned out his lights and headed up the foggy coast alone toward Kahili.

With McClurg on his wing, Chris flew inland and, after circling for a few minutes, managed to find Kara despite the low, 800-foot ceiling caused by the fog. Using hand signals, the pair soon got their bearings, then began a strafing run directly above the runway in the half-light of early morning. Dropping below the tops of the trees to avoid detection by anti-aircraft batteries, the two Corsairs were about midway down the strip when Chris saw a flash just off to one side and above the tree level. It came from the control tower, and he realized that had either he or McClurg been slightly out of position one or both of them could easily have run into it. Soon, they sighted the fully loaded bombers lined up on the end of the runway and proceeded to turn several of them into blazing infernos with well-aimed incendiary loads from their machine guns. In his post-mission briefing, Chris estimated the enemy losses as "five or six," while McClurg claimed "at least ten." Walton's official intelligence assessment based upon aerial reconnaissance photos taken later that day indicated eight bombers destroyed.

Because of the surprise attack and the low level at which they were flying, the AA fire was completely ineffective against the Marine fighters. It wasn't until the duo cleared land and were over the ocean that they faced any real peril. That's when the big enemy shore batteries began to open up on them, employing a tactic that both sides sometimes used against aircraft flying close to the water. The shells were aimed not at the speedy Corsairs but at the water's surface, where they would explode and throw huge "geysers" several hundred feet into the air. Such was the size and force of these giant walls of water, that one of them could easily knock a fighter plane out of the sky. The two pilots were quick to identify the danger, though, and climbed to a higher, safer altitude.

Chris found out later that Boyington was successful in locating Kahili in the fog, and, despite heavy ground fire, destroyed three bombers parked on the end of that strip. The squadron had to wait several hours to hear the skipper's report, however. It seems Pappy decided to make a side trip to Vella Lavella after learning someone had a bottle of booze waiting for him there.

Six of the Black Sheeps' eight aces pose in front of a Corsair in this publicity photo (total confirmed kills for each are in parentheses after their names). Standing (L to R) Paul Mullen (6 1/2), John Bolt (6), Bob McClurg (7). Kneeling (L to R) Ed Olander (5), Chris (9), Don "Mo" Fisher (6). Bolt would shoot down six MiGs during the Korean War, making him the Marine Corps' only two-war ace

Courtesy of Fred Losch

Their first tour complete, the Black Sheep flew their Corsairs back to the Russells on October 20 and rode a transport plane to Espiritu Santo two days later. The new camp contrasted sharply with Munda. It was located in a picturesque coconut grove, and the ground was covered with green grass instead of mud. The men were quartered in small groups in spacious, comfortable Dallas huts rather than a single overloaded facility. There were paved roads, a clean sandy beach, plenty of good food, an occasional USO band for entertainment on the other side of the island, and no mosquitoes.

For Chris, the return to Espiritu Santo also meant an opportunity to catch up on his reading and weight training, as that was where he'd been forced to store his books and barbells when the Black Sheep were sent to the forward bases.

One of Chris's most notable eccentricities, and the subject of considerable discussion among his comrades, was his choice of daytime apparel at the back area camp. He always seemed to be wearing the same pair of blue bathing trunks. Some speculated that he never took them off. Eventually, much to his consternation, the swim wear was stolen from his locker and reportedly buried for "hygienic reasons." Although the identity of the thief, or thieves, was never revealed, most of the pilots seemed to think Junior Heier was a likely culprit.

Only a run-in between Boyington and his group commander—a fat lieutenant colonel they called "Lard"—marred the men's enjoyment of Espiritu Santo. Lard fancied himself a "spit and polish" Marine and was determined to harass the squadron leader. His distaste for the casual, fun-loving Pappy dated back to well before the Black Sheep Squadron was formed.

When Lard pulled a surprise inspection on the VMF 214 camp at midnight of the very day they arrived, he chastised the weary Boyington for the encampment's slovenly appearance—a condition created by its just-departed former occupants—and the lack of mosquito netting over the bunks (there were no mosquitoes). The pilots picked up the grounds, then the next morning gave all the huts a thorough cleaning, and even set up the unnecessary mosquito nets. By afternoon the place was pristine. Lard still gave Boyington low marks on his next fitness report, noting "this officer is a good combat pilot, but can't command men because of his drinking."

In early November, Chris and his mates prepared to move out, again. This time, though, they wouldn't be taking any Corsairs. Their long awaited week of rest and recuperation in Sydney was about to begin.

Chapter 5

Sydney and the Second Tour

⌣

T o an American fighter pilot who had just completed a six-week combat tour, never certain that each dawning day wasn't going to be his last, a trip to Sydney took on the same sort of significance as a pilgrimage of the faithful.

Walton, Doc Reames, and the two dozen surviving pilots of the Black Sheep Squadron, including recently reinstated casualties Quill Groover and Rollie Rinabarger, packed themselves into two transport planes in the wee hours of the morning. During the almost 1,700 mile southern journey—which included a brief refueling stop in New Caledonia—the pilots had to virtually fly as cargo among bags, packages, and crates as well as their own gear. There were no seats, and the noise of the twin engines was so loud as to make conversation extremely difficult. It was up to each man to make himself as comfortable as possible during the twelve-hour trip. Chris, who could and frequently did snooze through midnight air raid warning sirens, had no problem getting his beauty rest and arrived at Sydney's airport refreshed and ready to paint the town—not that a lack of sleep was going to keep any of the Black Sheep from enjoying their first evening in Australia.

It was the policy of the Marine Corps to send its South Pacific island-based pilots to Sydney after each six-week combat tour—the other services had somewhat similar programs—but the Black Sheep saw the trip as a reward for surviving both the Japanese and Munda. Those completing their

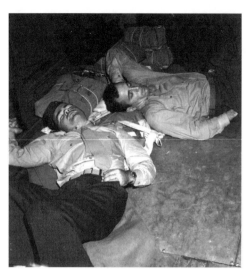

Despite less than luxurious accommodations on board the R4D Dakota, Chris (R) and Bill Case manage to nap during the long flight from Espiritu Santo to Sydney, Australia (November 1943)

Chris Magee Collection

second or third tours were, of course, already familiar with the pleasures awaiting them in the sprawling, modern city that contained some 1.5 million people. The Aussies hadn't forgotten that the U.S. Pacific Fleet had stopped the progress of the Japanese Navy at the Battle of the Coral Sea early in 1942, likely saving their continent from an invasion, and most of them welcomed the presence of the American servicemen.

For weeks, the veterans of previous Sydney visits filled the heads of the first timers with the glories of the great cosmopolitan city, especially its women. One of the better pieces of advice passed along and heeded by even non-smokers like Chris was to pack as many cartons of name brand American cigarettes as would fit in a parachute bag. The "coffin nails" were probably the hottest barter items in Australia. Although no one was supposed to take any more than what was considered necessary for personal use, most brought along about twenty cartons.

November was spring in the Land Down Under, an ideal time for sightseeing and taking in the beaches, the nightlife, and all the other attractions offered in Sydney. To ensure their enjoyment, Chris, Jim Hill, and Bob McClurg got together and rented the second floor rooms of a local residence. The Black Sheep had been warned about restrictions banning liquor and late night partying in the hotels, so most chose to lease rooms or apartments for the entire week.

American service personnel usually stayed in the King's Cross district of the city because that was where the action was. And nowhere was it greater than in the squadron's unofficial headquarters, the lobby and bar of the Australia Hotel where dozens and perhaps hundreds of eligible young women would flock every afternoon to enjoy the company of the "Yanks."

Holding court at this legendary watering hole—known throughout the Pacific Theater as the "passion pit"—was the equally legendary bartender, Frieda, a buxom fortyish gal known for her affability and quick wit. Frieda had a soft spot for American pilots in general and Marines in particular. She would even tolerate the boys' favorite bar game: trying to see who could toss the most Australian pennies in the big bowl lamps that hung from the ceiling. Unfortunately, city ordinances stated that hotels couldn't serve liquor after dark, so men who wanted to continue drinking had to relocate to one of the King's Cross nightclubs or purchase spirits and retire to their rented digs to party.

During an evening when several of the Black Sheep got together at one of the nightclubs, Chris stepped into the men's room and discovered an inebriated Boyington getting the worst of it in an altercation with two Army pilots. He immediately came to the aid of his squadron commander and dispatched both of his foes. Pappy often became belligerent when he got drunk and likely had instigated the fight, but that didn't matter to Chris. He did what any of the Black Sheep would have done in the sky or on the ground—protect his skipper.

It wasn't the only time Chris intervened to keep a drunken Boyington from hurting himself or others. Once, while returning in a crowded weapons carrier with several of his men from an Espiritu Santo officers' club, Pappy suddenly began waving a large bayonet. As the others backed away from their squadron commander, Chris grabbed his wrist and gave it a quick, hard twist, causing the weapon to drop harmlessly to the floor.

Like most of their comrades Magee, Hill, and McClurg had no wives or fiancees waiting for them back home, and they soon found very pleasant female companionship in Sydney. Chris and Jim dated a classy pair of sisters who were daughters of one of the city's leading politicians, and were invited to dinner at the family's big, lavish home. Chris and his favorite Aussie girlfriend Pat would get together again after the Black Sheeps' second tour.

Pat, Chris's favorite companion in Sydney (c. 1943)

Chris Magee Collection

The only occurrence that may have slightly marred an otherwise wonderful week was when Chris and his buddies decided to rent a car. They
put down a deposit of two hundred Australian dollars on a rather odd-
looking automobile the proprietor of the seedy rental office insisted was
roadworthy. Their first sight of the vehicle, which was powered by a primi-
tive, two-cycle engine that employed an external coke burner, should have
aroused the pilots' suspicions. It appeared to be of less value than the deposit. Chris had only recently learned to operate an auto, but since neither
of his companions felt comfortable about driving on the left side of the
road he took the wheel. Somehow, the car seemed to drive well enough to
get them where they wanted to go, which turned out to be a nearby bar.

After enjoying a beer or two with the locals, the three Marines stepped
back outside to discover the car was gone. When they returned to the bar
in dismay, their newfound drinking buddies were quick to advise them that
certain fly-by-night car rental agencies were known to perpetrate a con on
unknowing Americans. After leaving the rental site, customers would be
followed until they got out of the automobile, then the vehicles would be
"stolen" and returned to the rental agent. Thus, the client would lose his
deposit, and the unscrupulous agency could rent the same car to some
other poor sucker the next day.

The pilots soon found a cab and headed back to the agency. The proprietor, of course, wasn't about to admit to the con. However, after McClurg
advised him that his formidable buddy Magee had been "muscle" for the
Chicago mob and was ready to trash the office and anyone working there,
he had a change of heart and gave them another car.

Seven days passed all too quickly, and the twenty-six fun-weary Black
Sheep soon found themselves on a long transport flight back to Espiritu
Santo. Major changes awaited them upon arrival. Five of the pilots—Bailey,
Begert, Bourgeois, Case, and McCartney—had completed the required
three combat tours and were transferred to a squadron about to be rotated
back to the States. The Corps had recently instituted a new policy that
called for each squadron to carry a complement of forty pilots, instead of
twenty-six. Therefore on November 19, 1943, VMF 214 welcomed twenty-
one new faces, enough to not only replace the five men who transferred and
the four who had been lost in action, but also to fill the added billets.

Major Pierre Carnagey, a blond, solidly built native of South Dakota
who had been named for his home town, replaced Stan Bailey as executive
officer. He was a graduate of the University of Southern California and had

one previous combat tour. Major Henry Miller, a veteran of two tours in the old VMF 214 Swashbucklers, was the new flight officer. The Pennsylvania law school graduate quickly acquired the nickname "Notebook" because of his propensity for taking notes on almost everything. Others with combat experience were a tall, handsome Nebraskan, J. Cameron Dustin; Gelon Doswell, who had attended Tulane and had a wife and baby daughter in New Orleans; Fred Avey, who'd served in the RCAF and was, at thirty-one, the only Black Sheep pilot older than Boyington; Jimmy Brubaker, a twenty-one-year-old Floridian whose brother—a B-17 bombardier—was shot down over Germany the day Jimmy departed San Diego for the South Pacific; and Bruce Ffoulkes, a San Mateo, California, native who'd attended Stanford for three-and-one-half years prior to joining the Corps.

Beginning their first tour were Henry "Red" Bartl from Sacramento, California; Glenn Bowers, a former Penn State zoology major whose wife was expecting their second child; John Brown, a big, easy going ex-football player at Purdue; Rufus "Mack" Chatham, who had attended Texas A&M for three years; Ned Corman, a Penn State grad and soccer star; Bill Crocker of Worcester, Massachusetts; Bill Hobbs, a married Missourian who had attended his home state's university in Columbia; Herb Holden, a resident of New Jersey and graduate of Williams College; likeable, easy-going Perry Lane of Rutland, Vermont; feisty Fred Losch, a wiry, darkly handsome lad from western Pennsylvania; Marion "Rusty" March, who called Seattle home, but was a graduate of Stanford where he'd been a member of the track team; and Al Marker from Park Ridge, Illinois, who at twenty-one was one of the youngest of the Black Sheep. There were also two guys named Johnson among the new group: Al, a diminutive former New York University student known for his witty retorts; and Harry, a long, lean Alabaman from Birmingham whose accent rivaled even Doc Reames and earned him the title "Second Vice President of the Yamheads." Not surprisingly, the two Johnsons were dubbed "Shorty" and "Skinny" by the other pilots.

The pasty-faced Doswell, who always appeared in need of a transfusion, was another who soon received a nickname—"Corpuscle." Perhaps the most intriguing handle of all, though, was inadvertently bestowed upon Losch by Matheson. After seeing the skinny, deeply tanned newcomer seated cross-legged and shirtless on the floor of a hut and commenting that he looked like an Indian fakir, Mat jokingly asked Losch when he was going to perform his rope trick. The name stuck, and Fred was thereafter called "Rope Trick" or simply "Rope" by the other Black Sheep, although

Chris sometimes used the term "El Ropo." Losch would become one of Chris's closest friends in the months to come. Despite their vastly different backgrounds, the two shared a similar fighting spirit, and the twenty-two-year-old no doubt looked upon the older, combat seasoned "Maggie" as a role model of sorts.

Well aware of the squadron's reputation, the new men were excited about becoming Black Sheep. All had been trained in Corsairs and were looking forward to their indoctrination in Boyington's highly aggressive combat tactics. Unfortunately, their plans were put on hold by the skipper's old nemesis Lard, who decided to "ground" the quadruple ace and send him to Vella Lavella as group operations officer.

Pappy wasn't about to take this slap in the face lying down, however, so with Walton's encouragement he went over his group commander's head and directly to Major General James T. Moore, Assistant Commanding General of the First Marine Aircraft Wing. The general, it turned out, was never informed about Lard's orders for Boyington, and became highly incensed. Boyington had not only more than justified the confidence Moore placed in him by leading VMF 214 to a remarkable combat record, but also was becoming a "media darling" throughout the United States. The up-shot of the whole sordid affair was that Pappy left for Vella Lavella a few days later still in command of the Black Sheep, and Lieutenant Colonel Lard himself was ordered to take the operations officer job, normally a major's billet.

Shortly before departing for their new forward base, Chris, Jim Hill, and some of the other Black Sheep travelled to another part of Espiritu Santo near the naval base to watch a USO band perform. They were pleased to find several U.S. Navy nurses present in the hut where the band was playing. The women apparently were being transported to or from a South Pacific hospital facility, and their plane made an overnight stop at the island. It was likely to be the only opportunity the men would have to fraternize with the opposite sex outside of Australia, so Chris—an exceptionally good dancer—quickly selected an attractive partner and headed for what was being used as a dance floor. His enjoyment was soon interrupted, however, by a drunken, rather obnoxious Navy officer who insisted on trying to cut in. Neither Chris nor the young lady appreciated the persistent overtures, so when the Navy man decided to challenge the husky Marine to fight, he was happy to oblige. The fracas—if one could call it that—lasted just long enough for Chris to land a hard combination that left the gob sprawling on the floor. After the man's friends dragged him away, Chris returned to his dance partner and had a most enjoyable evening.

The second combat tour barely got underway before the Black Sheep lost two of its members for health reasons. When the transport plane carrying them to their new base on Vella Lavella made a stopover at Guadalcanal's Henderson Field, Rollie Rinabarger collapsed and was ordered to the island's hospital by Doc Reames. Realizing the young man had not allowed himself sufficient time to recover from the injuries he'd received on the first tour, Reames insisted Rollie be evacuated to New Zealand, then sent home. Not long after that incident, newcomer Al Marker suffered a broken arm in a crash landing. Over his strong protests he was shipped back to a rear area hospital, missing the rest of the tour.

Although the climatic conditions were similar to those on Munda—hot and humid—Vella Lavella was a far more hospitable place, with friendly natives eager to trade and an abundance of tropical fruit. Headquarters supplied the squadron with an ice flaking machine, so the men could enjoy cool, fresh limeade at every meal. The Seabees had blasted out the coastal edge of a large coconut grove that bordered Vella Bay and built an excellent coral runway for the pilots to use. Vella Lavella was at that time the most forward of the Solomons air bases, just 75 miles from the Kahili Airdrome and less than 400 from Fortress Rabaul on New Britain.

A group of Black Sheep gather at VMF 214s Vella Lavella camp site. Kneeling in front (L to R) Bruce Matheson, Burney Tucker, Harry Johnson. Others (L to R) are Perry Lane, Denmark Groover, Ed Olander, Bob McClurg, Jim Reames (in front of McClurg), Glen Bowers, Fred Losch, Ned Corman, Jim Hill, Bill Hobbs, Chris, Ed Harper   *Chris Magee Collection*

Not long after arriving at their new base, the Black Sheep received a surprise shipment of unusual cargo: St. Louis Cardinal baseball caps. Earlier, in what must be considered a true masterstroke in the history of military public relations, Walton wrote to the office of the Commissioner of Baseball asking for assistance. In the letter he explained that due to the rapid attrition caused by severe humidity, the squadron had run out of the sun shading ball caps they usually wore around camp. Walton then made a seemingly audacious proposal: the Black Sheep would shoot down one enemy plane for every cap sent them by a major league team. The publicity-savvy Cardinal organization agreed to furnish the headgear, although by the time the first twenty caps arrived Boyington and Co. had already accounted for forty-eight Japanese aircraft.

The first three weeks at Vella Lavella proved uneventful. Marines had landed on Bougainville on November 1, and were engaged in heavy fighting for almost a month, but thus far the Japanese had chosen not to contest the skies over that embattled island. Business began to pick up again one day in early December when the ground Marines requested air support to help reduce the deadly Japanese artillery and mortar fire that was making

In this publicity photo for the Caps for Zeros promotion, Chris (L) is presenting St. Louis Cardinal baseball caps to Greg "Pappy" Boyington in exchange for a like number of Japanese flag stickers used to symbolize each confirmed "kill" of an enemy aircraft
Chris Magee Collection

life miserable at their hard-won beachhead. The Black Sheep were more than happy to comply, making eight highly effective strafing runs that laid waste to countless enemy positions and personnel. Buoyed by that success, the flying Marines were determined to do everything they could to ease the burden of the "mud" Marines. After completing an unexciting patrol or escort mission, the pilots would take it upon themselves to go hunting around Bougainville for enemy targets rather than heading directly back to Vella Lavella. Nothing that belonged to the Japanese was safe. Ships, barges, anti-aircraft positions, troop encampments, bridges, and trucks all came under barrages of machine gun fire from "whistling death," the name enemy troops hung on those swift Corsairs.

VMF 214 Corsair in flight over South Pacific (early 1944)   *Chris Magee Collection*

From Vella Lavella, Marine aviators were within fighter range of Rabaul, but the armed forces bureaucracy had decreed that the island of New Britain was in a different "area of responsibility," thereby preventing the Black Sheep from striking the biggest Japanese stronghold in the South Pacific. Boyington was persistent, however, and finally convinced Air Command Headquarters to send a dispatch to General MacArthur requesting the area lines be revised. On December 16, the Black Sheep got the orders they wanted, and the next day Boyington led a strike force of eighty U.S. Marine, Navy, and New Zealand Air Force planes in a fighter sweep at the very heart of the enemy's air power. As luck would have it, the Japanese fighters refused to come out and play that day. Neither a disappointed Pappy nor Chris had any opportunities to increase their scores. A few enemy "strays" were out on patrol when the Americans arrived, however, and they were quickly pounced upon. Don Moore registered two kills, and Bob McClurg added another.

With heavily-fortified Rabaul now the prime target, Chris and Moore found themselves discussing contingency plans for a worst-case scenario where an aircraft was so seriously damaged by enemy fire that return to home base was impossible. The conventional wisdom had been to fly as far as possible in the direction of friendly territory, then parachute or ditch in the ocean and pray that an American seaplane or surface vessel got to you before the Japanese did. Since it was unlikely any potential rescuers would dare stray within two hundred miles or so of Rabaul, Chris suggested that the best chance for survival might be in the jungles of New Britain. If a pilot's worst nightmare should occur, he would fly as deep into the big island's interior as possible, bail out, then try to find a coast watcher who could radio allied forces and, perhaps, arrange for his escape. Chris had learned through intelligence reports of the contribution these unsung heroes—mostly Australians—were making to the war effort, including stories of missing-in-action pilots rescued at night by submarines after coded information had been radioed by coast watchers.

The Black Sheep would get another shot at Rabaul on December 23, when they were assigned along with U.S. Navy F6F Hellcats and Army Air Force P-38 Lightnings to escort two dozen B-24s in a bombing raid of the base and its harbor. The task force was divided into two groups of forty-eight fighters each. Six Black Sheep led by their executive officer Pierre Carnagey flew as low cover for the bombers as part of the first wave, while Boyington and nine others, including Chris, were to act as rear guard for the return trip.

The strike didn't go as planned. The rendezvous with the bombers was a half-hour late. When the formation reached New Britain and was pounced upon by Zeros, many of the fighters were out of position. In the intense battle that ensued, Carnagey and Jimmy Brubaker were both lost trying to protect the bombers. Additional carnage was likely prevented by Boyington's group, which was only fifteen minutes behind instead of the scheduled forty-five, thanks to the earlier delay. Chris got his eighth kill during the combat and Henry Miller scored his first. Bolt and McClurg moved into the "ace" category that day with two each, a number equalled by Heier, while Boyington shot down four Zekes, putting him at twenty-four—just two behind all-time Marine leader Joe Foss. The cost was high, however. In addition to Carnagey and Brubaker, Bruce Ffoulkes also failed to return to Vella Lavella.

On Christmas Eve, the Black Sheep celebrated with "milk punch," an eggnog-like concoction made from powdered eggs and milk, along with whiskey purchased in Sydney, and a few other ingredients. Chris wasn't scheduled for the fighter sweep the next day, but the eight who did tangled with forty Zeros and accounted for four more kills. What made Christmas Day really special for the squadron, though, was that all returned safely.

Chris was assigned escort duty on December 27, while Boyington was put in tactical command of large-scale sweep over Rabaul's Lakunai Airdrome. Once again all VMF 214 participants returned without mishap, this time with six more victories. Mo Fisher led the Black Sheep with two, giving him a total of six and making him the squadron's sixth ace. Boyington, Avey, and Harper managed singles, as did Mullen, who now had five-and-a-half, enough to elevate him to ace status as well.

That night, Associated Press correspondent Fred Hampson arrived on the island to interview Boyington. Pappy now had twenty-five kills, one less than Foss, and people back in the States were anxious to learn all they could about the Marine hero. What they didn't know was that the thirty-one-year-old pilot was now mentally and physically exhausted from the self-imposed pressure of daily missions and the malnutrition and other maladies of island life.

On December 28, Chris accompanied Boyington and ten other Black Sheep as part of another fighter sweep over Rabaul. Greg was not the tactical leader this time. The pilot who had that duty made the mistake of allowing the enemy planes to gain altitude advantage on his forty-six-plane fighter formation. In the melee that followed, Chris and his mates found themselves taking on about sixty Zeros. He destroyed one of the Zekes—making him the squadron's second leading ace with nine—while Matheson, McClurg, and Olander also added singles. However, the squadron would be reduced by three: Cameron Dustin, Harry Bartl and Don Moore. The loss of Moore was especially difficult for Chris. The two were close friends even before they left San Diego and shared a cabin together on the trip over with Bob Alexander, another Black Sheep who would never return to the flock.

The sad assignment of gathering up Don's personal effects and sending them home fell to his tent mate, Chris, who carefully arranged the cheerful Texan's belongings into three piles: one for valuables like money, jewelry, and watches; a second for uniforms, photos, and other memorabilia; and a third for flight gear and various equipment issued by the Corps. The first two were sent home to Don's parents, while the third was delivered to the quartermaster for reissue. Although it wasn't authorized, Chris decided to hang on to a few of the pictures of Don and his fiancée Barbara as a reminder of what he was fighting for. He figured his departed friend wouldn't mind.

Bad weather over the next few days kept the squadron from engaging in much activity. Ed Olander managed to score his fifth Zero on December 30, while escorting a bomber strike that was partially aborted due to the inclement climatic conditions. With time running out on what would surely be his final combat tour, Pappy continued to go out hunting for Zekes at every opportunity. The pressure to eclipse the Foss record was clearly getting to him.

On January 2, clear skies finally returned, and Boyington led three Black Sheep Corsairs and fifty-two other Navy and Marine aircraft in another fighter sweep over Rabaul. Unfortunately, the skipper's engine began spitting oil all over his canopy, and he never got a shot. Fred Losch would be the only Black Sheep to score a Zero that day. It was Rope Trick's first.

Chris was again on the sidelines the following morning when a contingent of VMF 214 Corsairs piloted by Matheson, Chatham, and Ashmun, led by a weary Boyington, left Vella Lavella as part of another major fighter sweep over Rabaul. This time they found plenty of action. Matheson knocked down one Zeke, but then had to escort his wingman, Chatham,

WAR HALTS FOR 100 PILOTS; THE SKIPPER'S GONE

ADVANCED SOUTH PACIFIC BASE, Jan. 4 [Delayed] (AP) – The skipper didn't get back.

The news spread like the chill wind from revetment to the "ready room" to the tent camp on the hill. The war stood still for a hundred pilots and 500 ground crewmen.

For Maj. Gregory Boyington, leader of the marine's "blacksheep squadron," had failed to return from a mission during which he shot down his 26th enemy plane to tie the all-time American record.

Three accompanying pilots saw the 31 year old Okanogan, Wash., ace send his 26th spinning down yesterday in a ball of fire into St. George's channel, that gateway to Rabaul.

Needed as Instructor

Lt. M.B. Miller then saw Boyington and Wingman Capt. G.M. Ashmun dive on a formation of Zeros below. "They disappeared below a cloud," he said. I don't see how Greg could have missed getting one or more, but I never saw him afterward.

Search planes sighted neither the wreckage of Boyington's Corsair nor the life raft that pilots carry.

Marine Maj. Gen. Ralph Mitchell of New Britain, Conn., commander of the Solomons air force, said: "Not only was Boyington of immense value as a pilot but his instructional ability was almost unmeasurable. We need men like him to "read the Bible, to the kids back home who don't know it yet."

Intelligence Officer Frank Walton, "father confessor" to Boyington, said:

"He may show up or he may not. If he doesn't, you ought to tell the American people they lost about the best and bravest guy that ever came out here to fight for them. The Japs know it already."

Accepted Any Odds

Boyington was a flyer's flyer. His squadron's esprit de corps fed on his skill and character. Like their leader, they considered themselves the hardest hitters in the Pacific (continued on page 75) home when the latter's electrical system failed. Mat reported to Walton that he'd seen Boyington and Ashmun attack a formation of fifteen Zeros, and Pappy had shot at least one down. The Black Sheep waited anxiously for their skipper's return that day, but it never happened. By late afternoon they knew that neither he nor Ashmun were coming back. Miller, who had taken over as executive officer after Carnagey was lost, went to see the base operations officer and cajoled him into letting some of the pilots search for their commanding officer. By the time the eight Corsairs reached the waters off New Britain, however, the surface was completely obscured by fog.

With only three days left in the tour, all the pilots took time after each mission to look for Greg and George, but their efforts were futile. Chris had no further opportunities to engage enemy aircraft, but inflicted plenty of damage on barges and coastal structures after a cancelled escort mission on January 5. Four of his mates—Mullen, Bolt, Groover, and Skinny Johnson—managed to score kills during that brief period. The first two were already aces while the latter pair drew blood for the first time.

The Black Sheep were relieved by another squadron on January 7 and transported to Espiritu Santo the following day. No one felt much like celebrating this time. They had lost eight pilots in combat—twice as many as on the first tour—and worst of all, one of them was their skipper. That they could boast of no less than eight aces and had set a Marine Corps kill record was little consolation.

(continued from page 74)

and accepted battles against any odds.

"He knew what a Corsair would and wouldn't do," said Capt. Kenneth Frasier, Burlington, N.Y., second Blacksheep ace with 12-1/2 planes, in commenting on Boyington's technical intimacy with airplanes.

At 31 the grandpappy of Pacific fighter pilots, altho he has never been decorated, this fighter was looking forward to ending his tour of duty in a week and returning home to "get acquainted" again with his three children.

A week ago he leaned across the mess hall table and bellowed, "Sure I want that record [of 26 planes downed]; who the hell wouldn't? I'd like to make it 35!"

Accepts Japs Challenge

Boyington chose his friends without regard for rank, and once was grounded for his attitude toward discipline — but he was too good to keep down.

Once at Kahili on Bougainville the Japanese found the allied fighters' radio wave length, and a servile voice said, "Maj. Boyington, what is your position, please?"

Recognizing the ruse, Boyington retorted, "Right over your damn airport. Why don't you yellowbellies come up and fight?"

"Maj. Boyington, why don't you come down!" came the Japanese voice.

Boyington and his wingman went down thru heavy anti-aircraft fire, strafed two gun positions and a couple of Zeros on the ground and shot up to fighter altitude.

"All right, you ——, I was down," yelled Boyington. "Now how about you coming up?"

No one came.

[Note: Capt. Frasier was not a Black Sheep]

Now they were hearing that the brass wanted to break up the squadron. Miller and Walton felt such an action would be a travesty and drafted a letter requesting that the Black Sheep be kept intact. General Moore not only endorsed the letter but urged Washington to "keep this combat unit intact" in his own handwriting. Unfortunately, the general was transferred soon afterward, and the Black Sheep were indeed broken up.

Chris emerged from his first two combat tours unscathed, but he'd certainly had his share of close calls. On three different occasions he ran out of fuel after a mission and was forced to make "dead stick" landings. A narrow escape over Bougainville was the cause of one of these incidents. Chris and his comrades had been separated during aerial combat, and he was flying near the water looking for targets in less than ideal visibility. Suddenly, he spotted four aircraft approaching in a formation that from a distance made them appear to be a U.S. Marine division. Chris decided to fly up to their level and join them for the journey back to Munda. As he reached the proper elevation, he ascertained first that the oncoming aircraft were not Corsairs and then that they didn't have radial engines. They were, in fact, in-line engined "Tonys," a new breed of Japanese fighters that reportedly were a match for Corsairs in speed and power.

Outgunned and too close to turn and run, Chris decided to surprise the Japanese pilots with a daring frontal "attack," and opened up with his machine guns from beyond what would be considered an effective distance. His tactics were designed to confuse the enemy, and they worked. Once past the scattered quartet, Chris rolled his plane into a long power dive through the clouds, not pulling up until he was almost at sea level. When he looked back he saw that none of his adversaries had chosen to follow him. The dive used up an alarming amount of fuel, however, and Chris had doubts whether there was enough left in his tanks to get him home. It turned out there wasn't.

As the Corsair approached the edge of the Munda strip with flaps down, the engine quit. Several Black Sheep were watching from the ready tent while the silent aircraft dropped slowly toward the coral reef in front of the airfield. They could see their buddy was in trouble. Thinking quickly, Chris pulled up his wheels to reduce drag and give his plane additional gliding distance. He slipped below the level of the trees between the runway and the ready tent, then—at the last possible second—yanked the toggle of the hydraulic bottle and "blew down" the wheels. The Corsair barely made the strip. Since the observers' view was obstructed by trees they didn't see the wheels drop, and feared Chris had crash landed. Their apprehension quickly turned to surprise and relief when the plane reappeared rolling quietly along the coral runway.

Chapter 6

Green Island Blues

—

Asecond sojourn to Sydney late in January helped the Black Sheep recover from the loss of their skipper and squadron. Chris, Bob McClurg, and Rope Trick Losch used their cigarette rations to barter a week's rental of a seventy-foot sailboat and its crew, and spent most of their R&R with female companions partying aboard the craft. Chris once again hooked up with the lovely and delightful Pat, whose presence certainly enhanced his enjoyment of the days and evenings on the waters of Sydney Harbor.

The seven days in Australia passed by all too quickly once again, and the marines found themselves back on Espiritu Santo. Although VMF 214 was officially disbanded and the squadron number sent back to the States for adoption by a soon-to-be-formed unit, the pilots would remain together for about a month, mostly ferrying planes from one island to another and engaging in gunnery practice or photo hops.

In mid-March the Marine Corps transferred Chris and fourteen other Black Sheep pilots to VMF 211 which was stationed on Green Island, halfway between Bougainville and Japanese-held New Ireland. Their new squadron—known as "The Wake Island Avengers"—had already established a notable combat record, although not on the lofty level of 214's. Major Tom Murto, the squadron commander was no Pappy Boyington either, but he had the good sense to leave well-enough alone and allow the ex-Black Sheep to form their own flying divisions under Hank Miller. The contingent from 214 soon found Executive Officer J.W. "Bucky" Ireland to be a man after their own hearts. He was a skilled, aggressive pilot who'd achieved "ace" status and was the true combat leader of 211.

Allied air power now controlled the skies unchallenged over New Britain and New Ireland. Even the Japanese Navy had all but deserted the area. The mighty fortress of Rabaul with its 85,000 heavily armed troops was neutralized, and U.S. forces had no reason to risk heavy losses by invading it. The route to Japan was now clear, and it was 211's job to make certain it stayed that way.

Chris (R) and division mates (L to R) Bob McClurg, Jim Hill, and Junior Heier appear to be comparing aerial combat techniques in this Green Island photo (early 1944). Notice the non-regulation facial hair   *Chris Magee Collection*

Not unexpectedly, the pilots had no opportunities to engage enemy aircraft during the six-week tour. They flew dawn patrols, task force cover, more ferrying assignments, escort for unchallenged bomber raids on Rabaul, and occasional missions to strafe enemy barges and trucks. Attacking Japanese trucks may not sound dangerous, but Ed Harper found out otherwise one day over New Britain. His four-plane division led by John Bolt had spotted several of the vehicles on a road below, and started making passes with their machine guns, receiving some groundfire in the process. With his ammunition almost used up, Harper made one final run, then gained altitude to join his comrades for the flight home.

It wasn't until Harpo jettisoned his canopy and pulled off his helmet that Bolt realized something was seriously wrong. Pulling alongside his troubled comrade, John could detect no bullet holes in the plane or blood on Harper, but he could see his buddy was having difficulty breathing and appeared to be on the verge of passing out. During the remainder of the trip back to Green Island, Bolt and the other two pilots, Tom Emrich and Burney Tucker, kept up close visual contact and a continuous radio conversation with the stricken Harper. After what seemed like an interminable period of time, but was really only several minutes, Harpo somehow managed to land safely, then he passed out. Later, the doctor on duty at the airfield determined he had taken a .50-caliber armor-piercing bullet through the rib cage and one lung, nicking the spine before exiting his back. Both legs had been partially paralyzed, forcing the wounded pilot to use his arms to lift them onto the pedals for landing. Harper remained unconscious for two days. He survived the ordeal despite his critical injuries, but his Pacific tour was over. It was six months before he could return to limited duty.

Jim Hill had a close call of a different sort while on Green Island. On a day when neither were scheduled to fly, he and Chris decided that a little beachcombing along the island's shore might help relieve the tedium they experienced since the demise of 214. To get to the beach near the airfield, the two pilots had to walk down several steps built into a sheer cliff separated from the ocean by a just a few yards of sand and coral. It was a pleasant way to pass a lazy afternoon. Jim had developed a tremendous admiration for his fellow Chicagoan. He usually flew in Chris's division, and the two shared some memorable times in Australia. Chris taught him plenty, and not just about fighter piloting. To Jim, his buddy was a fountain of knowledge, and he was sharing some of what he knew about the ocean and its flora and fauna as they walked farther and farther away from the airfield.

After an hour or so, they decided it was time to turn around and go back. Chris noticed the tide was starting to come in and suggested they speed up their pace. Jim quickly ascertained the reason for his friend's concern: at high tide there was no beach, just waves smashing against the rocky cliff. When they finally sighted the steps that had brought them down to the beach, the water was at knee level and the waves were getting bigger. Wading around a giant rock with just a few yards to go and water up to their waists, Chris looked out to sea and spotted a huge incoming wave that seemed to have deadly intentions. He yelled at Jim to follow his example as he spread both arms and flattened himself against the rock. The lanky Hill did as asked, realizing that it was safer to let the wave strike with full force against his body supported by the rock, than be thrown against the cliff. Still, the impact was so tremendous that Jim blacked out.

Seconds later, as he lay gasping for air beneath the warm water and in danger of either drowning or getting carried into the rocks by the next big wave, Jim felt two powerful arms lifting him above the surface. Chris half-pulled, half-carried Jim to the steps, where he recovered enough of his strength to climb to safety.

It was then that both men noticed the coral bottom had taken its toll on their skin: they were covered from head to toe with scrapes and cuts. Chris and Jim were given immediate medical attention upon returning to camp and became the objects of more than a little mirth when they emerged from the doctor's hut inundated in what was known as "the purple stuff," an all-purpose topical medication. Chris played down his heroics when Hill told the other pilots about their narrow escape, and years later would seem unable to recall most of the details. Jim, however, never forgot any part the experience.

Chris completed his third Pacific tour on April 26. Along with the other VMF 211 pilots who had finished their tours, he flew back to Espiritu Santo to prepare for his return to the States, then caught a seaplane flight in mid-May for Pearl Harbor. From there, the returning Marines were shipped via aircraft carrier to California for well-earned leaves. Like most returning veterans, Chris looked forward to seeing friends and family again. And yet there was something else on his mind as well. The two tours with the Black Sheep should have provided more than enough combat for any pilot, but not Chris. The experience only confirmed what he'd felt all along: he was a warrior, and as such he thirsted for battle. The enemy wouldn't be found in the United States; it was waiting somewhere out across the Pacific. The warrior inside Chris wouldn't be satisfied until he engaged that enemy in the skies again, and contributed to its ultimate defeat.

Chapter 7

Stateside Surprises

O ne of the first things Chris wanted to do after the ship docked at the Long Beach Naval Base was to catch a flight to San Francisco and call on Jean Scott. He hadn't received a letter from her in six months and was curious as to how she was adjusting to life in California. Of course, the possibility of romance now that he'd returned safely was certainly on his mind, as well. He didn't know whether Jean still had feelings for his brother, but that wasn't going to stop him from at least paying her a visit. Bud was busy fighting the Nazis in Europe, anyway.

Chris decided not to call ahead. His arrival at the home of Jean's parents would be a big surprise. But the biggest surprise of all was bestowed upon him, not Jean. The girl he'd been looking so forward to seeing was now a married woman. Years later, Jean said she was convinced, somehow, that neither Chris nor Bud were coming back from the war, so she wed the first eligible young man who asked. That her new husband's surname happened to be McKee was, she later admitted, perhaps a factor in her decision. Jean was only nineteen at the time.

After a long visit with his parents in Chicago, Chris moved on in August to his next assignment: Marine Corps Air Station, Cherry Point, North Carolina. He'd requested duty on the East Coast after asking other Marines who were supposedly "in the know" where he should go in order to make the quickest return to the combat zone. He was eventually ordered to a recently

HERO HOME ON LEAVE—Capt. Christopher Magee, marine fighter pilot hero of the South Pacific, and his parents at their home at 919 E. 50th st.

[Daily News photo.]

How a "100 to 1" retaliation attack on Jap-filled barges more than wiped out the score, following the loss of his air fighter squadron commander, Maj. Gregory Boyington, was related here today by Capt. Christopher Magee, Marine Corps. The captain won the Navy Cross and flew more than 90 combat missions in the South Pacific.

Capt. Magee is on leave visiting his parents, Mr. and Mrs. Fred M. Magee, 919 E. 50th st. The 26-year-old, former University of Chicago student served in the Royal Canadian Air Force before the entrance of the United States in the war enabled him to transfer to the Marines.

"A few days after Maj. Boying-ton, commanding our Black Sheep Squadron, was reported missing, we went out on a bomber escort mission in the Rabaul area," said the tall, brown-haired captain.

"We sighted two barges loaded with Jap soldiers and we let them have it with machine guns, sinking both barges and wiping out the Japs aboard. We estimate that we killed at least 100 Nips in this manner."

Capt. Magee, who attended Mount Carmel High School before becoming a Midway student, received the Navy Cross with a citation signed by Adm. W. F. Halsey, which records his "extraordinary heroism" while serving as a pilot of a fighter plane attached to a Marine aircraft group operating in the Solomon Islands.

formed replacement training squadron which was designated VMF 911. Joining him in his new unit were a couple of familiar faces: Hank "Notebook" Miller, who was the squadron commander, and Chris's close friend, Rope Trick Losch. Few Corsairs were available at first, so most of his flying time during August and September was in the ubiquitous SNJ trainers.

Although he still looked forward to getting back into the war, Chris wasn't complaining about life at Cherry Point. In Losch he had a good buddy to pal around with, and by October he was again getting hops in Corsairs, albeit mostly in the Goodyear-built FG-1A versions. Best of all, though, he'd met the girl of his dreams—a bright, pretty Navy nurse named Molly Cleary. Molly was a down-to-earth New Yorker with long, curly light brown hair and lively blue eyes. An Irish Catholic, she wore little makeup and seemed a young lady certain to meet the approval of his parents, not that it really made a difference. Chris wasn't one to choose anything or anybody based on his parents' opinion, or anyone else's for that matter. In addition to her good looks and fine character traits, Molly—like Chris—was an accomplished dancer. When they were out on the floor of the officers' club during a particularly lively number, other couples would often stop dancing to watch them perform.

Wedding photo of Chris and wife Molly (MCAS Cherry Point, fall 1944)
Courtesy of Zona Musser

Chris and Molly were married at the Cherry Point chapel that fall. Losch, a Protestant, was best man, even though the Catholic chaplain strongly suggested the groom bestow this honor on someone of his own faith. Chris had to take the priest aside and advise him, in no uncertain terms, that it was his wedding and his decision who would stand up for him. The newlyweds went to New York City for their honeymoon. Rope Trick and his fiancee accompanied them on the trip, which included an evening of dining and dancing at Billy Rose's Diamond Horseshoe in the Paramount Hotel. Chris also got to meet Molly's parents, both of whom were very pleased to have a bona fide hero in the family. No one, however, was more thrilled than Molly's thirteen-year-old kid brother Robert, the lucky recipient of a flight jacket complete with Black Sheep Squadron patch and a genuine St. Louis Cardinals ball cap from his sister's new husband.

Chris had few opportunities to fly in November and December, spending most of his time in Air Ordnance School at Turner Field, Quantico, Virginia. The only two hops he took during those months were in SBD-5 dive bombers. With the arrival of 1945 he was back in FG-1As, although by then the pilots of 911 were aware that there was an exciting new aircraft in their future. The planes arrived in late February, and, indeed, they were a different breed of cat—a Tigercat, that is. The Grumman F7F was a powerhouse of a fighter, with two of the same 2,000 horsepower radial engines used by the Corsair and armed with twenty-millimeter cannons as well as .50-caliber machine guns. The Tigercats could carry a good-sized load of rockets and bombs as well, making them true attack fighters. VMF 911 was the only Marine unit to receive the twin-engined newcomers and the sole "day" fighter squadron. The Navy versions were equipped with radar and designated "night" fighters.

All the pilots of 911 were duly impressed by the power of the F7F, none more so than Chris, who quickly learned all he could about his new mount. He used his early familiarization flights to test its capabilities. By late spring it became apparent that this otherwise remarkable aircraft had one glaring problem: its cannons had a tendency to overheat, causing the bullets to tumble out of the barrels rather than rotate in a spiral at high speed. In order to correct the flaw Marine officials decided to transfer the squadron to a place where the guns could be tested under the most severe conditions possible, a location very familiar to Chris: El Centro, California.

With Chris preparing to leave for California, Molly decided to move back to her parent's house to await the birth of their child, due early in the summer. Chris was not pleased about having to return to El Centro, especially with the summer approaching, but at least he was moving in the right direction—closer to the Pacific and the war. The squadron had been told that once the guns were fixed they would be deployed via aircraft carrier to the western Pacific.

Christopher Lyman Magee, Jr. arrived in New York just a few days before his father departed for California. While the idea of spending time with his wife and son had its appeal, Chris felt he still had a job to do, even if it meant first bearing up to a torrid summer in the desert.

A division of Grumman F7F Tigercats from VMF 911 flies in formation near MCAS Cherry Point, North Carolina (spring 1945)   *Chris Magee Collection*

By mid-August, the Tigercats were considered fully operational, so VMF 911 was sent to NAS Miramar for deployment to Okinawa and the planned invasion of the Japanese homeland. The pilots were in for a bit of a disappointment, however, because the ship never left the dock. The cause of this change of plans was something called the atomic bomb. Two of these instruments of mass destruction were dropped on the cities of Hiroshima and Nagasaki, respectively, and the Japanese quickly decided it was time to throw in the towel. Chris toasted the end of the war along with everyone else, although perhaps with a fraction less enthusiasm.

The real celebration for Chris and all who'd served in the Black Sheep Squadron came a few weeks later when what started as a pervasive rumor officially became fact: Greg Boyington had been found alive in a Japanese prison camp and was on his way back to the United States. Soon newspapers all over the country were telling how Pappy had tallied three Zeros before being shot down; how he was found floating on a raft by an enemy submarine; how he kept his identity a secret by jettisoning his dog tags and indicators of rank; and how he managed to survive more than a year and a half in captivity.

Chris and Rope Trick were just two of twenty-one Black Sheep stationed on the West Coast waiting to greet their famed squadron commander and Medal of Honor recipient when his plane landed at NAS Alameda early on the morning of September 12. Pappy was hoisted onto the shoulders of his men and carried into a reception room where dozens of reporters waited.

That night the pilots all got together again for a big party at San Francisco's St. Francis Hotel. Because of his prison camp ordeal the skipper was advised by doctors to lay off alcohol, and to everyone's surprise he did. In

Black Sheep welcoming party awaits arrival of newly-released POW Pappy Boyington at NAS Alameda. Kneeling (L to R) Fred Losch, Sandy Sims, Bruce Matheson, Ed Olander, Paul Mullen, Bill Case. Standing (L to R) Rollie Rinabarger, Stan Bailey, Hank Miller, Frank Walton, Bob Bragdon, June Little (Ground Officer), Chris, Herb Holden, Dr. Jim Reames, John Bergert, Hank Bourgeois, Rev. W. P. Paetznizk (Chaplain)   *Courtesy of Fred Losch*

Chris (far left) and three other Black Sheep aces listen to Greg Boyington relate some of his POW experiences during the September 1945 homecoming party for the squadron commander. Others are (L to R) Paul Mullen, Boyington, Ed Olander and Bill Case   *Courtesy of Anne York*

the national tour that followed he would more than make up for this lapse, however. *Life* magazine sent reporters and photographers to cover the festivities, and both Chris and Rope Trick were among those whose names and photos appeared in the October 1 issue. Chris was shown chatting with Boyington at the bar along with fellow aces Moon Mullen, Bill Case, and Ed Olander.

Losch was caught in a less flattering pose, crawling under a table to give a "hot foot" to one of his fellow pilots. The coverage of the party marked a first for *Life*. Never before had the magazine shown people consuming alcohol.

Chris (second from R) draws a laugh with his antics during the homecoming bash for Greg Boyington at San Francisco's St. Francis Hotel in September 1945. Other Black Sheep are Stan Bailey on the left, Bruce Matheson on the right, and Fred Losch, standing in back. The two civilians at the table are representatives from Chance Vought Aircraft, which sponsored the party   *Courtesy of Fred Losch*

Black Sheep serenade a jacketless Greg Boyington with their rendition of "The Wiffenpoof Song" during his homecoming gala. Chris is second from right of microphone   *Courtesy of Fred Losch*

For the Black Sheep, the get-together put an exclamation point not only on the war, but also on what, undoubtedly, would be the greatest experience of their lives. They had, after all, established a Marine Corps record with ninety-seven enemy planes confirmed shot down, and thirty-five more as probables. Perhaps even more significant was that ninety-four of the kills came over Japanese-held territory, where there was no margin for error.

When Chris returned to Miramar, he was told he had sufficient demobilization points to leave the Marine Corps, or he could remain with 911 and ship out to Okinawa. With no war left to fight and little desire to serve in the peacetime armed forces, he opted for the former. Thus on October 6, 1945, Captain Christopher L. Magee, USMCR, officially separated from the Corps, and headed back to New York to join his wife and their baby son. Chris had lived out his greatest boyhood dream. Now, could he settle into what most considered a "normal" life?

Chapter 8

A Postwar Odyssey

Chris drove Molly and Chris Jr. to Chicago in his newly purchased Lincoln Zephyr early in December 1945. The young
family moved into Fred and Marie Magee's spacious apartment on East 50th Street, where they received frequent visits from
old friends and neighbors pleased and excited to have a bona fide
hero back in their midst. His brother returned safely to Chicago as
well. Bud saw action as an infantryman in several major European
campaigns, but he didn't receive the sort of recognition the local press
gave Chris. He'd enjoyed the idea of fighting for his country and wearing a soldier's uniform, though, and decided to join the city's police
force when the war ended.

Chris's sister Zona and her husband Gus were expecting their first child.
Chris found out that his brother-in-law was flying PBY Catalina seaplanes in
the Solomons at the same time he was serving with the Black Sheep. Chris
recalled one incident off Cape St. George at the southern end of New Ireland when his four-plane division came to the rescue of a PBY. The big flying boat was on the water picking up survivors from a downed aircraft and
taking fire from a gun emplacement high on the cape. Chris circled around
the PBY to determine where the bullets were coming from, then led his
three comrades in a strafing attack on the enemy guns. The firing stopped
immediately after the Corsairs' first run, and the Catalina lumbered across
the surface and took off safely a few minutes later. That Gus could have

been at the controls of the PBY was certainly a possibility; he'd participated in his share of pilot recoveries. The brothers-in-law were never able to determine whether or not it was Gus's plane on that occasion, though.

Chris wasn't in any particular hurry to find a job, but there was no shortage of offers. Several major U.S. airlines contacted him. The idea of having a pilot in the cockpit of one of their aircraft who was not only an ace but a Navy Cross winner as well would have been a public relations bonanza for the management of any company in the commercial aviation industry. But Chris wasn't interested. He considered himself a fighter pilot, not an airborne bus driver. His war record was the subject of numerous articles in major Chicago newspapers and could have opened doors for him in any number of local companies, but—unlike so many others—Chris refused to exploit his heroics.

When Chris finally did accept a position early in 1946, the work was neither glamorous nor especially lucrative. He took a job as crewman on a New York-based Liberty ship bringing war brides back from Europe largely because he was interested in visiting that continent and seeing firsthand the effects of the war. Molly, pregnant with their second child, was pleased that her husband would be based in New York—life in Chicago had not been pleasant for her. While she genuinely liked Fred Sr., her mother-in-law was another matter. Shortly before Chris found employment she'd opted to move back to her parents' home, having had her fill of Marie Magee's frequent admonitions for her son to "get a job."

Chris's first return trip from England was a challenge to passengers and crew alike. Most of the British war brides had been malnourished for years, and their digestive systems couldn't handle the rich, plentiful food provided on the ship. To make matters worse, the voyage was a rough one with frequent gale force weather. Chris and the other crewmen spent a good part of their time cleaning up after the sick women, many of whom had babies with them.

During his many journeys across the Atlantic that spring, Chris utilized time ashore to explore postwar Europe. He soon became aware that a thriving black market existed. Because of his experience at bartering cigarettes in Australia, Chris recognized a solid, if slightly unethical business opportunity when he saw one. Tobacco products were a hot item, but he preferred to deal in something less bulky. It took just a few casual conversations with war brides for him to ascertain that cosmetics were almost impossible to find throughout Europe, and therefore at a premium. Chris soon seized upon the perfect commodity, something small and easy to bring aboard ship in large quantities: lipstick. The enterprise would prove quite lucrative, but it also created a lot of friction between Chris and his idealistic wife.

Chris left his seafaring job that summer and headed back to Chicago. Molly, Chris Jr., and newborn daughter Christine stayed in New York. Soon after his return home he was reunited with Ed Smart, who had remained in Europe after the war ended to further his education at the Biarritz School. The two men needed work, but were ready for a little adventure, too. They found both, but had to sojourn slightly off the straight and narrow to do so.

The new enterprise for the team of Magee and Smart was bootlegging. Their plan was to capitalize on laws in certain northern Michigan counties that prohibited the sale and distribution, if not consumption, of liquor. Before the duo could begin their illegal venture they modified their delivery vehicle, the big white Lincoln Zephyr, by removing the back seat for extra cargo space and beefing up the rear suspension. They also crudely "tinted" the side and back windows, using dark cellophane and scotch tape. Their clients were hotels that catered to the summer tourist trade. Since it was late in the season, the duo made only a few runs, but Ed would never forget one of them. The drop-off was a small resort hotel situated next door to a police station. When the Zephyr pulled up next to the hotel, the police were holding roll call outdoors, just a few yards away. Ed pointed out what was going on to Chris and suggested they exit promptly and return later when the situation was a little less risky. Chris just grinned, got out, and opened the trunk. He then removed four plain-packaged cases of liquor and carried them into the hotel. None of the cops even gave him a second glance. The same could not be said for his customer, the hotel's bell captain, who nearly went into shock when the delivery man casually strolled through the door into the lobby with all four cases. He hurriedly led Chris to a storage room and paid him $280 cash for the goods.

When the summer ended, Chris decided to move the operation to Kansas, a state that maintained prohibition laws similar to what existed in northern Michigan. He would pick up the booze in Kansas City, Missouri, and drive a loop of four or five hundred miles through rural Kansas, making several deliveries along the way. One of the most distant drop off spots was behind a church in the town of Pratt. The customer was the preacher. Ed was now engaged in the legitimate business of buying war surplus materials from the military and selling them to civilian companies. Since the work required him to make frequent trips to the U.S. Army Air Force Base near Pratt, he took Chris up on his offer to provide transportation. "If we're ever stopped by the cops," Chris advised him, "just tell them you didn't know about the booze."

Early one evening, a state trooper drew alongside the Zephyr and motioned Chris and Ed to pull over. Realizing the illegal cargo could be discovered if he stopped, Chris floored the accelerator. Since most of the whiskey had already been delivered and the big, powerful car was lightened considerably, they gradually put some daylight between themselves and the cop. Their pursuer was soon joined by others, however, and it wasn't long before a parade of sirens and flashing lights was following the big Lincoln down the usually quiet prairie highway. Luckily, the two Chicagoans weren't far from the state line, and managed to cross safely into Missouri. There were no "hot pursuit" laws at the time, so they were home free.

Chris and Ed weren't so lucky during a later trip. Waiting for a traffic light at a small town intersection, Chris was surprised to find a local sheriff standing next to his door and tapping on the window. He was ordered to step out of the car, then asked to open the trunk. The sheriff had become suspicious when he noticed the Zephyr was riding very low in the back. When the contents were discovered, Chris was immediately placed under arrest, and his car was confiscated. Ed proclaimed his innocence as Chris had advised him to do and was set free, but told he'd have to find his own transportation back to Chicago. Fearing his friend would be left to rot in the Kansas jail, Ed immediately sought out the town's nearest law office. The attorney he found informed him that it would cost $3,000 in fines, court costs, and other "expenses" to get Chris out of jail. Over Chris's protests, Ed returned to Chicago and borrowed the money from relatives. Chris was soon released, but he was anything but happy about gaining his freedom. "You should have saved your money," he told Ed. "I could have used a few months with nothing to do but read and write." His car was never returned to him.

Beginning in 1946, Chris and Ed also worked as couriers for a rather shadowy group of American "businessmen" interested in overthrowing certain Central American dictatorships and replacing them with democratic pro-American governments. The organization hoped to encourage commercial endeavors between the Latin countries and U.S. firms. Both Chris and Ed maintained a loose relationship with the group for several years.

Smart got married late in 1946 and shortly afterwards started his own taxicab business. Earlier, Bud Magee had also taken the marital plunge. His new bride, Helena, had been introduced to him as a pen pal by his older brother during the war. Chris, who by now realized he was not suited for marriage or family life, found work aboard a Lake Michigan ore boat while his wife remained in New York.

In May 1948, Chris learned through a newspaper article that the newly-declared nation of Israel was looking for volunteer pilots to serve in its struggle for independence. The story piqued his interest. He'd heard about the atrocities Hitler inflicted on European Jews, of course, but he'd been perturbed about their plight since the prewar St. Louis incident, when America and other Allied nations refused to allow asylum in their respective countries to a shipload of Jewish refugees. Now, with the British peace-keeping force about to depart Palestine, leaders of the surrounding Arab states vowed to push all Jews—both longtime residents and the rapidly expanding group of postwar settlers—into the Mediterranean Sea. The David Ben Gurion-led Haganah (Israel's defense force) had other ideas, however. Chris considered the Israeli cause a noble one and looked upon it as an opportunity to again use his fighter piloting skills. Ed wanted to go, too, but he was now the father of a son, and his wife convinced him otherwise. Chris contacted a front organization in downtown Chicago called the Land and Labor Office for Palestine, and arrangements were made to send him to a New York hotel where other volunteers were staying.

While in New York, Chris called on Molly for what turned out to be the last time. She was cordial, if a little cool, and intuitively commented she was surprised he wasn't involved in the Israeli situation. Later, Chris ironed out the details of his impending trip to Israel with recruiters at the hotel and applied for a passport. When told it would take a few days to process the application, he decided to return to Chicago to make certain his affairs were in order. He didn't bother telling anyone about his plans, though. When Chris flew back to New York, he discovered the volunteers had moved out of the hotel. He stayed around the place until he eventually spotted one of the recruiters, who reported to him that the others thought he'd been kidnapped by Arabs.

With passport finally in hand, Chris and the rest of the pilots boarded a KLM passenger plane for Amsterdam. The Dutch airline was unwittingly assisting in a smuggling operation. The contraband, though, was Americans who wanted to help Israel gain its independence, a noble endeavor no doubt supported by most of the people—if not officially by the government—of the United States.

The journey to Israel was anything but direct. Chris stayed in the Netherlands for a few days then was flown to Geneva. The volunteers remained in Switzerland a week while visas for travel into Czechoslovakia were processed. Chris used the time to take in the sights of Geneva, a beautiful city which—

because of the nation's neutrality—showed no ill effects from the recent war. After Geneva, it was off to Zurich for a brief stay then to Prague for another week of sightseeing and waiting. There Chris met Dr. Otto Felix, a lawyer who had organized the effort to supply the Israelis with much needed fighter planes in order to discourage daily raids on Tel Aviv by Arab bombers. Most of the volunteer pilots found Felix pompous and patronizing, but his contribution to the Israeli cause cannot be discounted. He reportedly paid $44,000 apiece from his own pocket for the first ten fighters sent to Israel, Czech-built versions of Germany's famed ME-109G Messerschmitt.

Eventually the pilots were taken by car to a nearby air base where they were checked out in the unfamiliar planes. Chris hadn't flown in nearly three years, but he quickly got the hang of the new aircraft—designated the Avia S-199—even though he was less than enthusiastic about its performance. The general consensus among the other volunteers was that the planes were accidents waiting to happen. There was no rudder trim tab, which meant the pilot would have to constantly fight for directional control. The original Messerschmitt engine had been replaced by a model used in the Heinkel dive bomber, and it was woefully underpowered—a shortcoming that was especially problematic to most of the flyers during takeoff from short airstrips. Worse still were the landing characteristics. The flaps were neither electrical nor hydraulic but manual. It took a minute of hard cranking by hand to get them into position.

Chris, who was just happy to be flying a combat aircraft again, didn't complain. He was accustomed to the long-nosed Corsair—an aircraft notorious for its lack of landing visibility from the cockpit—and had experienced the joys of hand-cranking during fighter training in the F4F Wildcats. Another drawback of the hybrid craft was its canopy, which had to be pushed out to open instead of simply sliding back. The pilots shuddered to think about how they would escape should the craft flip over on its back during takeoff or landing. Later, they would learn the hard way that the factory had often installed used or defective surplus parts in building the planes. Maintenance problems would be frequent, especially in the landing gear, which had a tendency to fold up when taking off, landing, or even taxiing. Decades afterwards, ex-Marine Lou Lenart—one of the first Americans to volunteer—would describe the Avia S-199 as "probably the worst airplane I've ever had the misfortune to fly."

Chris couldn't help musing about the irony of Nazi fighter planes being used by Israel in their fight for freedom from centuries of oppression and persecution. It was "the Nazi war machine furnishing fuel for the flames from which arose the reborn Jewish Phoenix," he would later write. "Could Dante have provided a sounder image . . . in his Inferno than that of Hitler staring madly at this worst of all retributions?"

The volunteers didn't know it at the time, but the little fighter had already proved its worth a few weeks before. On June 3, two slow-moving Egyptian Dakota transport planes, which had been modified as bombers, were making one of their daily unopposed attacks on Tel Aviv when the crews were shocked to see a Messerschmitt with unfamiliar markings closing in to intercept them. The pilot, an Israeli national and Royal Air Force veteran named Mordecai "Modi" Alon quickly sent one of the twin-engined craft smoking into the Mediterranean. He then chased the other Dakota southward beyond Tel Aviv, where it met a similar fate, this time finding a permanent resting place in Israeli soil. So stunned were the Arabs to discover that Israel suddenly had a real air force that the daylight aerial bombings ceased almost completely.

The new pilots were flown via a Lockheed Constellation from Prague to Tel Aviv, a city of 200,000 located on Israel's Mediterranean coast, arriving in the wee hours of a June morning. In addition to the pilots, the contraband on board the "Connie" included one complete disassembled Messerschmitt. Because of the blackness outside, the men had no idea they'd reached their destination until, suddenly, two rows of runway lights turned on below. Once the plane was on the ground and stopped, the lights immediately went off, and the new arrivals were escorted to cars by military personnel carrying flashlights. With Tel Aviv located just eleven miles from Arab lines, such precautions were certainly understandable. The pilots were then driven to the city's Park Hotel, where they remained for two nights before being assigned to Herzliya, an air base with a grass landing field. A day later, Chris flew his first mission. No contact with the enemy was made.

Chris's initial flight as a member of Israel's 101 Fighter Squadron—nicknamed the Angels of Death—was a harbinger for his entire stay in that country. He would never see an enemy aircraft and rarely had an opportunity to fire his weapons. This was perhaps a blessing in disguise as the two fuselage-mounted guns were poorly synchronized. Chris would later recall damaging and almost shooting off his propeller on one occasion. Another American, Bob Vickman, was lost in action presumably because he experienced the same problem. Most of the pilots soon wisely began to use only the two wing-mounted guns.

The reason for the lack of action during the summer of 1948 was the frequent periods of armistice. Chris had little to do militarily besides an occasional uneventful patrol. About the only thing in common from his Black Sheep days was the trademark bandanna—this time a red one—he nearly always wore around the airfield. He had plenty of free time and spent most of it either at the beach or enjoying the hospitality of the local residents and the camaraderie of fun-loving fellow American aviators such as Sid Antin, Giddy Lichtman, Red Finkel, Leo Nomis, Bill Pomerantz, and Leon Frankel. Like Chris, Frankel was a Navy Cross recipient, having torpedoed and sunk a Japanese cruiser from the TBF Avenger he was piloting.

While most of the men lived in military quarters, Chris stayed on the Mediterranean coast at a spacious villa owned by a small, charming young woman named Ofra and her frequently-absent army officer husband. There were also three female Israeli soldiers boarding there, one of whom was romantically involved with Frankel, who also stayed at the villa. Chris and the lady of the house were often seen together on the beach, leading to considerable speculation among his comrades. If there was anything untoward going on, however, he never admitted to it.

Chris, at thirty-one, was among the oldest of the pilots and one of a handful of Gentiles, not that anyone made a distinction. The volunteers of

Members of Israel's first fighter squadron with one of the Czech-built Messerschmitts they flew. Top (L to R) Maury Mann, Ezer Weizman, Aaron "Red" Finkel. Middle (L to R) Bill Pomerantz, Sandy Jacobs, Sid Antin. Standing on ground (L to R) Chris, Giddy Lichtman, Leon Frankel, Leo Nomis   *Chris Magee Collection*

Israel's 101 came from many countries—England, Canada, and South Africa as well as the United States. There were also pilots who actually were Israeli nationals, notably the popular Squadron Commander Alon— the air force's first real hero— and tall, bushy-haired Ezer Weizman, a young man known both for his geniality and wit. Alon was killed in a runway crash in mid-October, as his pregnant wife and many of the other pilots looked on in horror. His successor as leader was a burly South African, Syd Cohen, who went back to his homeland a few months later and was replaced by Weizman. Cohen returned to Israel with his family in 1965, settling there permanently. Weizman would eventually command the Israeli

During a visit to Herzliya Air Base, David Ben Gurion poses with Chris (R) and ground crewman (summer 1948)
Chris Magee Collection

Air Force. Later, he served as Minister of Defense and, in 1993, became the seventh President of Israel.

In the midst of still another cease fire early that October, Chris was told he would have to sign up for a full year if he wanted to remain in the country. He was enjoying himself, even if his $125 per month income was nothing to write home about, but he'd come to Israel to fight and wasn't getting the action he'd expected, so he opted to leave. He returned to the United States on a route that took him through Haifa, Athens, Rome, and Paris. Later, Chris learned, the conflict heated up considerably. The Avia S-199's were soon replaced by British-built Spitfires and American P-51 Mustangs. Several of his fellow pilots downed Arab aircraft. American Rudy Augarten and Canadian Jack Doyle tied as top scorers with four kills each, one more than Alon's total. Augarten's first score came in a Messerschmitt. His victim, ironically, was a British-built Egyptian Air Force Spitfire.

⚭

Back in New York, Chris tried to contact Molly but was told by her parents that she had divorced him, remarried, and moved away, taking their two children with her. They provided no other details beyond that. Chris would often think about his ex-wife and his son and daughter, but refused to dwell on what might have been and didn't attempt to locate them. He knew when he wasn't wanted. Forty years later he explained to interviewer Neal Gendler of the *Minneapolis Star-Tribune* that he was completely responsible for the failure of the marriage. "It was my fault for even getting involved. I knew better ... I wasn't about to be settled down somewhere."

Policeman Bud Magee wasn't any better at the marriage game than his older brother, just more persistent. Helena bore him twin girls, Barbara and Elizabeth, in 1948, then divorced him not long afterward. Later on, he occasionally visited his daughters but was not allowed to tell them who he really was. The twins were raised to believe their father was dead, and Bud was a "family friend." The younger Magee remarried in the early fifties. His second wife—a bright, petite secretary—coincidentally named Helen (last name Kirk) was employed by the same company as Helena, although the two never met. The union produced two daughters, Mary Kay and Connie, and a son, Michael, but also ended in divorce, as did a third marriage.

A new enterprise awaited Chris in Chicago upon his return from Israel. The entrepreneurial Smart offered him the opportunity to work for a recording business he was putting together with the assistance of his younger brother John. For lack of anything better to do, Chris decided to join the partnership. Prior to his leaving for Israel, Chris and Ed had developed some basic recording skills in another venture that found them taking on the roles of freelance broadcast journalists. Employing a police scanner in Ed's car along with a battery-powered tape recorder, they'd wait for reports of a fire, robbery, accident, or other breaking news event, then rush to the scene. Once there, Chris would conduct man-on-the-street interviews with victims or eyewitnesses while Ed recorded everything. Then, the duo would quickly drive to a local radio station and turn over the tape reel to the news director. Their fee varied depending upon the importance and immediacy of the story, and, of course, how much the station was willing to pay. Sometimes their client wasn't interested in the interview or made an offer they considered a little too frugal; then Chris and Ed would simply call other stations until they found the one that would pay the best price.

The recording studio, called Winchester Records, soon became a reality and was modestly successful in what were at the time relatively untapped markets: foreign language songs and American blues. Some of the biggest names in blues made studio cuts at Winchester, but in the late 1940s few in America were buying that type of music.

In the summer of 1949, Chris presented Ed with what he thought was a great idea for Winchester Records: tape the proceedings of the Goethe Bicentennial Festival in Aspen, Colorado. Smart no doubt had reservations. After all, this was pretty esoteric stuff. However, Chris felt that, with the world-renowned Dr. Albert Schweitzer as guest speaker, the recording certainly had potential to be a hit among intellectuals. After discussing the pros and cons, the partners finally decided to make the trip. They packed up their recording equipment and set out for Aspen, leaving Ed's wife, Myrtle, and young sons Kevin and Gary behind.

The event proved to be a memorable experience for Chris, and marked his introduction into what would later become known as "new age" philosophy. The recording process went well enough, and the unique 33 $1/3$ rpm two-record set of Schweitzer's speech later became a collector's item, but the duo realized little profit from their efforts. The visit to the sleepy little village of Aspen would prove most serendipitous for Smart, however. The enterprising redhead had developed an interest in precious metals and saw tremendous potential for mining gold and silver in the nearby mountain from which Aspen got its name. Not long afterward, he sold Winchester Records, moved his family to Colorado and began purchasing packages of mining land on Aspen Mountain. Chris found the town much too sedate and was soon back in Chicago. He and Ed would remain close friends, and stay in touch over the next few years, but they had no more business dealings.

When the Korean conflict began in 1950, Chris contacted the Marines to let them know he was interested in rejoining. The Corps had kept him "on the rolls" in an inactive status, and he figured they could use an experienced fighter pilot. Marine officials told him to wait, and they would get back to him; but the call never came. His age no doubt worked against him. Even though Greg Boyington had proved otherwise, it was still commonly believed that fighter pilots were over the hill after reaching thirty. Chris later learned that his old Black Sheep comrade John Bolt shot down six MiGs over Korea to become the Corps' first two-war ace. Bolt, a career Marine, turned twenty-nine in 1950.

After working aboard the ore boats for awhile, Chris signed on as part of the U.S. government construction crew building the Distant Early Warning (DEW) line, a series of radar outposts strung out across the western hemisphere above the Arctic Circle. He was sent to Greenland, one of the most desolate places on earth. The job paid well, but Chris was very happy to return to Chicago six months later when his contract was up.

A major source of income for Chris in the fifties was derived from work as a courier for the same covert organization he and Ed first became associated with in 1946. Most of his activities were based in the Chicago area, but he also made several trips to Latin America. During one trip to Cuba where Chris observed the type of conditions that prevailed under the dictator Batista, he decided to try to contact rebel leader Fidel Castro and offer his services. He was given an address for a training site in Mexico, but never went. Like almost everybody—including the U.S. government—Chris could not have foreseen that Castro would turn Cuba into a communist state after he came to power in 1959.

During the late forties and early fifties Chris maintained an on and off relationship with an attractive, vivacious legal secretary named Christine Codner. Sometime in 1954, however, he became involved with Joan Miller, a tall, dark-eyed librarian in her late thirties who was a neighbor of Fred and Marie Magee. Joan had three sons from a previous marriage, all teenaged or older. Her relationship with Chris would produce a daughter, Victoria, on June 25, 1955. Whether Christine knew about Joan and the baby is uncertain, as is the time of the final breakup of the two individuals with similar names, but no one in the Magee family ever really considered Chris and Joan a couple. Because he didn't marry their mother, Chris was not held in high esteem by Joan's sons, either. He did enjoy time with his daughter, Vicki, when he could.

Chapter 9

Crime and Punishment

——

After years of living on the edge, Chris finally plunged head-first into the abyss in 1955. Whether it was to help support Vicki, to pay off debts, or some other reason, Chris needed cash. The best place to find money, of course, is in a bank. So one day he disguised his appearance, walked into a branch of the Reserve Savings and Loan in Cicero, and asked for the manager.

He told the man he wanted to take out a loan. The manager walked Chris over to a desk and asked him to sit down. It was then that he handed the manager a note, opening his jacket to show him a military issue .45 automatic. Not unexpectedly the man became visibly frightened, so Chris calmed him down and quietly suggested they move to the back of the building where the cash was kept. There were two female employees sitting nearby as the manager removed the money, but neither paid any attention to what was going on. Chris said later, "I sure wasn't there to hurt anybody. I just wanted to get the money and get out …." which is exactly what he did. The gun he was carrying had no bullets. His take: about $3,000. In 1956, the Reserve Savings and Loan was held up again for a similar amount in a style much like that of the earlier incident, but the robber appeared to be a different man. Later, authorities decided Chris was responsible for that heist, as well.

The payoff was considerably more lucrative when Chris pulled his final bank job on January 15, 1957. This time the target was the Lincoln Way West Branch of the National Bank and Trust Company of South Bend,

Indiana. Chris discovered the bank during his trips to that city as a courier to deliver or pick up material from other agents and determined it was an easy mark. The disguise Chris used in South Bend was more elaborate than in Cicero: he wore a false moustache and eyebrows, stuffed his cheeks with cotton, and wore a heavy overcoat to make it impossible to tell what sort of body type he was. Later he said that if he'd looked into a mirror he wouldn't have recognized himself. His modus operandi in this robbery could be described as Dillingeresque. Once in the bank, he jumped over the counter and showed his gun, telling the five people inside to lay down on the floor. Surprisingly, the safe was wide open. Chris could simply, stuffing the bag he'd brought with him with stacks of tens and twenties.

In the midst of his activity he heard the front door open and turned to see a woman walk in. She quickly ascertained there was a robbery in progress and turned around and fled. Chris called to her, but she didn't stop. Realizing that he had to get out in a hurry, Chris ordered the others to the basement and left through the front door. He hustled down an alley, jumped into his car, and drove away toward the center of town. Several police cars with sirens and flashing lights passed him going the opposite direction. Later he pulled into a department store parking lot and disposed of his disguise and overcoat in a trash container. He hid most of the money at a construction site, removed and threw away the license plates he'd picked up at a junkyard, and replaced them with the originals before heading back to Chicago. He returned for the cash a day or so later. This time when he totalled up what he'd stolen it came to over $46,000.

Whatever debts Chris may have owed were soon paid off. Not wishing to call any undue attention to himself, he remained generally frugal in his monetary transactions. He did decide to buy a new automobile, however, travelling to Milwaukee to make the purchase. He paid cash, using $100 bills.

As the months went by, Chris tried to put his criminal past behind him. He reasoned that nobody had been hurt physically by his acts, and it appeared as if there would be no repercussions. Then, his luck ran out.

In October, he was at Sportsman's Park walking away from a betting window when two neatly dressed men stopped him and pulled out their badges: FBI. They asked him for identification, checked it carefully, and then apologized with the explanation that they thought he was "someone else." Two weeks after that, his car was pulled over in downtown Chicago by the same two men, and he was placed under arrest. He was told later that a woman who was present when the first robbery took place allegedly recognized him at the race track and called the authorities.

Chris smelled a rat. The chance someone could identify him after a very brief encounter two years before, when he'd been wearing a disguise, was highly unlikely. Decades later he would tell friends that he suspected the cops had been tipped off by a certain ex-con from his neighborhood who found out about the holdups, possibly through a verbal slip he could have made. He was locked in a Cook County Jail cell, but quickly made bail. Two weeks later, however, Chris was arrested for the South Bend robbery and sent to Indiana for incarceration. He would learn later that the FBI had been following him for months, and knew he was in South Bend at the time of the National Bank & Trust robbery.

After the arrest, FBI agents began hassling Ed Smart because of his longtime association with Chris. When they finally came to the realization Ed was actually at his home in Colorado during the time of the holdups, they decided to leave him alone. Chris learned of Ed's travails with the feds and figured it would be wise not to contact his friend for awhile.

Chris was put on trial for the South Bend holdup during April of 1958 and got an opportunity to experience the dark side of American justice. So certain was he that no one at the bank would recognize him in court, he even decided to grow a moustache just to show everyone he had nothing to hide. It didn't really matter. One by one, the obviously well-coached witnesses came forward and identified him as the bandit, even though their original descriptions of the perpetrator differed wildly from his appearance in court and none could identify him in a lineup following his arrest. Three men from the dealership where Chris had purchased the car all swore he'd paid in tens and twenties even though he'd taken care to use hundred dollar bills.

Despite the fact Chris wasn't being tried for that crime, the prosecution put a witness from the first Cicero robbery—the woman who allegedly had identified him at the race track—on the stand, a clear violation of U.S. court procedure. They even used prejudicial information about irregularities on his income tax returns. Deputy District Attorney Kenneth Raub referred to him as a "suave, slick, intellectual, smart sort of an operator who is at once Dr. Jekyll and Mr. Hyde." A statement by his own defense attorney, Richard Gorman, that Chris was "not the usual, ordinary kind of a person" probably didn't help his cause, either.

On April 29, Chris was convicted of bank robbery and sent to the Federal Penitentiary in Atlanta. His sentence was twenty-five years. Not long afterward he received an official-looking envelope addressed to Captain Christopher L. Magee, USMCR from Marine Corps Headquarters in Washington, D.C. Inside was an Honorable Discharge Certificate and the following:

A Marine Corps Reserve Officer Disposition Board . . . recently met at this Headquarters to make recommendations for retention in or discharge from the Marine Corps Reserve of those reserve officers who have been on the inactive Status List for three years or more. Your name was among those considered by the board . . . .

It is regretted that it is necessary to inform you that your name was not among those recommended by the Board for retention. As a consequence, it is necessary that you be separated from the Marine Corps Reserve. Accordingly . . . you are hereby honorably discharged from the U.S. Marine Corps Reserve effective this date. A certificate of discharge which reflects your honorable service in the Marine Corps Reserve is enclosed herewith . . . .

Was it coincidence that the letter was dated 30 April 1958, the day after his conviction was handed down?

The year 1958 was a very trying one for everyone in the Magee family, especially Zona. That summer, while her family of six was returning to their Mundelein home from a Florida vacation, her husband Gus was struck down by viral pneumonia and died within a few days in a southern Illinois hospital. Chris remained in the Atlanta facility for less than a year. While incarcerated, he taught educational courses to other inmates and took a Dale Carnegie course. Also, he befriended Soviet master spy Rudolf Abel, who was in charge of the linen room where Chris worked. Abel was later sent back to Russia, exchanged for downed U-2 pilot Francis Gary Powers. Because of the obvious prosecutorial violations during his trial, Chris's conviction was reversed and remanded for retrial early in 1959.

Despite the ruling, Chris was not a free man; he still had to stand trial for the Chicago robberies before retrial of the South Bend case. Then, he developed a different kind of problem—constant burning in his abdomen—a condition he first blamed on the greasy food he had to consume in prison. Exploratory surgery found something else, however: cancer in his colon. In a second operation at the prison hospital in Terre Haute, Indiana, the infected piece of that organ was removed. His weight dropped 50 pounds to 135, but he gradually returned to normal in the months following the surgery.

Chris stayed at the facility recuperating until fall when the Chicago trial was scheduled. While there, he became increasingly concerned about the disposition of his personal effects. He'd left many books and important documents in his apartment and given his brother both access to all his belongings and power of attorney over his affairs. Bud was the only Magee family member in attendance at the trial, and seemed to show concern for Chris's plight until he was convicted and sent to Atlanta. From that time on, the younger Magee didn't answer letters or make any attempt to keep Chris informed about other matters of interest to him, a malady that seemed to affect attorney Gorman, also. Especially frustrating to Chris was that Joan needed money to support Vicki and Bud wouldn't cooperate. Joan even began calling herself Joan Magee, claiming she was Chris's wife—with his blessing—in order to make it easier for her to communicate with him. Fortunately, Chris found an ally in Helen Magee, Bud's wife, who did her best to keep him apprised of what he wanted to know.

The date of the second trial finally arrived in the autumn of 1959. If Chris figured he had a decent chance of beating the rap this time, his hopes were dashed when he saw the name of his ex-con "friend" on the witness list. This confirmed what he already suspected: the stool pigeon was the one who tipped off the authorities in the beginning, no doubt to escape prosecution for his own transgressions. All Chris could do was cut his losses. Upon his attorney's advice he reluctantly accepted a plea bargain and was sentenced to a total of fifteen years for all three robberies, ten fewer than what had been imposed on him in the first trial for just one heist. He would serve his time in the notorious "hot house," Leavenworth Federal Penitentiary.

Despite its reputation, life behind the walls of Leavenworth in 1959 was far less severe than what was to be found in most maximum security penal institutions. James V. Bennett, Director of the U.S. Bureau of Prisons, was an optimistic sort who sincerely believed that most inmates could be rehabilitated if given the right conditions to do so. There were therefore plenty of opportunities available for anyone interested in acquiring job training or additional education.

Knowing he would be eligible for parole in just three years, Chris was determined to be a model prisoner, using the time to focus on his writing skills and advance his education in various academic areas. He enrolled in accredited classes taught by visiting instructors from nearby Highland College and Kansas University, and he took correspondence courses from other institutions of higher learning. He asked for and was assigned work in the prison library, giving him easy access to texts both useful in the classroom and for pleasure reading.

When Chris learned that inmates produced a quality literary magazine, *New Era*, he began contributing some of the short stories he was writing. Soon, he was invited to join the editorial staff as fiction editor. His byline would appear frequently on articles, essays, and poems. He also found time to teach high-school level courses in history and literature to other prisoners.

The distractions Chris faced came from outside the prison walls, where he was powerless to do anything. The health of his aging father had been in decline since the mid-1950s, and he was quite senile by the time Chris was incarcerated. Marie Magee was in only slightly better condition, having undergone a series of strokes that greatly incapacitated her. The burden of caring for the elderly Magees fell upon Zona, who was the sole support of four children from age seven to twelve, and Helen, mother of three preschoolers. Bud, dedicated to police work, was reluctant to get involved any more than necessary in the care of his parents.

Fred Magee, Sr. died of old age shortly after Chris was sent to Leavenworth, although Chris didn't learn about his passing for several weeks. Zona had a job teaching Catholic elementary school, thanks to the efforts of the sympathetic monsignor in her community's archdiocese. Despite the low wages paid by the school, Zona managed to keep her children sheltered, clothed, and fed. Also, she and Helen saw to it that Marie got the care she needed, which eventually meant moving her to a Catholic nursing facility. Once again, brother Bud was less than cooperative when it came to sharing the financial burden of caring for his mother.

Helen Magee received a letter from her brother-in-law shortly after Christmas 1962. She and Bud were no longer married, but she was the only person Chris could rely on to keep him abreast of family matters.

Greetings,

Thanks for the card and the snap of the kids …. I'm glad you let me know how my mother is. I hadn't heard anything from her in over a year, though I wrote several times. Thought perhaps she had given up and no one would tell me, as when my father died. I'm still puzzled over the motive behind that. Since I received your card, I wrote her a letter asking her to have one of the nuns where she is drop me a word now and then. Writing and receiving no answer is like talking into a dead phone.

Am continuing to teach six subjects (H.S.), mostly history and lit …. Taking on a new one now—really a college subject, but I have quite a bit of freedom in what I want to teach—Elements of Poetry and the Drama. Have been doing college work, too, on Saturdays and at night. Picked up about fifty credit hours so far. Besides that have been studying Modern Philosophy and am in my third year of work with the Great Books group. Am also fiction editor for our magazine, the New Era—so you see I never have time I don't have to snatch away from other demands. I do work out regularly with the weights and keep in shape.

Most of college work has been through Kansas U. They send their prof's over so it makes everything convenient. However, I've had about everything they offer in the subject I'm most interested in—writing (I've got twenty-one hours in English and composition). Soooo—I'm going to take a couple of courses in the drama from U. of California and one, in poetry, from U. of Chicago (corresp.). This will be a good arrangement because I am teaching these now—as I mentioned. After that, if I'm still here, I'll take Writing Poetry, Drama, and The Novel (three separate courses). Have already had Short Story Writing and Introduction to the Drama.

Went up for parole in October and they turned me down. Probably because I didn't have anyone to write to the parole board and ask them to turn me loose. I didn't ask because I just wanted to see what value a good record had without outside help. Obviously it means nothing. When I see that, it makes me feel better. Paradox? Yes I suppose so. Hope you had a very nice Christmas. Good luck to you and the kids . . . . Chris

Chris had more than enough time to take every course that interested him. He earned an Associate of Arts Degree from Highland College and, eventually, completed seventy-nine hours of college credit. He was promoted to managing editor on the *New Era* staff and by early 1964 was editor-in-chief. Perhaps the Federal Bureau of Prisons considered him too valuable to lose, as he was again turned down for parole. A close friend, author William Lichtman, volunteered to investigate possible reasons for the denials. His efforts to locate records of the arrest and trial proved extremely frustrating, however, as he explained in a letter to Chris dated April 8, 1964.

I spent a great deal of time over at the court house. Thank God I don't have to deal with them too often. They went through your file or at least some of it in front of me, and it was a mess. How in the world they could find anything is beyond me. I was getting mad as H— for what they were doing, and the waste and the time, and the stupid way they were doing things. All I can say (is) you can keep your civil service worker . . . . No one seems to know what the next one is doing . . . . You went to court . . . . You went through the whole business and there is not one person who can find a darn thing on you. Tell me, how in the devil did they get you into jail? Are they sure they have the right man? If they don't have your files and records then who in the H— would?

I'm sorry, Chris. I did want to be of help to you. Write when you can. Bill

Although the Magee family had once been a potent force on the Pittsburgh political scene, Chris had little regard for most elected officials—perhaps due to the pervasive graft and corruption he witnessed growing up in Chicago. In President John F. Kennedy he saw a different breed of politician, however, and quickly came to admire the young Commander-in-Chief. Chris could relate to the man. They were both born in 1917, were Irish Catholics, and had been decorated for their heroics in the South Pacific during World War II. That JFK was a man of letters also weighed in his favor. After Kennedy's assassination on November 22, 1963, Chris was inspired to honor his fallen leader with an original poem, "Toward Dusk." The piece was published in the Winter 1964 issue of *New Era*.

An incubus of disbelief squats on the chest of the Nation
  As it talks talks talks
Away thorny memories of its deeds that
  Evoked again among us
  Furies from Hadean night.

Heavy in its winding sheet of stricken silence
  looms that bronze casket,
Its shadow smothering with dread the remnants
  of a Nation's soul
Eaten hollow by ritual worms feasting
  on Hate and Greed
Within the bellies of the proud.

Heavy bells toll
  toll in the tragic gloom
Throwing their weight against advancing night.
Listen—do they mourn a man?
Or do they dirge for a people unaware
That effect must follow cause.
The Haunted, plagued by images of dread,
Hear ice grind in freezing veins
As frost of fallen ages
Ushers an iron foe
Come from the center of ancient night
To sit in wait for another wake.

Since
An opaque eye

Frozen to a cross-haired scope,
Like loveless Loki
Has hurled winged fury to smash into darkness
Another beacon that dared to thrust its lance of light
Against the creeping twilight
of the West.

The *New Era* often received laudatory mail from politicians, educators, literary figures, and other notables. The letters to the editor section in the Summer 1964 issue led off with the following note (as published):

... Mrs. Kennedy deeply appreciated ... memorial tribute to President
Kennedy, and I hope you will convey her special thanks to Mr. Magee ....
Pamela Turnure
Secretary to Mrs. Kennedy

Marie Magee died in Libertyville in 1964. She was buried next to her husband in a Catholic cemetery on the South Side. Zona, who'd taken on the full responsibility of caring for her, handled the funeral arrangements. That she managed to raise her children while taking care of most of the Magee family business on such a meager salary was due in no small part to her success in the stock market. Zona was the only child of Fred Magee to take an interest in his work, and she continued to educate herself about the ins and outs of the financial world through *The Wall Street Journal* and other publications. She never invested large amounts—just enough to realize the money needed to educate and provide for her family.

By the spring of 1966, Chris felt like a forgotten man. Eight years had passed since he was first sent to prison, and he was still serving time for crimes where no injuries had occurred. He lost both parents and his brother-in-law and heard nothing for years from either his brother or his sister. In the case of Zona, it was especially disappointing. Chris was, after all, the godfather of her eldest child, Kathy. He often visited the family before his incarceration and really enjoyed spending time with all the kids. Still, he had Joan and Vicki. His daughter was now ten. Joan sent pictures, of course, but he wondered how the little girl was handling life without a father. On April 7, feeling philosophical and perhaps a little bitter, he wrote:

Dear Joan,
Hope you and Vicki have (or had) a pleasant Easter. I suppose she gets all
enthusiastic about these holidays—school vacation and all that sort of

libertarianism and laxity. For me, they are all unreal, like something once glimpsed in another dimension by someone you were, but no longer are.

We've had no winter to speak of, so we speak of the winter we didn't have. The sun comes up and goes down regularly—well-trained, I suppose; although this has become a doubtful virtue. The moon I can't say much about, not having seen it at night for some light years (occasionally I have seen it early in the summer evenings or mornings; but this, of course, doesn't count). The wind continues to blow when and where it will, with the usual disregard for our wishes. What else is new? Wellll, they seem to have renovated a section of the wall, some new covering material they are testing out that's supposed to be effective for a hundred years. Meanwhile, politicians, sociologists, penologists, and other such wingless birds are spreading the joyful news that in less than 25 years there will be no more prisons such as we have today. But those who build walls are like burrowing animals who go on digging, digging, whether or not there is any purpose in it. Well, the money's there; so, of course, what else is there to do with it?

Perhaps, though, you don't dig "black humor." However, having the advantage of you at the moment, I'll force a bit more on you so there will be something profound for you to ponder while soaking your head in a schooner of suds .... It is so apt a symbol of everything we as a nation represent today in the world. For a long time we have had the Statue of Liberty standing in our front yard welcoming the peoples of the world. But what did we have, until very recently, in our backyard? Alcatraz, stashed away in San Francisco Bay. What piercing satire and irony. It fits our society as if it were done on purpose by some latter-day Voltaire. But to go even further, Alcatraz was staring at probably the most liberal-minded city in the nation. They raised so much hell for so long that finally the government had to close it—too much heat.

Tell Vicki I'd like to have her in my Easter basket. Love, Chris

Chris didn't know it when he wrote the letter, but his days as an inmate were soon to come to an end. Later that year during his annual parole hearing—his fifth—some discrepancies were apparently discovered in the system's record-keeping; errors that may have kept him in the penitentiary far longer than his crimes probably warranted. Chris finally was given his walking papers late in the fall of 1966. He had been confined in federal prisons for a total of eight-and-a-half years.

Chapter 10

Freedom and a New Direction

—

When Chris was released back into society his first challenge was to find a job. His field of choice, not surprisingly, was journalism. He now had plenty of experience, both as a writer and editor, and an impressive body of work. Still, there were two giant obstacles to overcome: his age—forty-nine is old for someone just getting started professionally in the field—and, of course, his prison background. That the institution where he gained most of his journalistic training was Leavenworth Federal Penitentiary wasn't likely to win over any potential employers.

Even with the two-headed albatross around his neck, it didn't take Chris long to convince someone in Chicago that he was worthy of an opportunity. The publishers of a twice-weekly community tabloid called the *Westside Times – Lawndale News* hired him on as editor. The editorial content of the paper was really a one-man operation. Chris was responsible for layout, photography, and writing the stories, in addition to his editing duties. The money was nothing to write home about, but—with both his parents gone—Chris didn't really have a home any more. He found a low-rent apartment in a less than fashionable section of the South Side—it was located above a seedy bar—and settled into his new career.

Chris kept in close contact with Joan and Vicki, who were now living in an old, but pleasant neighborhood on the North Side. He had no intentions of marrying, but they were, after all, family.

During his long imprisonment Joan wrote regularly, even if it was just to tell him how tough things were for her and her kids. Helen was also supportive of him, especially in the confusion of his early months of incarceration; and Chris made it a point to call on his former sister-in-law and her three children frequently. His brother was another matter, however. Bud essentially deserted Chris after receiving his power of attorney. He didn't answer any of Chris's letters and had generally been uncooperative in all matters pertaining to Joan and Vicki.

Zona and Chris had always been on good terms prior to his imprisonment. He'd visited her and Gus and their children often and was very fond of the family. But he heard nothing from his widowed sister for years—no letters, no phone calls. For several months after his release, Chris debated as to whether to call or visit her. What seemed an ideal opportunity for reconciliation soon presented itself. Through Helen he learned that Zona's eldest child, Kathy—his goddaughter—was about to graduate from nursing school, and her mother was throwing a big party to celebrate the event. Chris decided to surprise the family by making an appearance.

Kathy was astounded and delighted to see her long lost uncle at the ceremony. Zona's reaction was a little harder to gauge. She was certainly taken aback, at first, but seemed rather cool, at least on the surface. Chris began to feel uncomfortable. Perhaps he'd made a mistake in showing up uninvited. Maybe Zona didn't want anything to do with her brother, who was, after all, an ex-con. Why else would she be ignoring him? He decided his presence was probably an embarrassment to her and quietly slipped away without any good-byes, skipping the reception at Zona's home. Many years later he would learn that—except for Kathy—his sister's children were unaware he'd been incarcerated. Zona simply told them he'd moved away.

Chris was starting to feel like a pariah. His siblings seemingly wanted nothing to do with him, and he had little contact with friends from his pre-imprisonment days—with the notable exceptions of Joan and Helen. He lived on the edge for most of his first forty years and paid dearly when he finally fell. How long would he have to continue his penance?

Whether it came as a result of his experience in Leavenworth, the settling down that comes with middle age or some other form of evolution, Chris's lifelong thirst for adventure was transformed to a search for knowledge and spirituality. His guru—if one could call him that—was the late German philosopher Rudolf Steiner (1861–1925), founder of a school of thought during the early years of the 20th Century called anthroposophy.

The term, derived from Greek roots, literally means "wisdom concerning man," although Steiner defined anthroposophy as "a path of knowledge, to guide the spiritual in the human being to the spiritual in the universe." His teachings had tremendous influence on the abstract artists of his day and, decades later, on what would be known as New Age thinking. Chris was first introduced to Steiner's writings while attending the Goethe Bicentennial celebration at Aspen in 1949. He became a serious student of Steiner's work while in prison. During his first half-century of life, Chris read and absorbed countless volumes on philosophical subjects—everything from eastern religion to American Indian mysticism to existentialism—but nothing piqued his interest like Steiner's books and lectures. Beginning in the late 1960s and for many years thereafter, Chris was a regular attendee at the weekly gatherings of Chicago's Anthroposophical Society, which met in a house at 529 Grant Place. Joan often accompanied him to the sessions.

Late in 1968, Chris left his editor's job to accept a similar but better-paying position with the *Back of the Yards Journal*, a weekly broadsheet newspaper that served the working community of that area of the city. His new boss, Aaron Hurwitz, was owner, publisher, and founder of the forty-year-old journal that had a circulation of 120,000. Prior to taking on his new post, Chris and Joan visited Key West, Florida. It was his first vacation in many years and his last for some time to come. His duties at the *Journal* would keep him very busy; not only with writing, editing, photography, layout, and typography, but also supervising and participating in the composition of the paper at the print shop. In addition, it was his responsibility to publicize the activities of the Back of the Yards Neighborhood Council, nationally known for its expertise in using the democratic processes for community development.

As the decade of the seventies began, Chris was settling into a lifestyle that could easily be called conventional were it not for his rather esoteric intellectual interests. He had a steady job which brought him a certain amount of professional satisfaction and respect within journalistic circles. His income was hardly spectacular, but it was more than sufficient to meet his meager needs. Personal time was spent reading or attending meetings of the Anthroposophical Society or the Great Books of the Western World discussion group.

Chris's daughter Vicki—all grown up into a tall, beautiful teenager with long, lustrous dark hair—died suddenly in the spring of 1973, the victim of an apparent accidental drug overdose. The loss devastated Joan, and she began a long, slow decline marked by frequent health problems. Chris no doubt grieved as any parent would, but tried to deal with Vicki's death inwardly as much as possible. He seldom discussed the matter with anyone, except Joan, in the years that followed.

Aaron Hurwitz, owner-publisher of the *Back of the Yards Journal,* suffered a heart attack later in 1973 and turned over most administrative duties to his editor. Chris convinced his boss to change the paper's printing to the sharper looking, lower cost offset process and continued to turn out a quality product. Two years later, Hurwitz decided to sell the publication he had created over four decades before. The new owner brought along his own editor, and Chris was out of a job.

In October of 1975, Chris discovered a large manila envelope in his mailbox. It was postmarked "Denver, CO" and the return address was a suite in a bank building. Inside was the following letter:

> *C.L.*
>
> *Thought you had gone to another planet and decided not to return.*
>
> *Enclosed give a little insight into my nefarious activities.*
>
> *Also busy in Mexican projects which is really my first love along with my boats, planes and money.*
>
> *I now own Aspen Mountain which I lease to the ski corporation. Bought all the old mining companies, and they turned out to be real estate.*
>
> *Offspring in addition to Serya Sing (formerly Kevin) and Gary are Timothy and Mary. Same wife (I guess) . . . .*
>
> *Write!*
>
> *Come see us!*
>
> *Maybe I will get to Chicago in the near future.*
>
> > *Best,*
> >
> > *Ed*

The envelope included copies of several newspaper stories about Smart's various enterprises, along with a few photos, some of which were of Ed and his close friend, and sometime business partner, actor John Wayne.

Chris was, of course, very happy to hear from his old buddy. He knew that Ed had done very well for himself, with business interests around the world, but wasn't sure whether someone that successful really wanted to reestablish ties after so long. Now, he knew. Still, with Ed away from home so

Ed Smart (R) and business partners find a nugget in their gold pan at one of Ed's mining properties (1963)

Chris Magee Collection

much, it would be more than three years before the two friends would have an opportunity to get together again.

At the time he left the *Journal*, Chris hadn't taken a vacation in over six years, so, with the money he'd saved, he decided to travel for a while and visit places he'd always wanted to see, such as Santa Fe, New Mexico, the art and cultural center of the U.S. Southwest. Another excursion took him to Woodland Park, Colorado, for a series of New Age seminars where the principal speaker was the director of the teaching program at the Rudolf Steiner College in Sacramento, California. Chris lived in a tent during the eight-day outdoor event, which focused on the "Alchemy of Sense Perception—A Rosicrucian Path."

When Joan moved to the clean, picturesque suburb of Lake Forest, Chris took over the lease on her previous residence on Sunnyside Avenue. The apartment was located across from a park in a rather old section of town, but it was far more hospitable than the rapidly degenerating locale of his South Side digs. Best of all, it sat just two blocks from a branch of the Chicago Public Library where weekly Great Books of the Western World discussion group meetings were held. He and Joan continued to attend meetings of the Anthroposophical Society as well. One of the other members, Norm Pritchard, became a close friend. Since he resided in Lake Forest, Norm would often drive the couple back to Joan's apartment after the weekly gatherings, and the three of them would hold lively discussions of their own until well after midnight.

In mid-1976, several weeks after moving, Chris paid a visit to the bar beneath his old apartment to see if any mail had come his way. Mixed among the expected junk pieces was a large envelope with a return address in Hawaii, of all places. The name above the address was familiar—Frank

Walton. Could it be the same Walton he'd known in the South Pacific—the big, straight shooting, redheaded ex-cop who'd done so much to make the Black Sheep famous? Indeed it was, he quickly realized as he read the letter, which turned out to be an invitation to a VMF 214 reunion in Honolulu. The envelope also contained a questionnaire, plus information from the travel agent coordinating the reunion activities.

Chris had no idea how Frank managed to obtain his address, not that it really mattered. Reading the letter sent a wave of nostalgia through him, resurrecting many fond memories from the proudest and happiest time of his life. He knew he couldn't possibly afford to make the trip to Hawaii, as much as he would like to have spent some time with his old squadron mates. That did not stop Chris from granting Frank's request for updated information, though. When he got back to his apartment, he sat down and wrote his former air intelligence officer a long letter that included both the high and low points of his postwar career. He wondered what the other pilots would think of having an ex-con among their numbers—a real black sheep in their family.

∞

The efforts Chris made to find work as a journalist in the late 1970s were not successful. Despite the solid background he'd gained on community newspapers between 1966 and 1975, he was now past sixty and no amount of skill could overcome the age bias he faced at every turn. His prison record was no longer of any consequence, though. He'd even managed to hide his years of incarceration and turn the experience to his advantage, as evidenced by the completely factual information he provided in a letter applying for an editorial assistant position:

> … *Other editing-writing experience includes several years as associate editor and writer for a quarterly "little magazine" in Kansas while I was studying for my degree in English at Highland College and the University of Kansas. At that time I also conducted a writer's workshop for the inmates at Leavenworth penitentiary and led Great Books of the Western World discussion groups there.*

He didn't get the job, presumably because he was overqualified. Eventually, he settled for a position with a church bulletin, not writing or editing but selling advertising space over the phone.

Chapter 11

The Unexpected

The Skipper of *Silver Queen II*—a seventy-foot North Sea trawler docked in San Diego Harbor—was lounging on the deck one afternoon early in 1979 when he noticed someone striding along the pier toward his vessel. Something familiar about the erect, soldier-like walk made the seafarer stand up and take notice. As the figure came closer, the skipper ran a hand through his reddish gray hair and quietly chuckled at the man's appearance—somewhere between a modern version of Coleridge's *Ancient Mariner* and an aging Old Spice man. He wore a dark blue long-sleeved pullover and slacks with a matching wool navy watch cap and had a tote bag thrown over one shoulder. The man stopped next to the gangway, grinned, and heartily called out, "Permission to come aboard!"

"C.L., I can't believe it!" Captain Ed Smart exclaimed as he practically leaped out of his deck shoes to greet his old friend. It was a very special moment in the lives of both men.

Chris and Ed spent the rest of the day and evening trying to catch up on each other's doings. Ed was a wealthy man, but, despite the different paths their lives had taken, the friendship between the two Chicagoans withstood the years. Ed found Chris as agreeable and good-humored as ever, but somewhere along the way—perhaps in prison—he'd changed. The aggressive, devil-may-care risk-taker Ed had shared so many adventures with over the years just didn't seem to exist any more.

Ed was still officially a resident of Colorado, but had come to San Diego to pursue what had become much more than a simple interest in pleasure boating. *Silver Queen II*, which officially belonged to the Institute for Meso-american Studies—a non-profit organization Ed founded—was used as an oceanographic vessel and for exploring Latin American coastlines in search of mineral deposits and historical artifacts. One of Ed's successful projects was proving that—contrary to what was written in most history books—the fourth and final voyage of Christopher Columbus was a tremendous success. The explorer found a rich source of gold in Panama; enough to to keep his family wealthy for many generations to come.

Ed invited his buddy to join the crew, and Chris was happy to accept the offer. He'd always had an affinity for the sea, and he needed the job— not that there was a lot of work to do. Except for a couple of short voyages along both coasts of Baja California and up into the Sea of Cortez, the boat remained tied up at its dock in San Diego during his stay.

After a few months of the good life at sea and ashore in southern California, Chris began experiencing frequent pain in his abdominal area. A checkup at the San Diego V. A. Hospital confirmed what he suspected: the long dormant colon cancer had returned. Deciding not to burden Ed with his problems, Chris sat down with his friend one evening and told him it was time he returned to Chicago. He left the next day. Many years would pass before Smart learned the real reason for the sudden departure.

The operation was performed at Chicago's Westside V. A. Hospital and went off without a hitch. Chris recuperated quickly, with Joan's help, and was soon getting around as well as before. During the brief period before his retirement he earned a living selling the services of a moving company.

Chris retired at the age of sixty-five in 1982. Because his needs were simple and his apartment was rent-controlled, he could survive well enough on the meager five hundred dollars-plus of his monthly Social Security check. He no longer owned a car and—thanks to Chicago's fine public transportation system—didn't need one. His limited means prevented him from taking any vacations, of course, but Chris always found plenty of stimulating activities in and around the city.

In the spring of 1986, Chris received another large manila envelope, this time from an A. Finkel in Los Angeles. He couldn't place the name at first, but then a lot of good memories started coming back to him as he read the contents. The letter inside was from Aaron "Red" Finkel, one of his fellow volunteer pilots from Israel's war of independence. The purpose of the correspondence was to invite Chris to attend an Israeli government-sponsored reunion of the 101 squadron in Tel Aviv that summer. All the pilots were to be interviewed for a historical text being written about the nation's air force.

Wanting very much to go, but realizing he couldn't possibly afford such a trip, Chris called Finkel to pass along his regrets. Red, however, had other ideas. He told Chris not to worry about the cost and that everything would be taken care of. A few weeks later, Chris caught a flight to New York City, where he joined about a score of other American and Canadian citizens, all with ties to the 1948 war. The group was then taken to McGuire Air Force Base in New Jersey where they boarded an Israeli military transport plane for Tel Aviv.

The passengers on the 5,000 mile flight that July included nine others who had been forbidden cargo thirty-eight years before. This time, however, there would be no long stopovers in Amsterdam, Geneva, Zurich, or Prague. Chris spent the eleven-hour trip seated alongside Finkel and Minneapolis resident Leon Frankel, one of the pilots he was closest to in 1948. The lively discussions that took place kept all three men wide awake during the long flight. Red and Leon had remained in touch over the years, so Chris became the center of attention. The more the two successful businessmen could pry from him about his exploits, the more they wanted to hear. Under ordinary circumstances Chris didn't care to discuss the past, but his traveling companions were so good-natured and open about their own lives he soon began to feel comfortable recounting his checkered career, including the criminal activities that caused his long incarceration.

The landing in the bright sunshine at the big, modern Ben Gurion Airport was in sharp contrast to the last flight Chris made to Tel Aviv, when the four-engined Constellation carrying the volunteers slipped onto the runway at a tiny secret airfield in the darkness of early morning. This time they were greeted by Israeli Air Force officials upon debarking and hustled through customs, visa stamping, and the usual procedures. The former pilots were then given a festive reception before being driven to their headquarters hotel, the Dan-Panorama.

Later during the stay, everyone gathered at Ezer Weizman's elegant home in the ancient coastal city of Caeserea for a festive reunion party. It was there that Finkel got Chris to talk with the others about the bank robberies and prison experience, subjects he ordinarily avoided. His fellow fighter pilots seated themselves around the deck of the swimming pool and listened with great interest, seeming not the least bit uncomfortable or judgmental. In fact, the party proved to be a cathartic experience for Chris.

The 101 Squadron gathering lasted a week and included a four-day tour of the country, for some, and VIP excursions for all to the Air Force Museum and one of the newest bases. The ragtag volunteers were charter members of an air force four times as large as Great Britain's RAF and arguably the world's finest. It was an exciting and nostalgic time for all the visitors, both for the camaraderie and for the opportunity to experience the bustling, contemporary society they'd help create. Chris took many notes during his stay, in the event he decided to write about it later. He also promised Leon he'd take him up on his invitation to come and visit. Minneapolis was only an hour away from Chicago by commuter plane, and Chris looked forward to continuing their renewed friendship.

After returning from Israel, Chris settled back into his familiar inner-directed lifestyle. He kept in shape with long walks around his North Side neighborhood and continued to attend discussion groups and be the best customer of his local public library branch. Much of his time was also spent at Joan's place in Lake Forest. His longtime lady friend wasn't getting around all that well any more, due to various ailments that her doctors were unable to diagnose.

In 1987, Joan's sons—who were paying the rent on her apartment—decided the Lake Forest residence was getting a little too pricey and moved her to Mundelein, about twenty miles farther north. Neither Joan nor Chris cared much for the little town. Best known for its Catholic seminary, Mundelein had almost nothing to offer in the way of cultural attractions. Joan's new apartment was cozy and reasonably-priced, however, and one of her sons lived just a few miles away. Going to visit Joan turned out to be considerably less convenient for Chris, however. It meant taking a train to Libertyville then walking more than two miles, as there was no public transportation available. Still, he managed to get up to Mundelein almost every weekend.

Despite its less than desirable location for Chris, Joan's place was far more habitable than his own. A fire in the apartment above his unit had inspired a visit from the Chicago Fire Department, and the water damage resulted in a potentially dangerous sagging of his ceiling. The landlord refused to do anything about the situation, telling Chris he could move if he didn't like it. The apartment building owner's attitude came as no surprise to Chris. He'd refused to make even minor repairs for years, reasoning that since he was not permitted to raise the rent on his current tenants, he therefore should not be required to maintain the place. Building inspectors cited the landlord on several occasions, but he somehow managed to make the citations go away after a visit to City Hall.

Chris was now seventy years old. He had come to the realization that despite his robust physical condition he lacked the financial means to explore the country in search of new experiences whenever the spirit moved him, and he stoically accepted his lot. His was now a world of ideas rather than actions. He kept up on current events through television and newspapers and found fascination in the way the media was affecting and manipulating the everyday lives of the populace. His earlier triumphs and travails held little importance to him anymore.

"The past is something that's not going anywhere," he told Minneapolis newsman Neal Gendler during a visit to Leon Frankel's home in 1988—a rare sojourn from the Greater Chicago area. But then, when asked specifically about his experiences as a fighter pilot, he added, "Certain things are like something outside of time itself. It's like an enclave in which you lived in certain ways that are so different from the ways in which people generally live: the type of excitement . . . adventure . . . spirit. These . . . things put it in a category of its own. They do not really belong within . . . so-called normal ways of life because the normal ways of life are not to live like that. People are trying to avoid the very kinds of things you're looking for, so it's just a reversal. There's a discontinuity."

Chris (L) and fellow Israeli Air Force volunteer pilot Leon Frankel, during a visit to Frankel's home in Minneapolis (August 1988)   *Chris Magee Collection*

The past that Chris insisted was "not going anywhere" caught up to him during the spring of 1988 and changed the course of his future. It started late one April afternoon when he arrived home after spending several days in Mundelein. As he approached the front of his apartment, Chris noticed a small piece of paper wedged in the doorway just above the knob. It was a note from someone whose name was unfamiliar. The gist of its message was that the writer regretted missing him again, and hoped Chris would contact him. There was no address or phone number listed. Chris was perplexed, but soon forgot about the note.

Then, a week or so later as he was sweeping the kitchen floor near the two steps that led upward to the front door, he noticed a large envelope that had apparently slipped through the wide crack in the top step. How long had the envelope been there? A day or two? A week? A month? Chris had no idea as he fished it from beneath the steps. His name was spelled out on the front of the envelope in large block letters. Inside was a long letter written on seven six-by-nine-inch sheets of lined paper. The hand printing wasn't stylish but was easy to read, as if the writer was concerned that Chris understood every word.

It didn't take him long to find out why.

Part II

Kindred Spirits

Chapter 12

The Underachiever

M y earliest clear memory is of the time late in 1948 when Mom, Baby Sis, and I boarded a shiny diesel train bound for Missouri, leaving the big brick duplex in Jamaica, New York, we shared with my grandparents and teenaged uncle, Mickey. I was only three years old, so I didn't realize we were moving to a new home or how much I would miss my mother's family—especially her father, a stocky, good-natured fellow who always had a twinkle in his green eyes. Papa and all the residents of the home on 164th Place called me Thumper, as did the neighbors, so I, of course, assumed it was my given name.

After a journey that lasted all night, we got off the train in Chicago and boarded another one. A second lengthy rail trip ensued, although not as long as the first, and we eventually arrived in Kansas City. I don't remember the train ride, but I do remember my first sight of our new home in Liberty, Missouri, where we would live with Bill Reed, our dad. It was a rather modest trailer—this was before the more socially acceptable term "mobile home" became popular. Fortunately, three-year-olds are seldom concerned with appearances.

The mists of time seemed to have obscured any earlier memories of my father, a tall, lean man with wavy black hair. Later, I learned he'd been in the Navy, so I surmised he'd probably been at sea most of the time during my first three years. One of Dad's first decrees—there would be many—

was that Baby Sis would henceforth be known by her real name, Anne. She was, after all, two years old and no longer a baby. I was told that I had a real name, also: Robert Timothy Reed. This was a complete surprise to me. Fortunately, everyone still called me Thumper. After that, when adults would ask me what my full name was, I told them, "Thumper Robert Timothy Reed." That usually produced a chuckle.

Another change that occurred in the lives of my sister and I at this time was Dad's frequent employment of a hitherto unfamiliar practice called spanking. Actually, Anne seldom had to suffer the sting of Dad's palm, but I was the sort of kid who enjoyed going where I didn't belong, saying what I wasn't supposed to say, and other acts of questionable behavior that merited such corporal punishment, at least in his eyes. Dad almost never raised his voice. He was always in complete control. I came to live in almost constant fear of him. Through Dad's example, my mother also became a believer, although a somewhat reluctant one, in administering a little justice on my posterior when the situation called for it. Her spankings were considerably less painful than Dad's, however.

We resided in Liberty because that's where both my parents were going to school—at William Jewell College, a small liberal arts institution founded by the Baptist Church. Most of the residents of our trailer park were students. Many were ex-servicemen with wives and children, who—like Dad—were taking advantage of the G.I. Bill.

Dad was a very energetic individual, and when someone needed help he would spring into action. I recall one morning when Anne and I awoke to learn that Dad was in the hospital. My mother explained that there had been a fire in one of our neighbor's trailers. Dad told her to call the fire department from one of the park's phones—we didn't have one of our own—then ran to the burning trailer, which was engulfed in smoke, and banged on the door. When no one came, he moved quickly to a window and smashed it with his bare fist in order to get inside. Fortunately, the residents weren't home. It was then he discovered that his right forearm was bleeding profusely from a jagged cut caused by the broken window glass. Dad returned from the hospital with a long row of stitches in his arm. He carried the scars for the rest of his life.

The best part of living in Missouri was our frequent visits to the farm near the little town of Appleton City (population about 1,200) where Grandma and Grandpa Reed lived. Our first trip to the farm was via bus in 1949. Grandpa picked us up in his Chevy—he always had a Chevy of one vintage or another—at the Butler bus depot and drove us to the farm, about twenty-five miles away, where we were greeted by Grandma as we pulled into the barnyard. Jim Reed epitomized the term "rugged individual." He was a husky, ruddy-faced man with brown eyes, gunmetal hair, and well-calloused hands. He almost always wore blue overalls and rolled his own cigarettes. Bessie Reed was small with dark hair and blue eyes and never used makeup. She usually wore an apron over her utilitarian house dress, and was constantly in motion from dawn till dusk—gathering eggs, pumping water from the well (there was no running water or electricity the first time we visited the Reed farm), churning butter, and preparing the incredible multi-course meals we enjoyed every day. Anne and I would watch with fascination as she strolled into the chicken yard, selected a victim, and quickly wrung its neck. Sometimes we'd help her pluck the feathers—a job I found tedious—in preparation for dinner.

Grandma had to have a lot of energy. She and Grandpa raised nine children—seven boys and two girls—of which Dad was number four in line. The youngest of the brood, Uncle Glen, or "Popeye," as he was called, still lived at home. Like my mother's younger brother Mickey, Popeye was seldom around. On the other hand two people who were always in the house were Grandma's parents, "Little Grandma" and "Little Grandpa" Bledsoe, the oldest people I had ever known. Little Grandma was small and sweet. Little Grandpa was lanky and talked slowly. He was always offering Anne and me something called horehound candy. We accepted his generosity the first time, but never again after that. How could anything that tasted so bad be called candy?

In addition to chickens, there were pigs in a pen on the other side of the barnyard, and cattle and sheep in the fields. But my favorite farm animals were the horses. In 1949, there were three: Grandpa's draft team, Fred and Bolly, and his wonderful saddle horse, Rex. How well I remember Dad hoisting Anne and me up on Rex's long back and leading us around the barnyard as we clung to his mane. What a thrill for two city kids. Later, of course, we'd learn to ride him by ourselves. Old Rex, who lived to age twenty-seven, will always hold a special place in the hearts of the Reed kids. We also discovered we had uncles, aunts, and cousins nearby—lots of them—and we became better acquainted each trip to the farm.

In 1950, our family moved to Columbia, where my parents enrolled at the University of Missouri, my father to work for his Masters' Degree and my mother on her Bachelor of Science in nursing. By that time, Dad had purchased a car—a black 1948 Chevy Fleetline sedan. That automobile would serve us faithfully for six years and earn the nickname "The Turtle," after a famous U.S. Navy patrol plane, *The Truculent Turtle*, that set a long distance flying record. The Reed farm was changing with the times. Fred and Bolly were replaced by a big, shiny red Farmall tractor, and the house welcomed the second half of the twentieth century with the addition of electricity, running water, and indoor plumbing. The family of Bill and Mary Reed was expanding, too. Diana Lynne arrived on April 18, in Independence. There was no sibling rivalry. Anne and I were both thrilled to have a little sister, even if it meant our trailer was more cramped than ever.

In 1951, we received the news via telegram of the sudden death of my maternal grandfather. He'd suffered a heart attack. I can remember my mother crying and Dad comforting her. Anne and I were both old enough to comprehend what death was, and we cried, too, knowing we would never see Papa again. Mom took baby Diana and flew back to New York for the funeral. I wished I could have gone, too.

Later, in September of that year, my parents enrolled me in the first grade. I would never become an outstanding student, but I enjoyed the interaction with kids my age, and, of course, I learned how to read. This latter activity would prove to be a double-edged sword in future years. On the one hand, it enabled me to study my texts; on the other, I became such an avid reader that I would pore through any written work that interested me—a vast category that usually did not include school books.

In the summer of 1952, Dad sold the trailer and our family moved to the big city of St. Louis, where he went to work as a teacher at Bayliss High School. We moved into a unit of Jefferson Barracks, which had been military housing. Our new home wasn't exactly sprawling, but it was a lot bigger than the trailer. A good thing, too, because on October 17 that year my brother, Edward James Reed—named for both his grandfathers—came into the world kicking and screaming and joined us at home a few days later. To say I was happy to have a little brother would be a gross understatement. I was thrilled.

Our stay in St. Louis and Dad's teaching career came to an abrupt end after just six months due to President Truman's decision to "call up the reserves for service in Korea." I knew Dad was in the Naval Air Reserve. Every month or so he put on his officer's uniform and carried out his duties as a "weekend warrior." Flying seemed like the greatest thing in the world to me, and I made up my mind that I wanted to be a Navy pilot when I grew up.

Dad's return to active duty meant packing up and moving again, this time to Norfolk, Virginia. He bought a modest three-bedroom, one-bath home just a few blocks from the Chesapeake Bay. Behind our spacious backyard were woods and swampland, deep enough for a kid to hide in but not to get lost. Our four-year stay in Norfolk would be highlighted by frequent trips to the beach and generally nice weather, marred only by an occasional hurricane. We also had some terrific neighbors, especially the Nortons, who lived next door. Their daughter, Charlene—two years my senior—was an only child who was really excited about having a big family close by. She spent so much time at our place that all the Reed kids came to look upon her as a big sister.

I especially enjoyed our trips to the Naval Air Station, where I could examine the aircraft, particularly the fighters. I fell in love with them, from the World War II-vintage Corsairs and Bearcats to the jets. Often I dreamed of sitting in the cockpit of the Navy's hottest new jet—the sleek, swept-wing Grumman Cougar—roaring across the sky at 700 miles per hour.

My sisters, Nancy and Barbie, were born in Norfolk. I did not greet the arrival of either with the same enthusiasm I'd had for Diana and Eddie. Hey, having a bunch of sisters around is no picnic for a growing boy.

Early on, my school work at Bay View Elementary wasn't achieving the level expected of me by my parents and teachers. One day my second grade teacher noticed I was squinting at the blackboard. She told my parents, and recommended I get my eyesight tested. Sure enough, the tests showed I was nearsighted—very nearsighted. Soon I was sporting spectacles. I could see much better, but truly hated the idea of having to wear glasses. They were something only mild-mannered studious sorts wore, as far as I was concerned. They didn't really improve my school performance but the new impediments took away some of my aggressiveness. I avoided fights and rough-and-tumble play for fear of breaking my glasses and facing the ire of my dad, who considered the eyewear a costly necessity. Worst of all, I had to give up my fondest dream. My parents explained that anyone hoping to become a pilot in the U.S. Armed Forces had to have perfect vision.

The biggest event for the Reeds in 1956 was the family reunion that summer in Appleton City. Everyone attended, even the three families from the Pacific Coast. How forty people could hang out together in one modest-sized farm house for the better part of a week remains a mystery to me.

In the spring of 1957, Dad was transferred to the Naval Air Station in Olathe, Kansas, for an operations training school. During the seven months he was stationed there, our family lived in a rented house in Appleton City. It was a wonderful experience for all of us. Appleton City was and is a charming, unpretentious little town populated by warm, friendly people. Our family could visit relatives almost any time we wanted, and I would fish with my newfound friends at various local ponds and lakes.

Maybe best of all, Anne and I could spend lots of time at the Dari-Burg. It was Appleton City's only fast food restaurant and most popular meeting place. Luckily, it was owned and operated by our Uncle Earnest and Aunt Evon—two of my all-time favorite characters—who were generous to a fault. The Earnest Reeds had three very personable offspring. Roy, the eldest, was married and usually busy elsewhere, but Joe Jimmy and Dot both worked part-time at the Dari-Burg and, like their parents, happily distributed freebies to our brood. The Bill Reed kids consumed a lot of gratis hamburgers and cherry cokes that summer, much to the chagrin of our parents.

Dad finished his schooling in Olathe in late October, and our family was soon on the way to his next duty station, NAS Quonset Point, Rhode Island. Our new residence was a smart, three-bedroom gray ranch house in an almost-new neighborhood called "Austin Manor." It was easily the most attractive home we had ever lived in, but it was woefully inadequate for a family with six children. Worst of all, it had only one bathroom. The girls' room was like a cramped barrack with two sets of bunk beds. I, on the other hand, shared my room only with my little brother. For once, being in the minority didn't seem so bad.

As soon as we were settled—before we even had the opportunity to get to know the neighbor kids—Dad stunned me by announcing that I would no longer be called Thumper. He reasoned that I was now in junior high school, and it was time to lose my childhood nickname. I was traumatized. One more vestige of my individuality was stripped away. I didn't like it, of course, but I was in no position to defy my father's wishes. I was really upset, and that night I cried at the loss of a cherished possession: my identity.

Although we lived in the community of North Kingstown, my junior high school, Robert E. Peary, was a converted mess hall located on the Navy base. It marked the first time I was picked up daily by a school bus. It wasn't long before I forged a friendship with one of the kids in my home room, a tall, dark-haired boy named Chris Hartman. Chris lived with his mother and grandmother in a sprawling old three-story home just above the quaint, early American fishing village of Wickford. Along with another friend, Bob Hinson, we had some terrific times there, discovering, among other things, the visual delights of *Playboy* magazine. The walls in Chris's room were covered with pinups, something that would be unthinkable in the Reed household. Fortunately for my buddy, his mother had already raised two sons and understood junior high school-aged boys quite well.

Chris's elderly grandmother died toward the end of our eighth grade year, so his mother sold the house that summer and moved to California, settling near Lake Tahoe. We received one Christmas card from Mrs. Hartman, but never heard from her or Chris again. We didn't learn until years later that she died of cancer shortly thereafter.

Residing in Rhode Island meant more frequent visits to our maternal grandmother, who still lived in the Jamaica duplex. Grandma was understandably depressed during the latter part of 1957, a result of that greedy villain Walter O'Malley's announcement that he was moving her beloved Dodgers to Los Angeles. She'd followed the Brooklyn ballclub for years, dropping whatever she was doing and parking herself in front of the TV whenever a game was on.

In the summer of 1958, Dad was sent to Pensacola, Florida, for two months of helicopter training. Mom decided to join him after the first month, so we packed our luggage in the station wagon and headed south. It must have been a real challenge for Mom, trying to control six lively, noisy kids over such a long haul. We were seldom unruly on long trips with Dad, because we knew he had no qualms about reaching back and swatting us. I remember Pensacola as being hot and sticky with surfless white sand beaches. Many a day I spent fishing off those beaches watching schools of fish swim by, but never getting a nibble.

Not long after returning home to North Kingstown, Dad learned there was a paper route available in an adjoining neighborhood and ordered me to take the job. It turned out to be a grueling experience, especially during the snowy winters, but I managed to survive and, for the first time in my life, started to put away a little money. I'd never saved any cash before because I never had any. Dad simply didn't believe in allowances. However, once I started delivering the newspaper, he encouraged me to save by promising to match everything I put in the bank. Dad designated my account as a college fund, and I was not permitted to make any withdrawals.

Around the same time I started the paper route, my parents decided to do something about my moderate overbite. Dr. McKenna, the orthodontist they selected, was old and crusty. He was also cheap. The monthly twenty-mile drives we made to his Providence office were times of great trepidation for me, as Dr. McKenna was not a sympathetic sort, and gentleness was not a trait he considered necessary in his professional ministrations. A few months after my treatments began, it was determined that Anne's teeth would require similar action. Soon, she was joining me in regular visits to the man I not-so-affectionately referred to as "Mac the Knife."

While my junior high school work was never up to the lofty standards expected of me, at least it was mostly "B"s and "A"s. Dad encouraged me to do better. To ensure greater concentration on our studies, Mom and Dad restricted our television viewing. However, we never missed *Gunsmoke*, *Have Gun, Will Travel*, or *Bonanza* which were family favorites. Of course, our parents insisted that all homework be finished before we were allowed to watch these adventures. Homework was always a thorn in my side, but I'd dispense with it as quickly as possible and move on to more important things, like reading. Hitting the books, to me, meant war stories, adventure yarns, and *Field and Stream* magazines, not school texts.

I became actively involved in Boy Scouts during our stay in Rhode Island, even serving as patrol leader for awhile. North Kingstown also proved a great place to hone my angling skills. I'd been an avid fisherman for years but never had such easy access to spots where I could wet my line and sometimes even catch something. Also, I found the perfect partner, Tim Hofstetter, whose home was just a stone's throw from mine. Tim was my age, swarthy, and on the smallish side, but he was the star of the school basketball team and an excellent fisherman. We fished from the shore of the Hunt River—which passed just a quarter mile from our homes—three or four times a week, nine months out of the year. Our main quarry were trout in the springtime and pickerel or bass in the summer and fall.

On November 29, 1959, Mom gave birth to her seventh and last child, Virginia Sue. I was quick to express my disappointment to all about having another sister in the house. Dad took me aside and chided me for my immature behavior. I probably deserved even harsher punishment. Ginny grew to be a blonde charmer, full of wit, good humor, and love. I came to regret my selfish reaction to her arrival.

I entered the new, ultra-modern North Kingstown High School in the fall of 1960, and it wasn't long before Tim and I joined the Golf Club. Golf was a sport we had taken up the previous year and enjoyed almost as much as fishing. My afternoon paper deliveries precluded my taking part in anything after school, but Dad rejected any notion I had about quitting my route. All I could do was grit my teeth and persevere.

As 1960 wound down, Dad came home from work with a contented smile on his face. His request for transfer to a warm, dry climate—to alleviate a chronic back problem—was granted, and soon we'd be moving to El Centro, California. We jumped for joy. California! Even the name sounded wonderful as it rolled off our tongues. Sure, we liked Rhode Island, and we knew we'd miss our friends, but, hey, we were going to California, the land of sunshine and wide, beautiful beaches. We learned later that El Centro was in the middle of the desert, a two hour drive from the nearest beach.

Our cross-country trip to California in February 1961 was an eventful one. After a brief stop in New York to visit Grandma Cleary, we proceeded westward, only to be stalled in Indiana by one of the biggest blizzards of the century. Luckily, Dad found some nice folks named Gossage in the little town of Lewisville who put up our big family for the night. We exchanged Christmas cards with them for many years thereafter. The weather cleared enough the following day for us to proceed to the Reed farm in Missouri. I remember seeing many cars and trucks stuck in the snow alongside the highway as we passed through western Indiana and Illinois. We spent several days at the farm for what turned out to be our final stay there. Because of his failing health, Grandpa leased out the place the following year and moved with Grandma to a small house in Appleton City.

Three days after leaving our grandparents, we arrived in El Centro, population around 20,000, where we were greeted by a long row of tall palm trees in the highway divider. The pleasantly warm temperatures of the Imperial Valley were in sharp contrast to the weather we'd experienced during the trip, and the town was surrounded by agricultural greenery rather than the barren desert we'd expected.

Our new home, an attractive three-bedroom white house on Sandalwood Drive, was the first we'd ever lived in to have central air conditioning, something that is *de rigeur* in El Centro. The yard was full of fruit trees and other shrubbery. Best of all was the "maid's quarters" in back—the boys' room. Ed and I were thrilled. It even had a three-quarter bathroom. We were pleased, if a bit perplexed, to find that the previous owner left an antique eight-gauge shotgun mounted on the wall in our cottage. We learned later that his teenaged son was recently killed in a hunting accident.

Dad's job at Naval Air Facility, El Centro, was Operations Officer of the Parachute Facility, home of the Navy's crack skydiving team, "The 'Chuting Stars." He soon learned it was common practice for officers attached to the Parachute Facility to—at some time during their tour of duty—make a jump. Dad, who'd passed his fortieth birthday, would have nothing to do with that. Once, when another pilot asked him when he planned to take the plunge, Dad replied, "When both wings fall off the plane."

Central Union High School was made up of a hodgepodge of stucco classroom buildings interspersed with trees and desert vegetation to provide a little shelter from the constant, ferocious sun. The very first class I walked into at Central—Latin II—would acquaint me with the individual who would be the cause of more adolescent fantasies and heartaches than I ever could have imagined.

I initially noticed her after my teacher asked me to stand and introduce myself. While perusing the classroom, my eyes fell upon a honey blonde vision of beauty, with flawless skin and big, expressive blue eyes that sparkled like a mountain brook. I shyly smiled at her, and she confidently smiled right back. I was lost. Her name was Sally. It turned out Sally's family not only lived just a block away, but she attended the same church as ours. She was active in the Methodist Youth Fellowship, so I soon became a regular attendee at MYF's Sunday night meetings. The girl was out of my league, but that didn't stop me from hoping and dreaming.

My first real buddy in El Centro was Stan Moffitt, a student in my English class. Stan was a big-hearted kid with an occasional stutter and, like me, skinny and bespectacled. Also, he owned a car, and I became the beneficiary of a daily ride to my classes. Stan talked me into joining him on the track team as a distance runner. Unfortunately, my practice times were never fast enough to qualify for an interscholastic meet that spring. Training in the 100-plus degree spring heat was asking a lot of a scrawny kid who'd spent the last four years in New England, or at least that's the way I looked at it. The next year I decided to concentrate on a far less taxing event, the high jump, and managed to win a junior varsity letter.

Although I turned sixteen on June 26, 1961, Dad wouldn't allow me to take the state driver's exam until November. He was probably surprised when I passed both the written and driving tests on the first try, not that it really mattered. License or no, I would have few opportunities to be alone behind the wheel of the family's '59 Chevy wagon for some time to come. So much for any faint hopes of improving my meager social life.

Golf was still my favorite leisure activity. The Barbara Worth Country Club offered really low green fees for students. A fellow MYF member, Jim Waer, became my regular partner. He was a pretty fair golfer and had his own Volkswagen to facilitate our trips to the golf course.

In the fall of 1962, my senior year, I was invited to join honors seminars, which met once a week. At first I looked forward to the interesting guest speakers and lively discussions which took place at the weekly gatherings. However, soon I learned that each of us was expected to complete a special project by the end of the school year. When the day came for me to make my report, I quietly slipped into my guidance counselor's office and asked that I be dropped from the program. I was given my wish.

Later that year, a U.S. Navy chief petty officer visited Central to address interested students about educational opportunities offered by his service. My nearsightedness had, of course, demolished my dreams of becoming a pilot in the Navy—or any other branch of the military for that matter— but I still hoped to one day wear the uniform of a naval officer. I was familiar with the Naval Reserve Officer Training Corps (NROTC) scholarship program and thought this would be an excellent opportunity to learn more details. The idea of the Navy funding my college studies and making me an officer upon graduation sounded great to me. Unfortunately, the chief quashed this dream, too. When I queried him about the vision requirements of the program, he told me, "Twenty-twenty. Same as Annapolis." Deeply disappointed, I took his word for it—after all "the chiefs run the Navy," so who was I to question his expertise? Many years afterward I learned—too late—that one only needed vision "correctable to 20/20" to be eligible for an NROTC scholarship.

My adolescent heart was broken—or at least damaged—during Christmas vacation that year. Dick Pata, a friend from MYF, invited me to a holiday party at his parents' rural home, with the advisory that it was for couples only. I, who'd never asked a girl out on a date, decided the time had finally come to take that giant step in my social life. And, who would the lucky lady be? It was a foregone conclusion: I would start at the top. Summoning all the courage within me, I called Sally. She was kind enough to let me down easily, sort of. She thanked me for the invitation, but explained she had to stay home with her thirteen-year-old sister. I was crushed, of course, but a tiny, overly optimistic voice kept telling me, "Don't give up. You've lost a battle, not the war." Who was I kidding?

During my final semester of high school, I enrolled in a journalism course, thereby joining the school newspaper staff. It proved a serendipitous choice. I was assigned to the sports desk, a position I took to naturally. Soon, I was even hosting Central's weekly sports interview show on a local radio station, quite an accomplishment for a social nobody.

In May, I learned that the two colleges where I'd applied for admission, University of Missouri and San Jose State, accepted me. Missouri was always my first choice, but with no scholarship to assist me, I realized that attending school out of state would be very difficult financially, even with my college fund savings account. Naturally, I didn't attend the couples only senior prom, offering as a feeble excuse my need to hang on to every dollar for my higher education.

My high school graduation took place at night on the school's football field. Shortly thereafter, the Reeds sold their house again and moved away. Dad got his requested transfer: we were heading for San Jose.

San Jose was a very familiar place. Dad's brothers Herman and Earl resided there, along with their families, and we'd visited them on several occasions. Living in San Jose meant we were also closer to Mom's older brother Eddie and his brood, who lived in King City. We soon moved into a spacious two-story home in the east foothills, less than a half mile from both our Reed uncles. The Bill Reed kids were ecstatic to be living in San Jose—with the exception of Anne. She'd been a very popular student at El Centro and had to forego her senior year there because of the move.

While Anne would at least know one of her senior classmates—our cousin Doug—at James Lick High School, I was on my own at San Jose State. Although I still was uncertain about my major, I scored sufficiently high on my entrance exams to secure an invitation to an accelerated program called Humanities. I enrolled, but it proved to be a serious error because the course was impossible for someone with my atrocious study habits. As a result of poor grades in this honors course, I spent most of my first two years at SJS on academic probation.

Every American alive on November 22, 1963, remembers what he or she was doing. I was preparing to catch the city bus to my only class that day, when Mom called upstairs to tell me the President had been shot. The initial reports were sketchy, informing us only that Kennedy had been taken to a Dallas hospital. Not thinking clearly, I headed for the bus stop. By the time I got to the SJS campus, the news of his death had been announced, and I watched as small, somber groups of students—many in tears—gathered around portable radios. I walked in a daze to the room where my 12:30 class was to be held. When I saw the sign, "class cancelled" on the door, the tragic news finally sank in.

Death also touched the Reed family that year. After a long battle with heart problems and the infirmities of old age, Grandpa Jim Reed passed away in December at age seventy-three. Dad flew home to Missouri for the funeral. Like Grandma and both my parents, Grandpa had been a teetotaler, but his fondness for cigarettes was undeniable. Mom was quick to point the finger at tobacco for his demise. "Grandpa was too young to die of old age," she told us. Mom also blamed her own father's early death on his smoking habit, and often reminded us kids that nearly every lung cancer patient she had seen in her nursing career was a smoker. It was several years before the Surgeon General's office finally confirmed what she taught us from early childhood.

One teenaged rite of passage came early in 1964: I purchased my first automobile. It was a pale yellow (Coronna Cream) 1961 Chevrolet Corvair Monza sport coupe, and I was forced to employ a little stealth to get it. Dad made it clear to me that I wasn't ready to have my own car; but when I spotted the sleek little beauty on a bank repo lot and haggled its price down to a mere $875, a sure-fire plan came to mind. I went to my father and explained that I could buy the car, clean it up a little, and sell it for at least a $300 profit. Dad—always a champion of free enterprise—agreed, not realizing that once it was in my possession I'd sooner give up the big toe on my accelerator foot than surrender the car. It didn't hurt, either, that shortly thereafter I found a part-time $1.50 an hour job covering high school sports for a local community newspaper, a position that required the use of an automobile. During the next two-plus years, the little yellow peach proved to be a real lemon, dripping gallons of oil onto the driveway and nickel-and-diming me to death with repair bills.

Neither my first semester grades nor my decision to major in journalism met with any enthusiasm from my parents. For years, Dad had encouraged me to set my sights on a career as a physician or dentist, not for any humanitarian reasons but for the financial security such professions promised. I felt inclined toward becoming a writer, however, and journalism seemed like an appropriate way to go.

My social ineptness kept me from enjoying college life to any great extent during my freshman year; but by the time summer vacation arrived, I had made one very good friend, Gary Moore, a personable, blond sophomore from my physical science class lab. My cousin Doug, who enrolled at SJS the following fall, also became a close buddy. During the summer of 1964, I junked my hated spectacles in favor of contact lenses and went out on my first real date—with a flirtatious high-school girl from my church. She even gave me a good-night kiss. I felt so awkward that I never asked her out a second time, even though I liked her.

A solo car trip to El Centro to hang out for a few days with my old buddy Stan Moffitt brought 1964 to a memorable close. Stan found out about a New Year's Eve party at the house of one of Sally's best friends, Nina. All 1963 grads were invited. Sally was there, lovelier than ever. I had a nice conversation with her, but was careful not to make a nuisance of myself. When midnight finally arrived and kisses were being exchanged, I couldn't find Sally. Nina told me she'd gone home early. A sudden surge of foolishness overcame me, and I was soon in my car headed for Sally's house. When I confronted Sally at her front door, all I could do was express my disappointment at her early departure and wish her a "Happy New Year." The next day, I drove back to San Jose.

By the end of my sophomore year I was in serious danger of flunking out. To make matters worse, I was replaced on the community newspaper staff by a college intern who worked for free in the summer of 1965. My unemployed status was short-lived, however, because Dad was able to procure a full-time summer job for me as a stock clerk at the Moffett Field naval exchange. The pay was only $1.25 an hour, but it was steady work that would continue on Saturdays during the school year.

By the fall of 1965, all the Reed kids were in school. I joined the staff of the *Spartan Daily* as a sports writer, and Anne was in nursing schoool. High school sophomore Diana and fourth grader Barbie were both "A" students. Nancy, now a seventh grader, also performed quite respectably in the classroom, while eighth grade football hero Eddie was doing better than his college-man brother, but not much. Ginny, who entered first grade that year, was showing promise of becoming the biggest academic star of all. Not only did she demonstrate an exceptional ability to master her schoolwork, but the curly blonde dynamo had a great sense of humor and was quick to make friends among her peers. Of course, it came as no surprise to any of us. Even my uncles' families knew Ginny was very special.

If God in His infinite Grace were suddenly to appear before me and generously offer to perform one cosmically impossible task, I wouldn't hesitate a millisecond with my request. I would ask him to go back up the stream of time to October 31, 1965, and erase, forever, the horrible events of that Halloween night. Even more than three decades later it all seems surreal: Mom helping Nancy, Barbie, and Ginny with their costumes, taking special care to make sure the eye holes in Ginny's ghost outfit were extra wide for better vision; me walking down the hill to Uncle Herman's house to watch TV with Doug and Aunt Ruth that evening—Uncle Herman was on a hunting trip in Colorado—and, shortly after dark, the mournful sound of a siren as an ambulance rolled by on Alum Rock Avenue. "Oh, my," Aunt Ruth said worriedly, "I hope it's not a child."

Her fears had more substance than my aunt could have possibly imagined. Minutes later the phone rang, and she went into the kitchen to pick it up. Within seconds, she returned to the family room, a stunned look on her face. "It was Jimmy," she announced, momentarily forgetting I was there. "He says one of Uncle Bill's kids was hit by a car and might be dead. He thinks it was Barbie." Jimmy was my Uncle Earl's son.

The news hit the three of us like a thunderbolt. With such sketchy information, we decided to drive to San Jose City Hospital, thinking my parents were probably already there. Doug got behind the wheel of Aunt Ruth's big Impala, and we all rode in the front seat, me in the middle. The ten-minute drive seemed to take forever, but the effort would prove futile as the emergency room clerk knew of no young accident victims being brought in that evening. She then called Alexian Brothers Hospital, which was actually closer to our home, and reported that my sister was there but gave no further details. Again, the short drive seemed interminable, but eventually the three of us found ourselves in another waiting room. Our wait was all too brief, as a solemn faced doctor appeared. "Are you with the family of the little Reed girl?" he asked. We weakly told him we were. I was standing between Aunt Ruth and Doug, shaking like a leaf. "I'm sorry," he told us. "She's gone. She died before she got here."

By now, I was somewhat prepared for the bad news, but there was one more question to be answered. Jimmy had mentioned Barbie's name, but I still wasn't certain. "Which of my sisters is it?" I asked. "Three of them are out there tonight."

The question took the doctor by surprise. "I don't know her name," he answered. "It was a little blonde girl."

I knew immediately that Jimmy was wrong. It wasn't Barbie; she had brown hair. My next thought was that it must be Nancy, but I really didn't know. "Would you like to come look at her?" he inquired.

My reaction was momentary speechlessness. A hundred things must have passed through my mind in a few seconds. Then, Aunt Ruth spoke up, summoning strength beyond imagination. "I'll go," she stated.

My aunt followed the doctor down the hallway and through a door, as Doug and I stood silently and waited. My entire body continued to shiver uncontrollably. She was back within a minute. "It's Ginny," she announced softly. Then, the tears began to flow.

Death is a terrible way to bring families together. During the next few days, I saw firsthand how the loss of a child not only devastates parents, brothers, and sisters but uncles, aunts, and cousins, as well. Ginny was the youngest of the San Jose Reeds, and in a way she belonged to all of us. Since the circumstances of her death—a trick-or-treater struck down by a motorist—were so tragic, Ginny's story made the headlines in the city's newspapers. As a result, we received many cards and notes of condolence from people we'd never met. We buried Ginny in a local cemetery under a small marker inscribed with her name, the dates of her short, happy life, and the three-word title of a poem sent us by an unknown sympathizer— *A Child Loaned.*

Early in December, Dad announced we would all be going on a Navy-sponsored cruise to Hawaii during Christmas vacation. It would be a care-free time for healing, and everyone was excited by the news but me. For some reason, I really wanted to be alone for awhile. I suggested to Dad that someone ought to stay and watch the house, then quickly volunteered my services. He reluctantly went along with my plan, so I experienced two weeks of relative solitude for the first time in my life.

Mom and Dad and the rest of the kids came home tanned and smiling with the expected, "Boy, did you miss out on a great time," comments, then we all got on with our lives. I actually showed marked academic improvement, earning a 2.6 grade point average, which was good enough to get me off academic probation for the first time in a year-and-a-half.

With the spring semester came a new position for me on the *Spartan Daily* staff: photo editor. Assigning photographers to stories was simple work, and I performed it conscientiously; but I certainly missed the sports desk. By then, Dad had received orders to a new duty station. As soon as school was out in June, the movers came and the family departed for the long drive to Key West, Florida. Everybody but me, that is. I still had a year to go at SJS, and now I was truly on my own. With college friends, Tony Holland and Jon Erlandson, I rented an apartment near campus.

Before leaving for Florida, Dad had helped me trade in my temperamental Corvair for a 1962 Buick Special two-door sedan. Unfortunately, shortly after midnight on June 26—my twenty-first birthday—the light blue compact was heavily damaged in an accident. I had to fork over $500 of my meager savings to cover the repairs—a big outlay for a struggling college student—but I needed the vehicle for my full-time summer job at the Navy Exchange.

The rest of the summer of 1966 was much more enjoyable. I was legally an adult, so I could spend Friday evenings with my friends Gary Moore, Denny Anderson, and Ken "Crash" Molica at a popular beer and dancing hangout located in a south San Jose industrial park and aptly named The Warehouse. Denny, like Gary, was tall, blond, and appealing to the fair sex. Ken, a fellow student and race car driver, was a diminutive fellow who always seemed to enjoy himself. Saturday nights were often spent at the San Jose Speedway, rooting for Ken and his car number 69. Late in the summer, we discovered a place in Sunnyvale called the Brass Rail, where every Wednesday was amateur topless night. The featured star was Tara, the topless snake dancer, a lady with an apparent fondness for boa constrictors.

With the fall semester came new quarters for me. Tony joined the Navy, and Jon moved back in with his parents. I shared a one-bedroom apartment with Lou, a *Spartan Daily* staff photographer I'd worked with that spring. Except for a brief period when we were both enamored by a pretty, petite divorcee named Juanita, we got along well. Lou ended up with the girl.

In December that year, I decided to take the U.S. Navy Officer Candidate School exam. The draft reclassified me 1-S for no apparent reason the previous summer, which meant I had just one year to complete my studies before the Army got me. I always intended to join the Navy, no matter what, and I had no desire to serve as an enlisted man in any service. A letter informing me that I passed the OCS test came in January 1967, but I elected to wait a few months before taking the physical and having my interview—a decision I would come to regret.

Financial difficulties and a nineteen-unit academic load made my final semester the most challenging of my college career. Even though I borrowed $500 from my parents early on, I still couldn't afford to purchase books. I didn't do without them completely, however. A few days before a scheduled exam, I'd go to the campus bookstore and pay for the texts I needed. After completing the exam, I'd return them, along with my purchase receipt, for a full refund. I pulled this stunt more times than I can remember, but no one at the store called me on it

I graduated from SJS in June. *Los Angeles Times* publisher Otis Chandler gave the commencement address at Spartan Stadium. To my pleasant surprise, Mom and Diana flew in from Key West to attend the ceremonies.

With degree in hand, I drove to San Francisco for my final Navy Officer Candidate School physical and the all-important interview by a senior officer. I was told I'd be informed whether or not I was selected in two to three months. This presented a problem. On August 1, I was scheduled to be classified 1-A by my local Draft Board, and would probably receive an immediate induction notice. To avoid such a happening, I decided in July to sign up for the Navy on a 120-day delayed enlistment. This allowed me four months of freedom, and, I thought, sufficient time to have my OCS application processed.

Cousin Doug, two friends, and I rented a two bedroom apartment near the SJS campus and spent most of the summer partying. I tried not to let the two dull jobs I had interfere with my fun. An attractive junior-college coed named Barbara, who I met at a beach party during spring break, added to the enjoyment of this last carefree summer of my youth.

In mid-October, I quit my job, packed a suitcase and drove east, stopping in Missouri to visit Grandma and as many of the Reeds as possible before heading on to Key West. My biggest shock upon arriving at my parents home came with the first sight of my brother Eddie. He'd left San Jose a five-foot six-inch, eighth-grade graduate, but in sixteen months grew to a height of six feet and one inch. All my sisters were growing up, too. Nancy, now a freshman, played flute in the band; Diana, a senior, was an athlete and an honor student; and Barbie was at the top of her sixth grade class. Anne had enrolled in a local nursing school and would soon graduate. Mom was the same wonderful person as always, but Dad seemed to have undergone a subtle but significant change. The taskmaster I remembered was slipping away, slowly being replaced by a kinder, gentler, more nurturing person. I was surprised how happy it made me feel to see everyone, since I had never suffered a serious bout of homesickness while we were apart.

During the next two weeks, Mom showed me the sights of Key West and introduced me to many interesting people, most of them quite artistic. Then, after advising Dad that I was leaving my dependable little car to cover the $200 still owed him, I boarded a plane at the Key West airport for my journey back to San Jose. Two weeks later, perplexed and disappointed by the Navy's failure to give me any official word on the status of my OCS application, I took a bus to the Armed Services Recruitment Depot in San Francisco where I was put on a commercial flight to San Diego, site of the Navy's Recruit Training Center. My days of freedom ended on November 15, 1967.

Chapter 13

The Unnecessary for
the Ungrateful

—

The physical training aspects of Navy boot camp are no picnic, but they can hardly be compared to the sort of rigors expected of Marine recruits. On any given day we'd watch our green-clad brethren running up and down barren hills on the other side of the tall cyclone fence that separated us; and we'd thank our lucky stars we weren't among them. Still, we had to suffer a barrage of personal indignities, mostly from our company commander (CC), a brawny, florid faced boilerman first class (E-6) named Gardner and his adjutant, a sawed-off runt of a seaman apprentice (E-2), fresh out of boot camp himself. The first week or two was especially difficult for me, not because of any particular abuse of my body or psyche, but rather from the ridiculously early wake-up calls. Even roosters are sound asleep at 4:00 A.M.

Upon graduation from recruit training in February 1968, I was sent to the Naval Training Center's "com-hold" barracks, where sailors who applied for commissions were to await word on whether or not they'd been accepted at Officer Candidate School (OCS). Since I'd waived the service school that was guaranteed me in exchange for a "designated striker's" rating of journalist seaman (E-3), I was assigned temporary duty on the staff of NTC's weekly newspaper. The position kept me busy for the next two weeks, but one assignment was especially memorable. Our public affairs officer needed someone to photograph the honorary reviewer at a recruit graduation ceremony. He told us that several indoor photos of the guest, a retired reserve rear admiral, would be needed, and emphasized that no flash cameras be used. Since I was the only one in the office familiar with indoor "available light" photography, I got the job. The next day I had the privilege of photographing famed movie director John Ford, resplendent in black eye patch and well-worn World War II Navy officer's "blues," as he sat and chatted with two other admirals.

Whether or not my photos ever saw print I don't know. A few days earlier, I'd called Dad to ask him to check up on my application for OCS. He got back to me with the astounding news that the San Francisco Navy facility where I applied and was interviewed had no record of my ever having been in their office. Frustrated, I requested orders "to the fleet." This time, the Navy came through quickly. Within a week I was on my way to Long Beach, where the aircraft carrier USS *Hornet* was home ported.

Hornet, a much-decorated World War II relic, was a 900-foot-long floating city. Though not as big as the newer supercarriers, she was still an impressive sight to a sailor coming on board for the first time. As I reached the top of the after brow (enlisted men's gangplank) and reported aboard to the chief of the watch, I noticed that photographs of the commanding and executive officers were posted on a nearby bulkhead. To my pleasant surprise the skipper bore a familiar face. It was Captain Jackson A. Stockton, whose son, Jack, had been a good friend of mine in Rhode Island nearly a decade before. He now wore the uniform of a captain rather than a commander, but otherwise his appearance had changed very little.

As are all shipboard Navy journalists, I was assigned to the public affairs office (PAO), which was located immediately below the flight deck and just forward of the superstructure. Of the four fellow enlisted men in the office, only one, a skinny Oklahoman named Mike Wheat, was around for my entire twenty-five-month tour on *Hornet*. Wheat was not a fan of country music, and he'd often chide Charlie, a southerner and fellow journalist, for always having the office radio tuned to "that shitkicker stuff." I'd never heard that particular term used before, but it was obviously a favorite of Mike's.

Life as a Navy journalist was generally an easy one, especially when we were in port. My main function was writing news releases about the ship and its activities, or brief formatted stories on individuals who'd reported aboard recently. Not long after my arrival, a second class (E-5) journalist, Gary Froseth, joined us. Gary had an impressive background in broadcasting, and it became his job to get the ship's TV studio running smoothly.

I'd been on *Hornet* about four months when I went before a board of officers to determine whether I met the qualifications for OCS. I got a haircut, shined my shoes, and put on my best uniform. Sick and tired of being an enlisted man, I was determined to give the panel my best shot. In the finest acting performance of my naval career, I convinced three veteran officers that I was worthy of joining their elite membership. One rated me "above average" and the other two gave me "highest" recommendations. They'd have a tough time keeping me out of OCS now, or so I thought.

I reacquainted myself with Captain Stockton shortly after reporting aboard, so when his younger son, Herb, came to visit in June, he saw to it that the two of us got together. Herb was about to enter the Naval Academy. Like the other men in his family, Herb hoped to become a naval aviator, also. The skipper informed me later that his older son, Jack, was planning to come out as well; and, of course, I looked forward to that.

A few days before Jack's arrival in July, I flew to San Jose for the weekend. As usual, I stayed with Uncle Herman and Aunt Ruth. Saturday evening, law student Gary Moore and I arranged to go to San Jose Speedway to watch our good buddy, Ken Molica, in the supermodified races.

We never made it. Heading south on King Street, I could only watch in horror as an oncoming driver suddenly turned a hard left in front of us, and Gary's new Malibu SS broadsided him at about forty miles per hour. Gary was okay, but the next day I underwent surgery at Oak Knoll Naval Hospital in Oakland for a fractured superorbital bone and sinus repairs, which left me with a jagged scar above the bridge of my nose. I was released after eighteen days and happy to return to *Hornet*. I never got to see Jack.

Shortly after getting back on board, I learned that my application for OCS was rejected—a victim of bad timing. President Johnson had just announced all the military services would be making drastic manpower cuts as the war in Vietnam was supposedly winding down. Once again my hopes of becoming a naval officer had been derailed. In frustration, I gave up. All efforts to impress my superiors with a can-do attitude ceased. From that point on I did the absolute minimum expected of me. I was finished playing the Navy game. Although I didn't study, I took my examination for journalist third class (E-4) a few days later. In September, Wheat and I were informed that we both passed.

As I prepared for my first cruise to the Far East in the fall of 1968, Dad retired after twenty-six years of service—more than twenty of that on active duty. He'd already found a job as a high school guidance counselor in

Marysville, California, so the Reed family made one more cross-country move. Perhaps it was because he was an officer and a pilot that Dad really enjoyed his naval career. I, on the other hand, had more than my fill after less than a year—failing to get into OCS was really the last straw.

Following a series of short cruises to train the crew and test engines and boilers—most of which amounted to a seemingly endless circling of Santa Catalina and San Clemente Islands—*Hornet* finally set sail for the western Pacific (a.k.a. WestPac). Our first stop was Pearl Harbor, Hawaii, where I hit the beach with two of my favorite shipmates; slender, devil-may-care Kansan Bob Hill and Verdell "Tons of Fun" Tunson, a muscular, good na-tured preacher's son from Dallas. Both worked in the captain's office, which was located directly across the passageway from PAO. The island of Oahu was certainly pleasing to the senses, but it clearly catered more to tourists than to sailors. The nightlife was too rich for our meager budgets. It didn't take long for Hill to pronounce the island, "a nice place for the newly wed and the nearly dead." Fortunately for him, our stay was short and *Hornet* was soon underway again.

We arrived in Yokosuka, Japan, during the last week of October. The ship was now in a three-section duty arrangement which meant less liberty time. Sailors were welcome in Yokosuka, at least in the section of town near the U.S. Naval Base known as Thieves Alley. This area of several square blocks catered almost exclusively to American military personnel and con-sisted largely of noisy bars and nightclubs with a sprinkling of diners and hotels. Street vendors peddled their wares on every corner. Most of the clubs featured bands playing popular American music, and all had an ade-quate supply of what the sailors called bar hogs (attractive girls who were adept at separating a young serviceman from his paycheck.

Wheat and I went ashore on our first evening in port. During our tour of Thieves Alley, he suddenly broke out laughing for no apparent reason. When I inquired as to what was so funny, Mike pointed at the sign on a club which was emanating loud country music. It read, "Shitkickers Bar."

We stayed in Japan for less than a week before sailing to Yankee Station in the Gulf of Tonkin. *Hornet* was an anti-submarine warfare (ASW) air-craft carrier with three different types of ASW aircraft aboard, but the Gulf of Tonkin was too shallow for submarine operations. Our official function was "surface and subsurface surveillance," but because there was nothing below and only U.S. Navy ships and a few harmless junks on the surface, we found this a little hard to fathom. The ship's unofficial motto among enlisted man was: "the unqualified leading the unwilling to do the unnecessary for the ungrateful."

My personal function was cut and dried after we left Yokosuka. Jim Missett, the senior journalist in PAO, was transferred to shore duty back in the States, and I was given his job of putting out *Hornet*'s daily news sheet, *The Straight Skinny*, meaning the unvarnished truth—as opposed to scuttlebutt, meaning rumor, and mess deck information (MDI), shipboard terminology for "only in your dreams."

Missett, who was tall, thin, and bespectacled, had taken his function seriously and really enjoyed hunting down feature stories from among the crew. So popular was Jim throughout the ship, he was known as Skinny Man. Conversely, I found the job pure drudgery and particularly dreaded my daily battle with the temperamental mimeograph machine. Almost as big a challenge was trying to make sense of the usually garbled wire-service copy coming off the ship's teletype, then editing it into something the sailors could read.

Thanksgiving week found *Hornet* dropping anchor in beautiful Hong Kong Harbor. Liberty parties took small motorized passenger boats back and forth from the shore. With the notable exception of Sydney (or any place in Australia), Hong Kong was considered the best port city in the Far East. Even better, we went to a four-section watch and liberty commenced at 0800 every morning for non-duty personnel.

Hong Kong's Wanchai district, that catered to Americans and other foreign military personnel, featured as many tailor shops as bars. Tailors came out and offered sailors a beer if they'd stepped inside to sample the merchandise. Hong Kong suits were real bargains—good materials, expert tailoring, and ridiculously inexpensive. I'd been saving for something else, though, and soon was the proud owner of a new Canon 35mm camera.

Between stays on Yankee Station we visited Sasebo, Japan, over Christmas and New Year's and Subic Bay, Philippines, in late January. Sasebo was an attractive, friendly place. Many of the drinking establishments were pub-like places called stand bars. The bartenders were usually attractive women, but the conversational pleasures they provided were strictly platonic. Members of the local citizenry often frequented the stand bars as well. The populace had a significant Christian representation, which may have contributed to the somewhat different atmosphere.

Subic Bay was another sort of experience altogether. In an effort to lure servicemen away from the dubious pleasures of Olongapo, the local "sin city," the U.S. Naval Base and the Cubi Point Naval Air Station were two of the most sailor-friendly facilities anywhere. They offered such services as bowling, scuba diving instruction, go-karts, and any number of other recreational activities. However, wishing to escape from Navy life for awhile, Wheat I packed our overnight bags with caught a bus to Manila. The ninety-mile sojourn took three hours, and was eventful for the hilly rural scenery and for the ancient bus itself, which seemed to have no shock absorbers and nearly rattled the fillings out of our teeth. The new side of Manila where we stayed was laid back, quite attractive, and had some very nice, inexpensive restaurants.

Our next stop—after the usual three weeks in Vietnamese waters—was the exotic island nation of Singapore. On the way there, *Hornet* dipped below the Equator so those "pollywogs" aboard who had never made the crossing—the majority among the crew—could be initiated into the Realm of Neptunus Rex. The colorful crossing ceremonies gave "shellbacks" (those already initiated) the opportunity to administer various punishments and other indignities upon the rest of us, including officers. After crawling for several hundred feet along the flight deck through a garbage chute and a gauntlet of sadistic, hose-wielding sailors, kissing the "royal baby's" fat, greasy belly, and finally being dunked in a cleansing pool, I emerged a trusty shellback. Such are the rewards of spending far too much time at sea.

Singapore had little in common with our other ports of call. The British naval base where we docked was almost a half-hour cab drive from the city, and, although there were several interesting places to hang out—including the American Club, the Britannia Club, and the famed Raffles Hotel—no section of the city really catered to foreign sailors. As a result, it took almost all of our six days there to get a feel for the place.

During the latter part of March 1969, we docked in Subic Bay for twelve days for mandatory maintenance and taking on stores before returning to Yankee Station. Our WestPac deployment was supposed to be nearing its end—just three more weeks at sea, then a brief stop in Yokosuka before heading stateside—but an international incident changed all that.

Hornet was on station in the Tonkin Gulf when we received the news: a U.S. Air Force reconnaissance plane had been shot down, apparently over international waters, by the North Koreans. We were ordered to proceed immediately along with our six escort destroyers to the Sea of Japan in "a show of force." *Hornet* carried no fighters or attack aircraft, so she could hardly be expected to exercise a retaliatory strike. Still, our administrative officer called an emergency meeting and told us we might be going to war.

Of course nobody believed that for a second because the officer, a veteran lieutenant referred to not-so-affectionately as EEK (an acronym of his initials) had the reputation for being a "sweater." Petty problems caused him to break into a sweat, and big things sent him over the edge.

As with most cold war incidents, concern over the lost aircraft cooled after a couple of weeks and *Hornet* moved on to Yokosuka, then home. By then, I'd added a second chevron to my "crow," signifying my advancement to journalist second class—as high as a U.S. Navy sailor can expect to go without re-enlisting. I had been on active duty for just seventeen months.

When we got back to the states, I bought a 1962 Olds Cutlass convertible for $350. The car represented far more than transportation and status to me. It also became the closet for my civilian clothes. My hopes for a summer of top-down fun in Southern California were short-lived because we soon learned *Hornet* would be going to sea again for six weeks in June. Our assignment was an historic one: recover the *Apollo 11* astronauts—the first men on the moon—after their Pacific splashdown. The best part of the recovery mission was the camaraderie with the civilian media. Reporters representing the news services and several major dailies boarded in Hawaii, along with newsmen from the three major television networks and engineers and equipment from ABC. Our favorite was NBC's commentator, Ron Nessen. Ron was a friendly, unpretentious guy who kept everyone in stitches with his often warped sense of humor. Also brought on board was a dummy command module for use in the numerous practice recoveries that were to be carried out. PAO held a contest to choose a theme for the *Apollo 11* recovery, and the winner was "*Hornet* Plus Three." The civilian media took a liking to the slogan and spread the word.

On the evening of July 23, one day before the recovery was to take place, I was hanging out with Wheat, Froseth, Wilson, and a few others in the TV studio when there was a knock on the door. It was opened, and a snappy-looking Marine sergeant stepped through followed by a scrawny little white-haired guy with a weathered face and a hat that appeared to have been battered by gallons of sea spray from countless voyages. Both hands were thrust into the pockets of his bridge coat, and a huge green cigar protruded from his mouth. Wilson immediately shouted, "Attention on deck!" and everybody jumped. Our diminutive visitor was none other than Admiral John S. McCain, Jr., Commander-in-Chief of all U.S. Forces in the Pacific area (CINCPAC), a post considered second in authority only to the Chief of Naval Operations. The four star admiral walked up to the first man he saw, reached out his hand and, looking him squarely in the eye, said, "McCain's the name," a procedure he followed with everyone present, putting us all at ease. He gave the crew a televised pep talk over the closed circuit system before slipping away without fanfare. I'll always remember Admiral McCain as an "old salt" in the best sense of the expression.

President Nixon arrived on board early on the morning of the recovery, along with other VIPs. It was overcast when the actual splashdown took place about twelve miles from our location, making it difficult to see even with the most powerful binoculars. I was close enough, however, to get a good view of astronauts Armstrong, Aldrin, and Collins when they stepped from the recovery helicopter onto the hangar deck and walked into the Quonset hut-like mobile quarantine facility (MQF) which would be their home for the next month or so. A few days later the MQF was dropped off at Pearl Harbor, and *Hornet* headed back to Long Beach minus the "Plus Three" as well as most of the civilians from NASA and the news media.

The evening after our return from the *Apollo 11* recovery, I met a lovely, dark-haired Italian woman at a popular dance club well away from downtown Long Beach. Our developing romance was interrupted after less than three months because of *Hornet's* selection as recovery ship for *Apollo 12*, but I was not the only member of PAO unhappy about the honor. Mike Wheat married Judy, his longtime sweetheart from Oklahoma, and they'd just set up housekeeping in Long Beach.

The five weeks at sea required by the *Apollo 12* mission were among the longest of my life. The onboard activities were much like those for *Apollo 11* but without the excitement. My new girlfriend and I corresponded several times, but I worried she would lose interest in me while I was gone.

My fears were unfounded. When *Hornet* pulled up alongside the pier in Long Beach on December 4, 1969, Wheat and I scanned the large crowd and were surprised to locate his wife and my girlfriend standing together.

Upon our return, we learned that *Hornet* was scheduled for decommissioning the following spring and to be mothballed at Bremerton, Washington. Since this meant no more time at sea, I rented an apartment in Long Beach. I was sick of shipboard living and wanted to be closer to my girlfriend. The guys I hung out with were either out of the Navy (Hill), transferred (Tunson), or married (Wheat). The rent for the little studio was ninety dollars per month and well worth it.

Christmas 1969 was the first I spent with my family in five years, and I was determined to be home for that holiday every year thereafter, no matter what. By now, Dad was well-established in his school counselor position, and Mom had a part-time job as a school nurse. The Reeds lived in a nice, big ranch-style home south of Yuba City, which was not one of the liveliest places in California but much more pleasant than its sister city, Marysville, where Dad worked.

With *Hornet* slated for final decommissioning in June 1970, the Navy decided to keep the crew intact and to give those with less than a year to go an early out when the ship officially retired. I didn't qualify. My enlistment wasn't scheduled to end until November 1971, so a few months before the final voyage to Bremerton, Washington, I was transferred to Commander Antisubmarine Warfare Group Three in Long Beach where, it turned out, they already had their compliment of one journalist on board. Then, due to this snafu, I received orders to another Long Beach outfit, Commander Mine Forces Pacific Fleet (ComMinePac), where Eek was the administration officer. Fortunately, he was a pretty decent guy on dry land.

My main job was photography, which was great because I got to spend most of my time either shooting or hanging out in the photo lab. It wasn't long before another journalist arrived, a third class named Steve Busch, who was a reservist and a great guy, but there wasn't enough to do for both of us. That allowed me to take thirty days leave from mid-August to mid-September and go to Italy with my girlfriend.

If I live a hundred years, I will probably never have a better month than the one I enjoyed that summer in 1970. Seeing the sights, getting to know the Italian people, and experiencing living in another country all contributed to the good times; but being with the woman I loved was without a doubt the most satisfying part of the experience.

Shortly after my return from leave that September, I was given temporary orders to the public affairs office at Navy Base, Long Beach. It was a plum assignment, as I arrived to find a staff of true professionals and an almost civilian-style atmosphere where I actually felt comfortable most of the time. It would also prove to be my final duty station.

I was given an early release from the Navy on July 1, 1971. It was—and probably always will be—the happiest single day of my life. That morning I visited the base wine mess and picked up a couple bottles of cold champagne before officially checking out. Then I went to the PAO, found some paper cups, and toasted my imminent departure with all the naval and civilian personnel I knew. For the first time in almost four years I was free, and nobody was going to stop me from celebrating. Thus ended my naval career. As with nearly everything else in my life, I served without distinction, leaving nary a ripple in my wake.

Chapter 14

Family Secrets

The first I heard of any skeletons rattling in the family closet was in the mid-seventies during a visit from my brother. Ed, now a strapping six feet three inches and over 200 pounds, had completed his two-year active duty commitment in the Naval Reserve and was happily working as an FAA air controller in San Jose. During a casual conversation about his recent trip to the home of Mom's younger sister Liddy and her husband Norman Yorke in Florida, Ed related a curious incident. It seems he'd been thumbing through a family album when he spotted a picture of Mom in her Navy nurse's dress uniform with a U.S. Marine officer in what he believed was a wedding picture. Next to it was a photo of the famed Black Sheep Squadron. Ed quickly deduced that the Marine with Mom was a member of that illustrious group.

I asked my brother if he was certain that the first shot was indeed a wedding photo, but he admitted he wasn't. In fact, Aunt Liddy noticed his observing the picture and quickly pulled the album away from him, indicating verbally that he wasn't supposed to see it. Ed and I briefly discussed the possibility that Mom had been married or at least engaged to someone else before she met Dad, but decided it really wasn't any of our business.

I didn't think very much about my brother's discovery over the next two or three years, but then came the evening that turned my world upside down. I was in San Jose, staying with Ed for a day or two. We were visiting with our cousin Doug and his wife Melinda at their home in Los Altos when the subject of family history came up. Melinda was doing some research in that area because the Reeds were planning a family reunion in 1979. Somehow, a question from Ed led to Melinda's announcement that our mother had indeed been married once before. She added that I, especially, should talk with her about it. I indicated that if Mom thought it was important she would have told us about it long ago, but Melinda was persistent in her advice. After a while the truth began to dawn on me. Even though we moved on to a different subject, it continued to gnaw at me

I slept little, if any, that night. No one actually said the words, but I knew. My dad—the man I loved, admired, and feared for as long as I could remember—was not my natural father. Also, it seemed logical to assume that my sister Anne, just thirteen months my junior, was in the same boat. This hit me so hard I simply had no idea of how to deal with it.

The next day Ed rented one of the private planes that belonged to his flying club, and the two of us flew to our parent's place. We didn't discuss the conversation of the night before, but the flight was memorable for my seemingly inexplicable air sickness. It was my first and only bout ever with that malady, and thank heavens there were two barf bags aboard because I needed both of them. My unsympathetic brother's comment: "What a lightweight!" When Dad picked us up at the Marysville airport, he admonished Ed for his derogatory remarks to me, adding that he knew many experienced pilots who suffered the same fate at one time or another. I don't think I ever felt closer to my father than I did at that moment.

The subject Melinda considered so important was not discussed during the visit. Eventually, I pushed the dismay and the heartbreak of that crushing revelation to the back of my mind and got on with my life. Although not exactly in denial, I wasn't ready to come to terms with the truth.

The Reed family reunion in Appleton City went on as scheduled during the summer of 1979, with the Bill Reeds in 100 percent attendance, including Anne and her husband, Tom McNeil, and their two kids, four-year-old Tommy and baby Megan, just nine months. The happiness of the occasion was tempered only by Grandma's death earlier that year. Despite the diabetes that plagued her since middle age, she led an extremely active life that ended peacefully after eighty-three years. Shortly before her passing, this remarkable woman had the rare privilege of holding her first great-great grandchild in her arms. One of the last things she said was that she was looking forward to seeing Jim again.

Mom finally came around to telling me about my true paternity in 1981. It was a very tearful phone call. I admitted I already suspected the truth, thanks to the conversation Ed and I had with Doug and Melinda. When she asked me if I had any questions about my birth father I told her no and that, as far as I was concerned, Dad was my only father. I didn't even ask what her first husband's name was. Later I learned that Mom was seeing a therapist about recurring bouts with clinical depression, and my sister Nancy—who drove her to the doctor—overheard a conversation about her first marriage through the paper-thin doors of the doctor's office. On the way home my irrepressible sister told our mother what she heard. I guess Mom decided, now that the cat was out of the bag, it was probably a good idea to pass along the information to Anne and me.

Even though I saw my parents at least once a year, I avoided discussing the subject with them. In fact, many years passed before I talked about it with any of my siblings. One thing I did do, though, was check out a copy of Pappy Boyington's book, *Baa, Baa Black Sheep*, from my local library. It was a fascinating story. What the text lacked in literary style was more than made up for in content. Although the famed Marine ace didn't delve very deeply into the personalities of his Black Sheep, one individual struck me as a likely candidate to be my birth father—partly because of his physical description and partly due to his somewhat mysterious character traits. Boyington referred to this pilot as "McGee."

Not long after finishing the Boyington book, I decided to do a little more research on the subject and discovered a multi-page pictorial in the October 1, 1945, issue of *Life* magazine about Boyington's welcome home party in San Francisco. One photo featured Pappy at a bar surrounded by four of his aces, including one identified as "Captain C.L. Magee," a muscular, ruggedly handsome fellow who was standing in right profile to the camera. I thought he looked a lot like my sister Anne and became even more convinced my impression from the book was correct.

I chose not to pursue the matter any further, however. My feeling was that if my birth father were still alive—a big if—and he never bothered to contact my sister and me, why take the trouble to try to find him? What kind of father abandons his children after a divorce? If there existed even a remote possibility of my ever becoming a family man, it vanished with the knowledge that I would pass on his genes to another generation. Also, there was the matter of loyalty. I was a Reed and proud of it. When I was growing up, my father never said anything to me that hinted otherwise, neither had his parents nor any of his brothers and sisters, all of whom knew of my origins. At least some of my cousins must have known as well, but they, too, kept the secret and always treated me as a full-fledged Reed. Different bloodlines or not, the Reeds were and always would be—along with the Clearys—my true family.

It was my sister Barbie who got me started on the quest that would change my life. The date was December 26, 1987. She and her boyfriend Mark were driving me from Yuba City to the Sacramento Airport in Mark's Citroen, along with her daughter Paige. For reasons still unknown, Barbie began out of the blue to question me concerning how much I knew about my birth father. When I told her, "very little, not that I really care," she suddenly began blurting out bits of unsolicited information, such as his war record as a Marine fighter pilot, that he—like myself—had been a journalism major in college, then later became a mercenary, and, oh yes, he went to prison for bank robbery.

So, that's why Mom was so reluctant to tell us about the existence of the man, I thought. Barbie added that my sister and brother-in-law, Anne and Tom, stumbled upon some information about him a year or so earlier. Tom contacted several members of the Black Sheep squadron, trying to locate him, but nobody seemed to know whether he was alive or dead. I tried to feign disinterest in Barbie's revelations, but my heart was pounding. Finally, she asked me, "Don't you even want to know his name?"

"You're probably going to tell me anyway, so go ahead," was my chagrined reply.

"It's Chris Magee," she stated. "And when you were born your name was Chris Junior."

Chapter 15

The Quest

For years, any interest I had in my beginnings lay dormant, and likely would have remained so had Barbie not insisted on passing along the information she knew. The fact my birth father's name was Chris Magee came as no great surprise, but that I had been born Christopher Jr. was a real shocker. Barbie told me Mom had changed the names of both her children when she married Dad and he adopted us. She didn't have to look far to find the new handles. I was re-christened Robert after her kid brother, whom the Cleary family always called Mickey. My sister, originally named Christine, became Anne, the given name of our Aunt Liddy, Mom's younger sister. Since we were always called by our nicknames, Thumper and Baby Sis, the transition didn't affect us at the time. Now, however, at age forty-two, it really bothered me to learn that my siblings knew things about me that I wasn't aware of. I had to learn more and the sooner the better.

A day or so after returning to Huntington Beach, I paid a visit to my friend Forrest Pharaoh, an aviation buff who was working as a bartender at a local watering hole. He took an immediate interest in my story and recommended I talk with the folks at the Planes of Fame Museum in Chino.

My trip netted an important piece of information: a comprehensive book about the Black Sheep existed, and it included information about their postwar careers. The title was *Once They Were Eagles: The Men of the Black Sheep Squadron*, and the author was Frank Walton, the squadron's intelligence officer. A few days later I found the book at Huntington Beach Central Library. I read it cover-to-cover in one sitting. What a story! By the time I read the final page, I felt I knew all the pilots personally. Many had gone on to lead extraordinary lives, but none more so than Chris Magee, whom Walton called, "perhaps the ultimate combat fighter pilot."

Chris's letter to Frank and the poem that accompanied it really knocked me for a loop. Although the eventful life described in the epistle bore little resemblance to mine, I felt an intense spiritual connection with the man. My interest in my birth father was no longer one of mild curiosity. I resolved then and there that if Chris had not, as the book suggested, "passed on to Fighter Pilot's Heaven," I would find him no matter how long it took or how far I had to travel.

My search began early in January 1988 with a letter to Frank Walton, who resided in Honolulu. I introduced myself, told him how much I enjoyed his book and asked him if he'd heard anything more from Chris since *Once They Were Eagles* had been published two years earlier. I didn't have to wait long for Frank's reply, as this letter arrived less than a week later.

7 January 1988

Dear Mr. Reed:

Everything about Chris Magee is amazing and, it appears that more amazing things turn up all the time.

For example, I got a call from a man here in Honolulu after the book came out; his name is Christopher Magee. He is the son of your father's father's brother. In other words, Chris Magee, the Black Sheep pilot, is the son of Chris Magee of Honolulu's father's brother.

A few months ago, an article appeared in a Chicago newspaper reporting from Israel, that Chris Magee had finally been awarded his Israeli Air Force wings. He had flown for the Israeli Air Force against the Arabs.

The Honolulu Chris Magee tells me that the Black Sheep Chris Magee (your father) has a sister:

Zona Marie Magee Musser

Libertyville, Illinois

A letter addressed that way would probably reach her. Or, you might try information and get a telephone number.

The Honolulu Chris Magee also suggests that you correspond with:

Chris Magee Steel

Box 177

Costa Mesa, CA 92627

The local Chris says that Steel is an avid genealogist and might be of help.

Some of the Black Sheep pilots came home from the South Pacific with Black Sheep pilot Chris Magee and one, who lives here in Honolulu, recalls attending a dance at the Trianon Ballroom with Chris and either a girlfriend or his wife; that was probably your mother.

Another Black Sheep, Fred Losch, stood up with Chris when he was married ... Fred can give you details about Chris at that time. His address is:

Fred Losch

555 New York Drive

Altadena, CA 91001

Let me know if you find out anything as to our Chris Magee's whereabouts.

Hope this has been of some help.

> *Best Regards,*
> *Frank Walton*

"Some help," indeed. Frank's letter not only provided what I considered valuable leads, but motivated me even more to find Chris, not that I really needed additional inspiration at this point. With the help of telephone directory assistance operators, I soon obtained the phone numbers of Fred Losch, Zona Musser, and Chris Steel. Steel, who lived in Costa Mesa—a community that borders Huntington Beach—wasn't home, so I left a message. Fred seemed delighted to hear from me, and we made an appointment to get together at his home in Altadena. Zona, who I telephoned on January 17, was completely taken aback—and perhaps a bit suspicious about the motives of my call—but soon recovered and became reasonably cooperative. She told me she hadn't talked with her brother in about twenty years and didn't have a clue where he resided or even if he was still alive, but she really wanted to see him again. I told her she would be among the first to know when I learned of his whereabouts.

A couple days later I called Zona's eldest daughter Kathy Lunardi, who lived with her family in a San Diego suburb. Kathy said she hadn't seen or heard from Uncle C.L. since he showed up unexpectedly at her nursing school graduation in 1967, not long after his release from prison. She suggested that if I were to go to Chicago, I should contact Helen Magee, former wife of Chris's late brother Fred or, as he was better known, Bud.

Another call went to my sister and brother-in-law, Anne and Tom McNeil, in Massachusetts. Anne seemed surprised at my sudden interest in my birth father, indicating she'd heard that I didn't care to know anything about him. She told me she and Tom had read the Walton book about a year before, and he'd made several inquiries into Chris's whereabouts, speaking on the phone with Black Sheep pilots Jim Hill, Ed Olander, and Pappy Boyington. The trail, however, went cold. I felt as if I'd been presented a great challenge, so I promised my sister what I already had vowed to myself: if Chris was still among the living, I'd find him.

I made the hour drive to Fred Losch's beautiful estate in the Los Angeles foothills a few days later. I'd never been to Altadena before, but it was easy enough to find—just a few miles west on the 210 freeway from the Santa Anita race track, a place with which I was quite familiar. Fred, a successful semi-retired businessman in his late sixties, greeted me warmly and quickly escorted me to his comfortable home office, which was filled with photos, plaques, and other Black Sheep memorabilia. He told me, among other things, that he and Chris were transferred to the same squadron after the Black Sheep broke up, and he had, indeed, served as best man at Chris's wedding to my mother. He even accompanied them—along with his fiancee at the time—on their honeymoon in New York. A wave of nostalgia seemed to hit Fred as he explained how much he would love to see Chris again, and Molly, too. "Next time you talk with your mother, tell her Rope Trick said hello," he beamed. I told Fred, regretfully, my mother didn't know I was trying to find Chris, so I couldn't mention our meeting.

"Chris was the original hippie," Fred said to me later that day while we enjoyed lunch at his country club. His dark eyes lit up as he reminisced about the Black Sheep days. "Not that he was into drugs or anything like that. He was a great guy, just different. If you needed him, he was there. But if Chris wanted to do something, he did it and never worried about the consequences." Fred recalled a conversation with Chris in which they discussed their plans for making a living after the war. Chris seemed to have no delusions about becoming a wealthy man, saying the only way he'd ever get rich would be by robbing a bank.

Before I left for home, Fred gave me several photos of Chris and the other VMF 214 pilots at leisure in the Solomons and a copy of a column from the Chicago *Sun-Times* dated July 24, 1986, that told of Chris flying to Israel with other American volunteer pilots to belatedly receive their Israeli Air Force wings. The article even included an address for Chris on Sunnyside in the Chicago suburb of Lake Forest, but Fred advised me that fellow Black Sheep Jim Hill checked with the Lake Forest police and learned the address didn't exist. Still, I was excited to see the story. It meant Chris was alive and well just eighteen months earlier and probably still resided in the greater Chicago area.

A week or so after my visit with Fred, I received a phone call from Chris Steel, who told me he was in Pittsburgh when I tried to reach him. He seemed actually thrilled that I contacted him and wanted to know all about me and my sister. The reason for his excitement soon became apparent. Steel is the unofficial Magee family historian and a second cousin to my birth father. He'd tried unsuccessfully to locate Chris, my sister, and me for years. He was very serious about the genealogical work he had chosen to undertake, as I discovered at his home a few days later.

During the afternoon of our meeting I answered Steel's questions about my own life while he tape recorded our conversation. Then I listened as he expounded about the six prior generations of Magees in America. He had a lot to say about the original Christopher Lyman Magee, whom he said ran the city of Pittsburgh for many years and was one of the most powerful leaders in the national Republican Party at the turn of the century. Steel was, of course, dying to talk with "Black Sheep" Chris and wished me well in my endeavor to find him. He had, in fact, already corresponded with the Marine Corps Association and several government agencies in his attempt, without success, to locate his elusive kinsman. I left Steel's house with the realization I knew more about the family history of the Magees than I did about that of the Clearys and the Reeds combined. It was an eerie feeling, to say the least.

By February, I was busy writing letters to anyone whom I thought might be able to assist me in my search for Chris. Unfortunately, Pappy Boyington would not be one of them. The news of his death in a Fresno cancer hospice was announced by the television network news and all major newspapers at the end of January. Fred Losch and another Black Sheep, Ned Corman, had visited their old skipper the day before he died. The hospice, according to Fred, had the atmosphere of a funeral home, and he told Corman, "We've got to get Greg out of here."

When they found Boyington's room, an attending nurse tried to shoo them away. Pappy, though barely a shell of his former self, managed to motion the two men to approach his bed, telling the nurse, "Just a couple of my boys coming to say good-bye." It was an emotional moment for Fred and Ned, who tried their best but couldn't completely hold back the tears.

Boyington died before they could arrange to have him moved to a cheerier place. Fred flew to Washington, D.C., to attend the funeral at Arlington National Cemetery. He told me the ceremony—as befitting a Medal of Honor winner—was quite impressive. Two months later I called Pappy's widow, Jo, and had an engaging conversation with a truly delightful lady. Jo told me her husband had greatly admired Chris's adventurous spirit and "really liked him." She kept apologizing for not being able to provide any information about his current whereabouts.

It was around this time I began to notice a change in myself. For more than a decade I had felt lethargic and aimless. All my jobs had been uninspiring and short lived, and my writing career was going nowhere. My life was in the doldrums. To put it succinctly, I felt lost. Now, all of a sudden I had a single-minded purpose: I was on a mission to find Chris Magee.

Since I had the equivalent of two weeks vacation time coming from my job, I decided to use some of it in April to visit Anne and Tom and my nieces and nephew. My flight included a four-day stop in Chicago, where I would attempt to learn more about the whereabouts of the elusive Mr. Magee. I was hoping to receive a reply, to a letter I'd written earlier, from the Israeli Embassy in Chicago prior to my departure. Because they had located Chris in 1986, I felt the Israelis were probably my best shot for finding him. I checked my mail the day before I left but found only the usual junk. It looked as though I'd be winging it once I got to Chicago.

I caught an evening flight to O'Hare International Airport on Wednesday, April 20, and arrived at 12:45 A.M. After renting a car, I drove around until I found a reasonably priced motel in Skokie. I probably shouldn't have bothered—I got very little sleep that night. In the morning I made a list of places to investigate in hopes of finding a lead or two concerning the whereabouts of my quarry. These included the Chicago Police Department, the U.S. Postal Service, the local V.A. Hospital, and the Israeli Embassy. My maternal grandfather Ed Cleary had been a highly respected private detective—he'd even been called in on the Lindbergh kidnapping—and I hoped, perhaps, that I may have inherited some of the traits that made him such a great sleuth.

Before checking out at noon, I perused a Chicago metropolitan area map. That the "Sunnyside" address in the 1986 *Sun-Times* article did not exist in Lake Forest was certainly not discouraging. There seemed no reason for Chris to mislead the reporter, so I concluded, logically, that either the street name was misunderstood—it could have been "Sunnyslope," "Sunnydale," or something similar—or the actual city was wrong. None of the information I had gleaned about Chris indicated that he could afford to live in an upscale village like Lake Forest anyway. However, a brief inspection of the map revealed a street called Sunnyside on Chicago's North Side, just a few miles from where I was staying. I decided to take a drive down that avenue before visiting the various agencies on my list on the off chance that 2316—the street number in the article—existed. First, however, I called Jim Hill to let him know I was in town. No one was home, so I left a message on his answering machine.

Although unfamiliar with the city, I quickly learned finding one's way around Chicago is not difficult (except, perhaps, for the huge industrial area on the West Side). It didn't take long to locate Sunnyside, a narrow, one-way eastbound street. Turning east off Western, I saw a big, grassy city park on my right, then a modern-looking Catholic church on the left that sat alongside a series of aging four-level apartment buildings, all built on narrow frames. One of them had the number 2316 over its entrance.

I parked my rented car as close to the apartment as I could and walked through the glass door into the foyer. Seven mailboxes were lined up on the left wall, each with its owner's name clearly visible. The one on the far right said "Magee." My heart was pounding like a bass drum. I'd struck oil with my first well. Still, I wondered how the *Sun-Times* columnist had placed Chris in the exclusive community of Lake Forest instead of this aging, rather austere Chicago neighborhood.

Now, I had to figure out which apartment was the right one, as none of the mailboxes were numbered. I started knocking. No one answered at the lone ground floor apartment, nor at either first story unit. Then, I found a young man at home on the next level, but he'd moved in only recently and didn't know his neighbors very well. He did tell me, however, that there was an older man living in the ground floor unit. I went downstairs and knocked again, harder this time, but got the same non-response. This time I noticed a small paper bag against the outer wall. Curious, I examined the contents. Inside was a well-worn paperback novel about World War II combat flying by Ernest K. Gann.

So, I'd located Chris, but he wasn't home. I didn't have the slightest idea where he was or when he'd be back, so I decided to grab some lunch at a local diner and check again afterwards. Three hours later, I gave up for the afternoon, and called Jim Hill. This time he answered, and invited me over. Ironically, he lived only five miles or so from Chris.

The youthful Jim and Muriel Hill turned out to be two of the warmest, most generous people I've ever met, and both seemed amazed I could find Chris's place so quickly. Jim had been looking for his old Black Sheep buddy for well over a decade, and was disappointed two years earlier when the Lake Forest address didn't pan out.

Jim related a strange occurrence that took place around the same time the *Sun-Times* article appeared. It seems someone claiming to be "Chris Magee" had called him and written to Walton, Boyington and other squadron members asking for "reference letters" to help him get certain criminal charges reduced. Money wasn't mentioned in the notes, but it was obvious the writer would have accepted a handout if one were offered. Since the return address on the envelopes was for a Chicago-area jail, Jim decided to investigate. When a guard pointed out the cell occupied by the man claiming to be Chris, Jim took one look, then turned to the jailer and said, "That's not Chris Magee!" His flimsy impersonation exposed, the man then wrote to Boyington and others claiming his name was really "Chris Bolt" and he was a close friend of Magee's from Leavenworth. He tried to further arouse sympathy by claiming he had "prostrate" *[sic]* cancer and his wife was ailing. Later, it was discovered the imposter had somehow managed to pass himself off as John Bolt, another Black Sheep ace, and run up bogus credit expenses that were charged to the real Bolt. Jim told me he seriously doubted this phony ever knew Chris, but simply obtained his information from Walton's book.

Not wishing to impose on the Hills for dinner, I stayed only two hours before going back to check on the Sunnyside apartment. Although I returned again and again that evening, no one answered my knocks and I never saw a light in any of the windows.

The next morning, after again failing to find Chris in residence, I called Helen Magee, who invited me over. Helen's home was located near Midway Airport on the West Side, some distance from where I was staying. Helen, a small, neat, energetic woman in her early sixties, greeted me warmly at the door and quickly made me feel at home. The youngest of her three children, Mike—a strapping young man of thirty-two with movie star good looks—was also there. Mike was quiet and shy, in sharp contrast to his extroverted mother. Helen had recently taken early retirement from her job due to a noticeably disabling ailment in her spine, but she refused to allow her physical problems to slow her down around the house.

Helen told me she was Bud Magee's second wife, having met him some time after spouse number one—who, oddly enough, was named Helena—had divorced him. The twin daughters from his first marriage were told their father was dead, and even though Bud occasionally visited the girls when they were children, his ex-wife wouldn't allow him to reveal his relationship to them. His third wife was named Sammi, but that marriage failed as well. Bud served as a street cop with the Chicago Police Force for over thirty years and died on the job of a massive heart attack in 1979.

As it turned out, Helen and Chris got along very well both during and after her marriage to Bud. They corresponded while he was in prison, and he visited her and the kids several times during the first few years after his release. I was surprised to learn that Chris had developed colon cancer while awaiting his second trial for bank robbery as an inmate at Atlanta Federal Penitentiary. He was only forty-one at the time, and at first believed that the intense fire in his digestive tract was due to the "greasy" food prisoners were served. An operation to remove the malignant area was performed, and no further complications occurred during his years behind bars. Helen also told me about Vicki, the daughter Chris had with a woman named Joan Miller in the mid-1950s, who died of a drug overdose while still in her teens. It was around that time that Chris stopped coming around. Helen said she hadn't heard from her brother-in-law in more than fifteen years.

The three of us enjoyed a pizza that night, not that I was really very hungry; Helen had fed us various tasty snacks all afternoon. Before I left, she gave me some old photos along with copies of Chris's letters and the newspaper clippings she'd saved from his bank robbery trial. I especially liked one picture of Chris and his mother seated at the dining room table. In his late thirties, his hair was clearly receding, but he had a twinkle in his eyes and was still physically imposing with a muscular, broad-shouldered torso. That night I checked into a different motel, but not before another unfruitful visit to 2316 Sunnyside.

On Saturday morning the mysterious paper bag and and its literary contents were gone, but my knocking at the door still brought no response. I called on Zona later that day at her ranch-style home in Libertyville. She was sharing the residence with second daughter Sue, construction worker

Chris and his mother Marie, Chicago (c. 1954)   *Courtesy of Helen Magee*

son-in-law George Eberhardt, and their three kids in what appeared to be a very amicable arrangement. Zona had seemed a little distant in our first phone conversation, but I found her to be warm, talkative, and highly intelligent. Although in her late sixties she was still teaching grade school, a profession she entered at age forty to support her four young children after the sudden death of her husband, Gus.

Zona told me she'd seen Chris only once during the past four decades— that being his surprise appearance at the 1967 nursing school graduation of Kathy, his goddaughter. She added that now she wished she'd spent more time with him at that event, instead of being so busy with the other guests. Among the more interesting memories she related was how Chris's literary tastes were so advanced that at age twelve he was actually reading a book written by Thomas Aquinas. I recalled being assigned a book by Aquinas in my college humanities course, but never really delving into it. Before I left, Zona gave me a studio portrait of Chris and my mother in uniform. I told her I would accept the gift gladly, but only until I could get it copied and return the original to her. Zona invited me to spend the night with her and the family, but I declined because I wanted to remain as close as possible to Chris's place until the time my plane was due to leave the next day.

As it turned out I would not get to meet Chris on this trip. Prior to departing for O'Hare on Sunday afternoon, however, I did have an opportunity to talk with a sixty-ish lady who lived on the third floor of his building.

Yes, she was familiar with the gentleman in the lower level apartment, even though she didn't know his name. To her, he was simply "the cowboy," because she often saw him walking around the neighborhood wearing a "cowboy" hat. She seemed surprised when I told her he was seventy years old, for he appeared much younger, and—in her words—"walked like a soldier, very straight." I took the lady's phone number, telling her I might call in a few days to find out if she'd seen him since our conversation. Before leaving, however, I hand printed a long letter and sealed it in a large envelope, then pushed it under his door. The letter began:

Sunday, April 24, '88

Dear Chris Magee,

I'm sorry I have to write this letter, as I was hoping to speak with you in person.

My name is Bob Reed, and I live in Huntington Beach, California. That name probably doesn't ring a bell with you, but a long time ago in another life (or so it seems) you knew me as "Thumper . . ."

I went on to tell the story of how I found out about him and the individuals who helped me in my quest, emphasizing that there were many people—including his family and members of the Black Sheep—who were really hoping to see him again. I also listed the dates I would be staying at Anne's home, along with her address and phone number as well as my own.

My first stop after leaving Chicago was New York City, where I stayed with my sister, Nancy. Nancy was going to drama school and living in a rather spartan upstairs apartment just a stone's throw from the Wall Street financial district. That evening we went to what she called a "trendy" part of Manhattan for dinner at a tiny Chinese restaurant, avoiding sleeping bums and aggressive panhandlers along the way. Although I was a native of the New York area, one day in the city was more than enough for me.

The following morning I caught a northbound train out of Grand Central Station. My next destination was Bridgeport, Connecticut, where I was picked up by my uncle, Bob Cleary, Mom's younger brother—no one except his surviving siblings called him "Mickey" anymore. Bob's hair was gray now, but he was still tall, slim, and handsome. Although only in his mid-fifties, he was already retired, thanks to a generous "golden handshake" he and other senior executives at his insurance company had received a couple years before. Bob's "retirement" allowed him to work as a part-time writer for a local newspaper, a job he really enjoyed. We drove to his lovely rural home to join my trim, youthful Aunt Connie, who was in charge of the children's library in a nearby city, and the youngest of their three daughters, Annemarie, then nineteen and a straight-A student in college.

Bob and I discussed Chris at great length. My uncle was in junior high when he met his sister's husband and was duly impressed by both the man's heroic war record and his astounding physical strength. "Chris Magee was without a doubt the strongest man I've ever known," Bob told me, explaining how easily he lifted heavy objects most men could barely budge. My uncle actually saw his brother-in-law on only a few occasions, but recalled Chris giving him a St. Louis Cardinal cap and a leather flying jacket with the Black Sheep insignia, both of which Bob wore proudly all the way through his high school years. The treasured items disappeared, however, while he was away from home in the Army. Bob also remembered Chris driving him around in a big Lincoln with little regard for speed limits. He showed me his only photo of Chris. In it, the muscular Marine was happily hoisting a smiling, blond-haired baby into the air. The little guy was me.

Chris with Chris Jr. in front of the Cleary's home in the fall of 1945. Within a year, Chris left for more adventures, never to return.   *Courtesy of Bob Cleary*

On Tuesday I took a picturesque journey via Amtrak to the home of my sister and her family near the village of Medfield, Massachusetts. Both Anne and Tom were very interested in what I'd learned of Chris, but we had to wait until all four of their kids were put to bed before we could discuss the subject. Anne rightfully felt there was no need yet for the youngsters to find out they had another grandfather. Once we were alone, my sister and brother-in-law started telling me about the weird coincidence of Anne perusing through Tom's magazine and discovering the existence of Frank Walton's book. Tom wasn't one to read the publication cover-to-cover, and likely would not have noticed the book review if Anne hadn't pointed it out to him.

During the next few days I had a thoroughly enjoyable experience acquainting myself with the McNeil children. Because they were busy with school and other activities, I didn't get to spend very much time with twelve-year-old Tommy and nine-year-old Megan, but energetic little ones Emily, age five and Julie, four, made my brief stay memorable.

My return plane flight wasn't scheduled until the following Tuesday, but on Friday night I decided to telephone the lady who lived in Chris's building. She reported that she thought there'd been a light on in his apartment the night before. That was enough for me. I quickly called to schedule a commuter flight from Boston's Logan Airport to O'Hare the next day and returning Monday. It cost $215, but I felt the money would be well spent if I found Chris at home.

I didn't. However, the time was not wasted as Jim and Muriel Hill were kind enough to invite me to stay at their home all three nights I was in town. It was a truly serendipitous opportunity to get to know these two delightful people, who remain my friends to this day. Jim was always happy to relate adventures he and Chris had shared. Especially impressive to me was the story of how Chris had saved him from drowning during an afternoon of beachcombing on Green Island. We drove the five miles or so to Sunnyside on the day I left, and I showed Jim the apartment. He told me he'd check on the place regularly until he found Chris at home.

After flying back to Boston and staying one more night with the McNeils, I returned home on Tuesday, May 3. It had been a memorable trip, full of surprises and good times with great folks. I had achieved all my objectives save one, but that single failure gnawed at me.

I was soon cheered up considerably by a phone call from a gentleman named Aaron "Red" Finkel, himself a volunteer fighter pilot in the 1948 Israeli War of Independence. Red was contacted by the Israeli Embassy in Chicago and told about my letter. The purpose of his call was to pass along Chris's address, information I no longer required, but the man was so thoroughly likeable I accepted his invitation to visit him in his San Fernando Valley home.

Red turned out to be a real character—witty, opinionated, and forthright. When I called him from the phone at the entrance gate to his secured condominium building he gave me directions, then added, "I'll meet you in the hall. Just look for the bald headed old son of a bitch." During my afternoon at Red's place, he had plenty to say about the 1948 war and the other pilots in Israel's famed 101 fighter squadron, as well as the long conversation he'd had with Chris when they flew back to receive their wings in 1986. We looked through a photo album that included several shots of Chris in his trademark bandanna, and viewed a videotape of the wings presentation ceremony, which Red was kind enough to copy for me. Before I left, he advised me that it was possible I wouldn't hear from Chris because of the shame he may have felt from having served time in prison. I prayed this wasn't the case.

Chapter 16

Contact

―

Almost two weeks after my return from vacation, I came home early one afternoon to find the light on my answering machine blinking. The aging Panasonic unit had become more and more cantankerous in recent months, so I wasn't surprised to discover the first part of the message hadn't been picked up. What I heard was an articulate, though unfamiliar male voice slowly delivering an equally unfamiliar phone number, then stating he would try again later. It occurred to me, of course, that the caller might be Chris, but since he left no area code, I dialed the number as if it were local. The person who picked up the phone was obviously not the same one who'd called; and no, he didn't know anyone with my name or phone number.

Next I called the Chicago area code, 312, with the number. This time, a soft, rather strained female voice answered. A little perplexed, I asked if anyone had placed a call to California from her phone earlier that day. She said, "Just a minute." After what seemed like an eternity, I heard the unknown voice from my answering machine say, "Hello." It was Chris. His voice had an open, almost jovial quality and great warmth.

I don't think I've ever felt more animated than I did during the next hour or so, as Chris and I tried to catch up on the previous forty years of our separate lives. Interestingly, he'd only discovered my letter a day or so before, as it had somehow fallen behind a broken wooden step that led down into his apartment. Since Chris had no phone of his own, he had to wait until he was back at the home of his lady friend in Mundelein to call me. He admitted he spent as much time at her place as his own and was visiting there when I was in Chicago. The only sad moment during our conversation came when Chris asked about his brother, and I had to inform him that he'd died of a heart attack in 1979. Chris took the news in stride, saying only that he wasn't surprised because Bud, "always smoked and drank too much." Before our talk concluded, I promised Chris I'd get back to Chicago sometime during the summer.

A few days later I put together some photos I had taken in April of both Zona's and Anne's families plus a shot of my girlfriend and one of me posing with my recently purchased, Japanese-built Chevy Turbo Sprint, and sent them to Chris along with the following letter:

May 24, 1988

Dear Chris,

Please forgive the word processor. I realize it can make a letter seem cold and impersonal, but anything is preferable to my atrocious, often illegible penmanship.

1988 has certainly been an eventful year for me, and having the opportunity to talk with you on the phone really tops it all. There are, of course, many other things I hope to converse with you about, but what's important is we have made contact, and can keep in touch.

I attended a MAHAL [sic] banquet Sunday, May 15, at the invitation of Aaron Finkel, and met several old friends of yours . . . . It was a delightful evening, filled with the kind of humorous kibitzing that makes Jews so special. Not surprisingly, Aaron was right in the middle of everything. The man re-defines the word "irrepressible." You are remembered fondly by all the pilots, and you can expect a big reunion party if you come out to the coast.

Fred Losch called a few days ago, having recently returned from several weeks in Brazil. He was very pleased to learn you had been located, so don't be surprised to hear from him in the near future. I hope you've been in touch with Jim Hill since we talked. He related several stories about your exploits to me while I was in Chicago, including one about the time you probably saved his life during a beachcombing misadventure. Jim sure speaks highly of you, but then so do all the guys who knew you when . . . .

I hope you like the enclosed photos. Anne and all her kids appear in the shots, but unfortunately there are none of her husband Tom. The only one I have—taken by Anne—shows Tom, Tommy and me at breakfast (7 A.M.), and all of us look like warmed-over death. Anne is a wonderful wife and mother, but a photographer she isn't . . . . You probably recognize most of the other folks, except the compact Italiana (my girlfriend) and the skinny guy in shorts (yours truly).

Guess it's time to get back to my current read, TEXASVILLE by Larry McMurtry. Not a bad book, but certainly a far cry from LONESOME DOVE, his last effort. I just finished WATCHERS, a highly imaginative work about a dog with human intelligence, the result of genetic engineering. The author is Dean Koontz, a local guy who is a real master of suspense.

I'll see you in early August, unless you get out my way sooner. Please write, and send a recent photo of yourself, if you have one. I am really looking forward to getting to know you.

I had to wait almost a month to hear from Chris, and the handwritten note he sent was surprisingly short, though beautifully crafted. It arrived just a few days after I'd mailed him a birthday card.

6/14/88

Dear Bob,

Thanks for the grand pix: fun-happy kids bursting with nature and young vitality. And Anne—a flower in full bloom with her buds unfolding around her. How radiant they all are!

Our world may seem old and weary to many, but such snapshots show that it's always new and exciting, too—always miraculous. So Woody Allen comments: "I'm not afraid of death, I just don't want to be there when it happens."

Tho human consciousness ordinarily functions between polarities and we strive to impose a mechanistic causal order upon what is essentially indeterminate. Happenings have their ways of ripping holes in the fabric of sequence, turning known into unknown, familiar into unfamiliar, triggering a sense of greater wholes than the senses can know, of the sacred in the secular, of the mysteries in the facts.

I'd better stop here before I vanish thru a crack in the floorboards of Limitation into an unstructured Infinity.

Just wanted to get this note off to let you know that I received the pix. Will follow up with more info and a photo . . . .

Chris wasn't exaggerating when he used the term "more info." Four weeks later his seven-page letter arrived, once again stylishly produced by hand. An excerpted version follows.

7/10/88

Dear Bob,

Thanks for your card . . . . Signs of the times: in this age of highly-touted instant information it took 10 days for your card to travel from California to Chicago. The old Pony Express could have done better. Like Chicago's CTA the more the fare is upped the worse the service becomes . . . .

My outer activities aren't much to write home—or from home—about these days: one long linear lethargy, like the stall on WWI's Western Front. But life works behind those scenes and in other dimensions, and there one can find endless pursuits in the wanderings of silent thought: like Tennyson's Ulysses: ". . . to sail beyond the sunset, and the baths of all the western stars . . . ." These ways are endless and forever green no matter how archaic, and the more you delve to plumb, the more hints there are that open onto other paths into other mysteries.

Such a view is reinforced when one sees and hears Bill Moyers interviewing Joseph Campbell for five hours on PBS-TV . . . . His pursuit, of course, is seen through a mythic lens, one he has developed thru many years and many volumes concerned with myths as masks of God. I could add to this that one might also say that myths are a means by which the perennial mysteries manifest themselves to human modes of knowing. Campbell died late last year at 83, shortly after the last interviews in this series. You'd never take him for that age because he was alive inside and that life kept bursting out of him, as if from a pagan source that had become free of dogma and categories—perhaps the "savage source" that Wallace Stevens heard chanting in Sunday Morning.

As for me, I manage to get along on what Social Security pays out—helped by low rent on my apartment, which I mainly use as an oversized storehouse for my impediments (junk), principally books, mags and other media items, plus my own scribbling of whatever Abraxas (a Gnostic god who made an appearance in Herman Hesse's Damien) *decides to boil in my mental pot.*

Anyway the place isn't fit for extended habitation. A year or so ago, perhaps three (time is not only relative, it often also becomes irrelevant, a victim of black holes in memory or overloaded, broken-down synapses) while I was off somewhere, the tenants above me (also off, but not spatially) had a fire; and in their zeal to overcome it the firemen ignored the rainbow promise to Noah and tried to outdo the Biblical downpour. Luckily (for me) result did not match intention, but they did succeed in altering the geometry of my ceiling from a brave rectangular plane to a disheartened conic curve that soon became a full-blown sag, reminiscent of aging actresses once celebrated for their fleshy appeal. However, in this instance there was no former glory to arouse present pity, so the owner offered no attempt at cosmetic revival, and eventually the sag evolved into a split which has slowly widened, allowing intermittent showers of fireproofing materials, segments of wooden laths and other bits of unclassified substances that old buildings usually manage to keep hidden from public view.

I should mention that this condition had been foreshadowed by the presence of two women who had lived above me for some time and were probably at the bottom—or top—of the fire (I being at the bottom of its consequences). The older of the twain may have been a candidate for Alzheimer's, or perhaps had adopted certain of its symptoms as a kind of camouflage behind which to withdraw from the assaults of her daughter's full-blown nuttiness amplified by menopausal side-effects. The younger woman, apparently substituting physical strength for absent rationality, seems to have frequently engaged some large piece of her furniture in a wrestling bout which inevitably was climaxed by her lifting her opponent as high as she could from the floor and then smashing it down with a body slam so professionally accomplished that it would have delighted the fans of any star TV grappler. Of course, the final victim of this mayhem was my ceiling which managed to survive intact until the firemen added their expertise.

So much for the adventure of my main room—but do not consider that the tale is ended there. It is but an episode, an incident, a mere moment in the ageless feud between Apollonian formative restrictions and Dionysian free-swinging elusiveness.

Eventually the mayhem above me earned the two dolls enough points to be evicted, and for a time a sort of Pax Romano prevailed—however, I would encounter occasionally this veteran of the furniture wars and she would mutter dark formulas at me and flash a mal ocho, but I was prepared to repulse such archaic deviltry by raising against it the equally antique sign of the fist with thumb thrust between index and middle finger, a once well-known protection against the strega.

The Pax, tho, was not of long duration. Soon, the ancient system responsible for circulating water into and out of my kitchen and bathroom began (and has intermittently continued) to suffer various afflictions . . .. The bathroom pipes, which are overhead, adapt to weather changes by allowing their seams to open small holes here and there, which results in anything from heavy dripping to a fine spray of hot water. And that periodically converts the entire bathroom into a sort of impromptu sauna that over time has brought down portions of the ceiling into the tub and sink—especially during one period when I was away for several weeks. That incident left the tub and shower in such a condition that since then I take my showers— when I'm around, which is infrequent—in the park field house across the street, which has a swimming pool (the field house, not the street). There is a certain advantage in all this. Because the owner has done little to correct the situation or to repair the damages, I have declined to accept any raise in rent. Since I'm not around most of the time but do need somewhere to keep all my things, the arrangement does have a certain felicity. This, plus walking or using public transportation—I haven't driven in several years—allows me to get along on my income, so I don't rock any boats unnecessarily.

All this is intended to warn you of what you can expect to see when you enter my version of a modern old Stone Age habitation. I wouldn't want you to go into shock at an unexpected disclosure or to feel uncertain as to whether or not you had wandered into a lost world. So—like an experienced Boy Scout: "Be Prepared."

I will now depart the lower depths for more pleasant climes—several days after meeting with Jim Hill I received a phone call from Frank Walton in Hawaii and he told me of a Black Sheep reunion to be held there in May '89. Have also received two letters from Bob McClurg . . ..

Hope to hear from you soon.

Chris enclosed a recent photo with the letter. The outdoor shot, which was from the chest up, revealed a man with close-cropped white hair wearing a white planter's hat of moderate size and a dark blue, long-sleeved shirt that was partially opened to reveal a blue and white striped tank top underneath. He appeared quite muscular and had a solid jaw line, a large face with rather soft features, and very kindly eyes. His mouth looked especially familiar, mainly because I see a nearly identical one in the mirror every morning. So, this is Chris, I thought—a stranger, and yet someone who had been a part of me for my entire life. How much I looked forward to the day when we would finally meet face-to-face, the condition of his residence notwithstanding.

Chris in Mundelein, Illinois (spring 1988)
Chris Magee Collection

August 1988 was a month that produced a record heat wave all over the midwestern United States. I hardly noticed it, though when I arrived at O'Hare; I was much too excited by the prospect of meeting Chris. Although he was expecting me to arrive at about four, the process of getting a rental car and battling heavier-than-expected traffic caused me to be more than a half hour late. Chris wasn't in when I arrived at his apartment; however, he left me a note on the door that said to come in and make myself at home and that there was juice in the refrigerator if I was thirsty.

The first thing I noticed upon opening the door was the two wooden steps leading down into the place; and yes, there was a wide crack running lengthwise in the top step. It was now obvious to me how this gap had swallowed up the large envelope that contained my original note to Chris and delayed our initial contact. I soon became aware of the sagging ceiling whose history Chris had so eloquently described in his letter, and the piles of books and other reading materials he warned me about. What surprised me was that the apartment was actually quite spacious and, probably, a most habitable place, once.

After dropping my luggage and getting a glass of juice, I sat down on the somewhat dilapidated sofa and waited. Before I could get comfortable, however, the door swung open and a solidly-built fellow in a light-blue long-sleeved shirt and—yes—a white planter's hat came through and bounded down the steps, a full laundry basket under one arm. He dropped his burden and reached out his hand, a big grin revealing some gaps in his yellowed teeth. "You must be Bob," he said merrily, shaking my hand. I was, indeed, and extremely happy to be finally meeting this mysterious, enigmatic individual named Chris Magee.

Chris had an aura of eternal youth about him, even when he removed his hat to reveal that the dark, thick wavy hair described in both Boyington's and Walton's books was now pure white and almost completely gone on top. His blue eyes had a warm, expressive quality and the skin on his face held no prominent wrinkles, nor did it sag in the way one might expect of a septuagenarian. I was not surprised to learn he had never used tobacco and consumed alcohol only moderately on rare occasions. One aspect of Chris's persona that did surprise me a little was the laid back, rather passive quality he seemed to display as we talked. It wasn't quite what I expected from an adventurous ex-fighter pilot known for his aggressiveness. Still, there was an unmistakable impression that he could quickly turn into a man of action should the situation call for it.

Even though I had a rental car and the weather was miserable, we spent a lot of time walking around the North Side neighborhood. As the lady upstairs had told me, Chris had the carriage and long, even stride of a young soldier. There was no hint of a strut or swagger, just the confident, purposeful moves of a man who knew exactly where he was going and intended to get there as expeditiously as possible. While climbing stairs he always took two steps at a time. When there was more than one flight, he would seize the inside handrail and swing around to maintain his momentum as he proceeded up the next stairway. Since he usually appeared rather unbalanced during this maneuver, I came to worry that he might lose his grip for a split second and centrifugal force would cause him to take a bad tumble. Of course, that never happened.

I stayed with Chris three days, and during that time we discussed many areas of interest to both of us. Chris told me he had never remarried, making it clear that he simply wasn't cut out for the job of family provider. He willingly talked about his past, including his prison term and two additional bouts with colon maladies in the years after his release: one cancerous, one not, but both requiring surgery. Chris seemed more interested, however, in discussing art, classic literature, philosophy, media, and trends in contemporary society. In fact, he could speak eloquently on almost any topic.

I soon realized his mind was like a computer. He'd accumulated a vast storehouse of knowledge that could seemingly be recalled whenever he wished. On one occasion we were discussing poetry and our mutual affection for the works of Tennyson. I mentioned how impressed I was by the poet's amazing prophetic vision of aviation in *Locksley Hall* (written in 1842) but was unable to remember any of it. Chris concentrated for about five seconds, then began an uninterrupted recitation of the lines.

> *"For I dipped into the future, far as human eye could see,*
> *Saw the vision of the world, and all the wonder that would be;*
> *Saw the heavens fill with commerce, argosies of magic sails,*
> *Pilots of the purple twilight, dropping down with costly bales;*
> *Heard the heavens fill with shouting, and there rained a ghastly dew*
> *From the nations' airy navies grappling in the central blue ...."*

Many intellectuals are so pleased with their own brilliance they use every opportunity to make those around them aware of it. Such was not the case with Chris. While it was impossible to hide his mastery of the language—especially in the letters he wrote—he was an excellent listener who saw no need to impress others with his knowledge and recall. His eloquent observations about a limitless variety of subjects were usually only provided after asking him a leading question, as I did about the Tennyson poem.

Chris read at least two different newspapers every day in addition to the large number of books he borrowed regularly from a branch of the city library located just a block away. He also attended certain literary discussion groups that held regular weekly or monthly meetings in the field house of Welles Park across the street. Chris obviously enjoyed living in Chicago, an energetic city with much to offer culturally and plenty of "action"—an all-encompassing term he often used.

Such was not the case in Mundelein, where Chris's lady friend, Joan Allen, lived, and where he spent much of his time. He advised me that Mundelein was the kind of place that rolled up the sidewalks as soon as the sun went down. On the second day of my stay, we made the thirty-odd mile drive to that quiet town. The floor space in the small, one bedroom apartment Joan occupied was reduced in size even further by the presence of numerous boxes of books stacked along the living room wall. Almost all, I suspect, belonged to Chris.

Joan, who was around the same age as Chris, had dark eyes and long, thick hair that was either off-white or very pale blond, depending on the light. She was quite tall when she stood up, which wasn't very often, as various ailments had made her a semi-invalid. She said she enjoyed walking with Chris on her better days, but these were becoming less and less frequent. She also said she missed living in Lake Forest, where she'd had an apartment up until the previous year, but had to move when the rent was raised to a price she couldn't afford. Joan had obviously been a real beauty in her youth and still looked good for her age, but I couldn't help get the feeling that—unless her condition changed radically—she wasn't long for this world. Fortunately, Joan felt well enough that day to join Chris and me for our three-mile drive to Zona's home in Libertyville.

The reunion of Chris and Zona was surprisingly low key. Neither showed any noticeable emotion after greeting each other for the first time in over twenty-one years; they acted like two people who'd been apart for only twenty-one days. Despite the rather tentative start, I sensed no hostility between them, and it soon became apparent these two really cared for each other. Zona invited us to dinner, and we accepted. Sue, George, and their three children joined us. Not long after the meal, Joan started looking a little peaked, and told Zona she wasn't feeling well. George kindly offered to take her home. Chris accompanied them. With the trio departed and the kids in another room, Zona quietly told me, "She's the one."

"What?" I inquired, more than a little perplexed by her statement.

"She's the one Chris had a daughter with," Zona explained, adding that Joan had been a divorcee with three sons who lived in Fred and Marie Magee's apartment building at the time she met Chris and began their relationship. It was then that I remembered Helen telling me about a woman named "Joan Miller," and quickly realized that Joan Allen was the same person. Had she reverted to her maiden name? It seemed unlikely, as Joan told me she was of Lithuanian parentage. I would never discuss the matter with her or Chris.

I could imagine Joan's predicament: a single mother of three in a nice middle class neighborhood—and a Catholic at that—being with child during the unenlightened 1950s and with a man who had no intention of ever marrying her, or anybody else for that matter. What a neighborhood scandal that must have been! Worse still, Chris had gone to prison when their daughter was still a toddler and didn't get out until she was in the sixth grade. Yet, somehow, after all those years, his being away in prison, and the tragedy of losing their daughter, Joan and Chris were still close. She must really love the guy, I thought. I could tell Zona had a rather low opinion of

Chris's longtime companion, but Joan just gained greater respect in my eyes. I found it interesting that Zona never brought up the subject of Chris's other child during our previous conversations. It was, in fact, her sister-in-law Helen who told me about Vicki, the ill-starred daughter of Chris and Joan.

Chris and I went to see Helen the following afternoon. In addition to Mike, Helen's two daughters Mary Kay and Connie, Connie's husband John, and Helen's three grandchildren were anxiously awaiting the reunion with their uncle. The recent addition of air conditioning to the home was a welcome relief from the sweltering Chicago weather, and added to the already congenial atmosphere.

That evening, my last before returning home, we paid a visit to Jim and Muriel Hill. We were joined by their son and daughter, both of whom wanted to meet Chris. Since my previous trip to Chicago, Chris and Jim had gotten together on several occasions and clearly enjoyed each other's company. Listening to these two fighter jocks reminisce about the amazing adventures they'd shared was enthralling for me and the younger Hills, as well. Not that either man was living in the past, both were quite adept

Jim Hill and Chris in Hill's den, Stokie, Illnois (August 1988). Note the Black Sheep memorabilia in background   *Photo by author*

at discussing contemporary issues during the course of the evening. That Jim and Muriel—two outgoing but rather conventional individuals—could so thoroughly and sincerely welcome the friendship of the free-spirited Chris really did my heart good.

Any fears that Chris had become bitter and withdrawn after years of separation from family and friends were put to rest during my brief stay. His austere lifestyle seemed to support the main focus of his life: an unending pursuit of knowledge. One could describe Chris as stoic, but such a term would hardly do justice to this complex, fascinating man. In a short time, I came to look upon him as a kindred spirit, perhaps much like an older brother. I also sensed that—even in his seventies and living on a Social Security pension—Chris would welcome the opportunity to get away from the familiar sights and sounds of Chicago from time to time and, perhaps, rekindle some old friendships. I was determined to make it happen.

Chapter 17

Back with the Flock

—

Thirteen senior gentlemen were gathered in a suite of Oahu's Hawaiian Regent Hotel on the evening of May 4, 1989, along with nine of their wives. The men came from many walks of life—retired military officers, airline pilots, civil servants, businessmen, legal and medical professionals—but even in their casual aloha-style dress, all carried the unmistakable look of success and prosperity; all, that is, save one: a smiling, muscular man wearing a gaudy yellow-and-black-striped rugby shirt and straw planter's hat and appearing in need of some dental work. An outsider observing how the individual in the killer-bee pullover seemed the center of attention could have concluded he was some sort of eccentric multimillionaire, and the others were all seeking to curry his favor. But, as usual, appearances tend to deceive.

What was happening, in fact, was a reunion of the most famous of all Marine fighter squadrons, the Black Sheep, and the man in the middle was a long lost comrade whom they hadn't seen in over four decades. The preceding years had done nothing to diminish the esteem in which he was held by his fellow pilots. If anything, time had enhanced the mystique of the fearless warrior they had known. Even the wives—all of whom had heard the stories of his prowess but were meeting him for the first time—looked upon the prodigal Sheep with something resembling awe. As several

Attending the Black Sheep Hawaiian cruise in May 1989 were (seated L to R) Bruce Matheson, Ed Olander, John Bolt, Ed Harper, Frank Walton, Bill Heier; (standing) Jim Reames, Denmark Groover, Fred Losch, Ned Corman, Tom Emrich, and Chris   *Chris Magee Collection*

of the pilots would relate to me later, it was truly an "unforgettable moment" for everyone present when Chris Magee stepped through the door of Ned Corman's suite.

That Chris could join his fellow warriors at the Waikiki reception and enjoy the following weeklong cruise of the Islands was due in no small part to the generosity of Frank Walton and the others. Knowing his old friend didn't have the financial resources for a luxury cruise and probably wouldn't accept charity, Frank informed Chris that the group had enough participants to qualify for a free-bonus cabin. He added that the others had discussed the matter and decided to award the cabin to Chris as an enticement for him to attend the reunion.

"All of us shared Chris on that cruise," Bruce Matheson would tell me later. "[We] wanted to update ourselves on what he had been doing." And, as the other Black Sheep soon found out, Chris had been doing things most of the others hadn't even dreamed of, much less actually considered trying.

One story related to me by Fred Losch was particularly amusing. The cruise ship was docked in Lahaina, Maui, for the day, and Chris joined Denmark Groover—a Georgia state legislator—and his wife for an informal tour of that picturesque whaling village's many art galleries. At one particularly exclusive shop specializing in pricey statuary, Chris engaged the operator in a conversation about the different pieces. So knowledgeable did

he prove to be about art in general and the shop's merchandise in particular that the operator became convinced he was a wealthy collector. Soon,
they were haggling over prices, with Chris querying him about multi-unit
discounts and the availability of certain works that were not on display. No
transactions were made, of course, but Groover got a big chuckle out of the
entire proceeding.

I picked up Chris at Los Angeles International Airport (LAX) the
evening of May 13. His Hawaiian vacation had obviously agreed with him.
He was in excellent spirits, but—as I would learn—Chris was always in
good humor. Still, I would like to have had a nicer place for him to stay
than my rather puny one-bedroom apartment. I offered to take the sleeper
sofa and let him sleep on my waterbed, but he wouldn't hear of it, insisting
he could get a good night's rest on anything. Having spent a night or two
on the thin-mattressed convertible unit, I figured that ability was in for a
severe test, but he slept just fine. I envied him. Insomnia has been a frequent bedtime companion most of my life. Too bad I wasn't lucky enough
to inherit Chris's ability to sleep.

The next day, Sunday, was spent enjoying the ambience of Huntington
Beach, including lunch with my girlfriend at a small restaurant alongside
Huntington Central Park Lake and a visit to Sunset Beach's annual outdoor
art festival. Chris was quite taken by my girl, and always asked about her
whenever we talked on the phone afterwards.

That afternoon I decided, for better or worse, to call Anne and Tom in
Massachusetts. Even though my sister and brother-in-law knew Chris's address, thus far they hadn't written to him. After managing to get them both
on the line at the same time, I introduced Chris and handed him the
phone. He seemed a little reluctant at first, but was soon engaged in a
pleasant conversation that lasted about ten minutes. Tom would thank me
for the opportunity to talk with Chris, but the McNeils never attempted to
contact him again. It seemed ironic to me because, from the time we first
heard about the existence of our birth father, Anne was the one who expressed interest in learning more about him.

Sunday evening we went to Sunset Beach again, this time to visit my
bartender friend Forrest at work at King Neptune's Restaurant. I was hoping
to introduce Chris to the owner, Dick Harrison, another much-decorated
World War II Marine, but he was elsewhere that night. A good buddy, mu-
sician Les Crawford, did drop by in a slightly inebriated state, however.
Everyone at the bar had a great time with Chris.

May 15, Chris's last full day at my place, was a busy one. In the morning we drove south to northeastern San Diego County for a visit with Kathy Lunardi, Zona's eldest child and Chris's goddaughter. Kathy hadn't heard from Chris for more than twenty-one years, but was delighted to see him. Her husband, Dan, was at work and her kids were in school. Unfortunately, we couldn't stay long enough to see them because of previous commitments. Kathy did bring out an old photo album, though, and one shot from the 1950s caught my attention. It was of Zona's family, including her late husband Gus, at a dining room table. Chris was there, too, and seated next to him was a very attractive lady who bore more than a passing resemblance to my mother. Kathy told me the woman's name was Christine, and that she was his steady girlfriend for a long period of time. As with much of Chris's personal life, I didn't pry any further into the matter, but I still wonder whatever happened to Christine. It seems likely that she probably just got tired of waiting for him to commit to a permanent relationship.

On our way north we stopped for a couple hours at Dr. Jim Reames' newly purchased home in Laguna Niguel. Doc, an immensely likeable gentleman with a charming deep-south accent and his lovely, petite wife Rosalita—who described herself as the last of the southern belles—were two of the most hospitable people I've ever had the pleasure to meet, and both were tremendously fond of Chris.

After apologizing for the condition of their house, which they hadn't completely moved into yet, Rosalita invited Chris and I to join her in a cocktail. Chris accepted, while Doc and I settled for soft drinks as we enjoyed the "million dollar view" of mountains and ocean beyond the backyard. While we perused Doc's Black Sheep photo albums, he related a very funny story about a wild pig hunt he'd had with Pappy Boyington; then we set off for our final destination of the day.

Twilight had descended on Southern California by the time Chris and I pulled up at the West Los Angeles home of Mitchell "Mike" Flint, prominent attorney and former U.S. Navy and Israeli Air Force fighter pilot. Red Finkel had promised me that if Chris were ever in L.A. he would get all the volunteer pilots from the 1948 War who resided in the area together for a big party, and he came through in flying colors. Mike—an incredibly youthful guy with a full head of flaming red hair—proved a most genial host. I kiddingly asked Finkel why he, and not the decidedly more hirsute Flint, had been nicknamed "Red" by the other pilots. His answer: "I got there first, and I had a lot more hair in those days than I do now."

Among many others in attendance were Lou Lenart, leader of the first aerial raid into Arab-held territory; Rudy Augarten, who shot down four Egyptian aircraft—the most of any IAF pilot; and Leo Nomis, one of the handful of other Gentile volunteers in the 101 Squadron. Flint's wife Joyce had prepared some tasty traditional Jewish hors d'oeuvres, and there was an ample supply of liquid refreshment. Very little alcohol was consumed, however; the entire group was so full of good spirits that further stimulation was simply unnecessary.

I drove Chris to LAX the following morning. We'd had a marvelous time together, but it had been all too short.

The inevitable disaster perpetrated itself upon the ground floor apartment at 2316 Sunnyside that summer, as the long suffering ceiling finally came crashing down onto Chris's living room. Fortunately, he was in Mundelein at the time. Not unexpectedly, the deadbeat landlord chose to not make the expensive repairs, leaving Chris no choice but to move permanently into Joan's already tight living quarters. One major change in the relationship between Chris and myself was that he now had a telephone available full time. This would prove to be a double-edged sword: it was much easier to reach him whenever I wanted, but our written correspondence would cease almost completely. His informative, exquisitely-worded letters were always something special, and I'd saved them all.

I remember my weeklong visit with Chris in October of 1989 as our cultural tour of Chicago. Zona was nice enough to put me up in her basement bedroom, allowing me the opportunity to get to know both her and daughter Sue's family much better.

Each day followed the same pattern. Zona—who had recently retired from teaching—and I would spend most of the morning conversing about current events and other subjects. Like her brother she was an exceptionally knowledgeable person, although she seemed more interested in the practical than the esoteric matter Chris was so fond of. Around 10:30 A.M., I would depart for Mundelein in my rented wheels and pick up Chris. I always invited Joan, but she never felt well enough to travel. From there, it was off to Chicago for a day of sightseeing and enlightenment at the Art Institute, the planetarium, the Shedd Aquarium, or one of the fabulous museums that have earned the city its reputation as a center for science, culture, and the arts. Here Chris was truly in his element. I felt blessed to have such a well-versed guide on our excursions through these fascinating places.

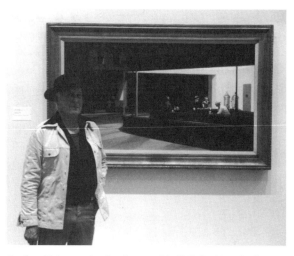

At the Chicago Art Institute with "Night Hawks," one of Chris's favorite paintings (October 1989)

Photo by author

Zona came along on one of our trips into the city—a visit to the Museum of Science and Industry—and Chris suggested we make a side trip to the Magee family's old South Side neighborhood.

The Kenwood area, as it turned out, had seen better days. An apartment building where Chris and Zona once dwelled as children was abandoned and boarded up, but neither Magee seemed noticeably perturbed by the disintegration of their childhood home. However, the adjoining Hyde Park neighborhood remained mostly unchanged from the 1930s. The huge, impressive brownstone homes looked as though they were built to last five hundred years, and most had well-manicured lawns. Chris commented that many of the current residents were administrators and faculty members of the nearby University of Chicago. He also pointed out the former residences of some notables who had been a part of the faculty.

Some of our liveliest and—for me—most enlightening conversations took place while we were driving back to Mundelein every evening. Chris never lectured, but he certainly knew how to stimulate discussions on any number of subjects. He had strong opinions, too, especially on such foibles of contemporary society as postmodern art and historical revisionism, and the staggering power and influence of the broadcast media.

He could analyze the words and ideas of eighteenth and nineteenth century poets and philosophers one moment, then quote such modern luminaries as Andy Warhol and Marshall MacLuhan the next. Often, his discourses would move beyond the range of my intellectual capacity, but I continued to listen attentively in hopes of absorbing at least a little.

Not long after I returned home to California I learned from Fred Losch that the Black Sheep were planning another cruise—this time in the Caribbean—for May 1990. Chris said he probably wouldn't be able to make it, but I had other ideas. I discussed the matter with both Fred and Frank, inquiring as to whether it was possible for me to pay a full fare and get Chris aboard at a discount if we shared a cabin. It was a long shot play on my part, but everything worked out, thanks to the generosity of Fred, Ed Olander, and some of the other pilots who kicked in the necessary funds to make Chris part of the group. I insisted on paying his $200 deposit in addition to my own fare, and it turned out to be money well spent. A letter Chris wrote to Fred two weeks before the cruise indicates he was aware that the generosity of his friends helped make him a part of the reunion:

Greetings,

So now the Marine Hymn is never far from my thoughts and by extension only an engram away from my Black Sheep memory bank. Thanks again for making the past present, for revitalizing that part so that it has a presence in the contemporary scene and is thereby saved from being swallowed up in some Black Hole of the Forgotten.

When I write—even in letters—I tend to go inward, as if some guide were leading me and pointing out this and that thought form or idea for my attention. I think that at least some of this is attributable to my years under federal censorship. Most of what was going on outside of myself was not okay for mailing and so much of what was had little interest for me.

So I would go inward—automatically, as if my pen had taken over—and look into the caves of mystery or kick over rocks to find the hidden, and drag whatever attracted my attention squirming and squalling into the light of consciousness.

And I continue to do so when what is going on around me becomes obviously repetitious and is too much a product of patterns too well known. But there are always new adventures and new places one can reach within and through your self. And you can always be the wide-eyed tourist there—and even move in for awhile, or return again for an extended visit.

So much for that for now...

See you soon,
Chris

Chris (L) with Ed Harper and the author on board SS *Starward* (May 1990)   *Courtesy of Fred Losch*

Losch would tell Chris later that he could not understand half the things Chris talked about in his letters, but he still loved reading them, "so keep writing."

The Norwegian Cruise Lines' SS *Starward* set sail from San Juan, Puerto Rico, one sultry Sunday afternoon in May, with twelve Black Sheep among the several hundred passengers on board. The party—and it was a party in both senses of the word—also included nine wives, one girlfriend, and me.

From the very beginning of the weeklong voyage, I was made to feel part of the Black Sheep family. Fighter pilots, I would discover, are a special

Chris and the author on Martinique. Historic Fort St. Louis in background (May 1990)   *Photo by author*

breed of men even decades after they last sat in a cockpit. In the days we were together, I had the opportunity to chat at some length with each pilot, and in every instance I detected a merry twinkle in the man's eyes and an unmistakable *joie de vivre*. These qualities were especially obvious in Chris's fellow aces: erudite attorney John Bolt (who also shot down six MiGs during the Korean conflict, making him the Marine Corps' first two-war ace), easygoing Don Fisher, and the eternally youthful Ed Olander. Due in no small part to their fame as warriors, Don and Ed were elected mayor of their respective communities after the war. If anyone seemed a little down at times it was Frank

On board an excursion boat in Martinique Bay, Chris enjoys the sea air (May 1990)   *Photo by author*

Walton. It was only a few months earlier that he lost Carol, his wife of over fifty years. It was obvious that Frank—at eighty-one, the eldest member of the group and only non-pilot—was both leader and father figure to the other Black Sheep. When he had something to say, everybody listened.

As *Starward* sailed from one exotic island to the next, Chris and I tried to pass each day ashore with as many different members of the group as possible. In Barbados we hung out with retired Pan Am captain "Long Tom" Emrich and his lady friend Helen, a former flight attendant.

On Martinique, we toured the island and the historic Fort St. Louis then went on an excursion boat with McDonnell Douglas executive Ed Harper and Arizona State University business professor Bill "Junior" Heier and their wives, Jane and Carolyn.

Chris was easy to spot during these sojourns on land, because he always wore matching dark blue slacks and long-sleeved shirts—not exactly a popular (or practical) fashion in the tropics. He seemed comfortable enough, though. Only his omnipresent headgear would change—light-colored planter's hat some days, navy blue sailor's stocking cap on others.

By rotating seats each night at the four dinner tables assigned to us, I had the opportunity to get to know all the couples, including Chris's fellow Chicagoan, retired Colonel Bruce Matheson and wife Jo, who resided in Hawaii; Perry and Carmen Lane; Al and Nancy Marker; John and Dottie Bolt; Don and Betty Fisher; and Ed and Flo Olander. Fred and Jean Losch were, of course, already familiar to me. We had some nice times with all of them. Some of my most rewarding moments came during private conversations with Bolt, Matheson, and Olander—all highly successful men—who confided in me how much they liked and admired Chris for his comportment during the war, both in the air and on the ground.

Chris and I seldom talked much about his wartime exploits during my visits to his home, and I noticed that the other pilots had little to say about their individual heroics, preferring instead to recall narrow escapes and humorous off-duty episodes. However, during one particularly memorable discussion among a group of the Sheep, Chris got very philosophical in expressing his opinion about what it takes to be successful as a fighter pilot.

"The best pilots aren't necessarily the best fighter pilots, and vice versa," he said. "The key word here is 'fighter': a killer instinct is often more important than technical virtuosity." This opinion came from the man Frank Walton credited in his book as having "complete mastery of the airplane; he could do things no other pilot could."

Prior to the cruise, Les Crawford surprised me with a gift: a copy of Pappy Boyington's *Baa Baa Black Sheep*. Les found the book—a first-print edition in excellent condition—at a garage sale and paid a dollar for it. After taking it home he started thumbing through the pages and discovered that Boyington had signed it, thereby increasing its value substantially. While on board *Starward* and in the years to follow, twenty-two members of the original Black Sheep Squadron autographed the volume. Sometimes the least expensive of gifts are the most thoughtful, and can become the most precious, as well.

Chris and I continued to keep in touch every month or two via telephone. Our discussions always lasted more than a half-hour. Often in conversations with other friends and relatives, I would find myself pausing because I wasn't sure what to say or ask next. This was never the case with Chris. Time seemed to accelerate whenever we talked.

It was only the reminder about the phone bill that would bring the talks to a conclusion, albeit usually not a rapid one.

Shortly before my departure for another Reed family reunion in Branson to be followed by a three-day stay with Chris, I received this letter.

July 20, '91

Dear Bob,

We are hurtling thru summer and soon, very soon it will be August—and you will be here: the seal on the torrid season and the harbinger of fall. This little planet seems to set new speed records every year in its circumnavigation of our ancient sun.

Meanwhile, from the cosmic to the mundane: Mundelein is dawdling, puttering, sputtering along on a too-lean mixture of dynamic change. And its muses slumber in Hypnos' cave, incapable of providing inspiration or images from beyond the realm of sleep.

So a summing of what may—or may not—be news seems to be in order: Suzy, George and progeny have long settled in their old-new home (Mundelein vintage—a mile or so from Joan's location), and Zona has her cat for company. They commiserate together over the loss of collie Kelly, who suddenly collapsed, for reasons unknown, and took some two hours, with her head in Zona's lap, to complete her departure. But Zona has acquired one of a new generation of canines to solace her grief and to provide a new source of interests. . .

As for myself—I've shed about 23 pounds on my way down to a goal of 175: seven more pounds to go. Last winter I reached a top of about 205 lbs. These figures are all sans clothing. I've found that the best way for me to lose weight is exercise. So I started by cutting out lunch and then walk and do calisthenics after each of the other meals, thus burning off calories after each meal—not giving them a chance to "take root." This routine takes place for about an hour twice a day—morning or early P.M. and about 10 or 10:30 at night. Have worked up to about 500 movements per session and use three pound weights for the night workout. All of this is done outside because I walk to begin with, then exercise, then combine walking and exercise, then about 15 minutes more of a workout. As a finale, I walk about another half mile, combining extra movements for legs, etc., with the walking. The 500-plus movements each session are all waist exercises, and I will add to them as I go along. Have been at this, or working up to it, for the last 3–4 months. (I use the weights only to provide leverage for stretching waist and other trunk areas). . .

Haven't heard much from Helen except that Mike is a fireman and happily learning the ways of a full-fledged "smoke-eater."

So that's about the extent of the local action. . .

Chris never appeared to have had a weight problem, but I applauded his determination to lose several pounds and get into the healthiest possible condition. How many seventy-four-year-olds would even consider such a demanding daily regimen? Christmas was still several months away, but the letter helped me decide upon the ideal present—a pair of quality cross training shoes. I began sending Chris birthday and Christmas gifts in 1988, the year we got together, and he responded in kind. I tried to choose practical things—a fan to help cool his place in the summer, a microwave, and even my old yet serviceable VCR. The latter selection came about when I discovered he was taping his favorite PBS-TV shows, such as "Joseph Campbell and The Power of Myth," on audio cassettes. Chris, on the other hand, sent me imagination-stimulating gifts like books on abstract art and frameable prints by Escher and Magritte.

I flew to Chicago for brief but enjoyable stays in '91 and '92, but the best and most memorable time we spent together was in the following year. It was neither in Chris's home town nor mine, but in a city known for good times—New Orleans.

Chapter 18

The Golden Gathering

—

New Orleans was one of those places I'd always wanted to visit, but the opportunity had never presented itself for one reason or another. So, when I learned that the Black Sheep were planning to hold their fiftieth anniversary reunion at that Mississippi Delta city I was eager to include Chris and myself in the festivities. Chris was a little reluctant at first. He didn't come out and say so, but I was almost certain that financial considerations had something to do with his attitude. Eventually, he was persuaded by my reasoning that I intended to go anyway, and the cost for the hotel room was the same whether it was occupied by one or two individuals; plus the airline I was using offered senior discounts and had a "friends fly free" promotion in effect. In other words, my cost would be about the same whether I attended the event alone or if Chris came along, too.

Still, Chris almost missed the reunion. He started experiencing some problems in his digestive system a few weeks before the event, and advised me that the doctors at the Chicago V.A. Hospital could veto his participation if tests showed that the condition was serious—meaning the insidious colon cancer had returned. Fortunately this proved not to be the case. He happily reported the good news to me by phone just days before our scheduled departure.

We met at the New Orleans airport on May 10. On that cloudy, muggy afternoon, we took a taxi to the Black Sheep's headquarters hotel, the fine, old Chateau Le Moyne in the French Quarter. It was drizzling by the time we'd changed into our evening wear and moved downstairs to the atrium where the rest of the group were gathering. What an impressive turnout it was: no less than twenty-two of the twenty-eight living members of the squadron attended. One finds it hard to imagine any high school or college class with an eighty-percent turnout at their fifty-year reunion. And these guys had been together as a unit for only a few months, not four years.

I was happy to see Jim and Muriel Hill were present this time, along with their closest friends from the Black Sheep family, the vivacious Bob and Julie McClurg. My fellow Orange Countians, Dr. Jim and Rosalita Reames, were there, too, along with several new (to me) faces including the Ned Cormans, the Denmark Groovers, the Al Johnsons, Hank Bourgeois, Bill Case, Harry Johnson, and Sandy Sims. Another new face—and a very lovely one at that—was Virginia Walton, Frank's new wife. The Waltons had been married earlier that year, and were on their honeymoon. Frank, now eighty-four, had recently been operated on for cancer, but was obviously in remission and in great spirits. No doubt his youthful, charming bride had a lot to do with that.

After group photos were taken, everyone moved into the hotel's banquet room where John Bolt eloquently offered the following toast:

Celebrating the Black Sheep Squadron's fifty year reunion in New Orleans during May 1993 were (seated L to R) Fred Losch, Al Marker, Frank Walton, Jim Reames, and Hank Bourgeois; (second row) Al Johnson, Chris, Ned Corman, Jim Hill, Perry Lane, Bruce Matheson, Ed Harper, and Tom Emrich; (top row) Bob McClurg, Denmark Groover, Bill Heier, Ed Olander, Don Fisher, Bill Case, Harry Johnson, John Bolt, and Sandy Sims   *Chris Magee Collection*

"To our fallen companions whose bones rest on the bottom of the sea in the Solomon Islands, cut down in the bloom of youth, denied the pleasures of life, which by chance, the rest of us have enjoyed.

"To Gregory Boyington, the courageous, charismatic leader of our days of glory.

"To Frank Walton, who from our early days has not only been our Boswell, our biographer, in creating the Black Sheep legend, but by his own life has been a friend, inspiration, and role model to all.

"To Jim Reames our compassionate squadron doctor, whose medical treatment, Lejon brandy, and cheerful good humor helped each of us to bear the stress of combat when death was a frequent visitor to our squadron.

"To our wives and ladies without whom life would have been a fruitless, cheerless existence without meaning.

"To each of us, once a proud, brave brotherhood in arms, today we are bound by our own actions in the Black Sheep legend, as friends forever.

"Last to our beloved Marine Corps. We all knew when we put on the forest green uniform that it would ask us to put our lives at risk, which it did, and it would give us only pride and self respect, which it has."

Everyone seemed moved by the toast, even an ex-Navy man like myself who hadn't been born when the men of VMF 214 were battling not only a stubborn, deadly enemy but also the elements, pesky insects, dangerous reptiles and various tropical maladies, all of which would be discussed at length during the next four days.

The cocktail party and banquet that followed were first rate. In the finest tradition of the Corps, a Marine guard presented the colors and music was provided by a Marine band. The formality of the proceedings was to be expected: Bourgeois, Bolt, and Fisher, three of the chief architects of the reunion were retired career Marines, as were Case, Harper, Heier, and Matheson. I heard later that the commanding officer of the local USMC facility balked at the Black Sheep's request for a band and color guard, but did a quick about face after Bolt made a courtesy telephone call to a good friend in Washington, the Commandant of the Marine Corps.

Bolt also brought three special guests to the reunion: Bruce Gamble of Pensacola's Naval Aviation Museum, his wife Margaret, and his toddler daughter Rachel. Bruce was putting together an exhibit for the museum that would feature historical information about the Black Sheep, and planned to spend a half-hour or so interviewing each pilot on audio tape. As it turned out, his session with Chris lasted over two hours.

Nearly all the attendees went on to impressive postwar careers. The seven retired Marines moved successfully into other fields after leaving the Corps. Three of the pilots who left the service after the war—Ned Corman, Tom Emrich, and Al Johnson—became captains with major airlines, while Perry Lane served as an FAA official. Harry Johnson, Fred Losch, Al Marker, Bob McClurg, and Ed Olander went into business for themselves. Olander was twice elected mayor of his hometown, Northhampton, Massachusetts, and Fisher served as city manager and later mayor of Beaufort, South Carolina. Denmark Groover had recently been reelected for another term in the Georgia state legislature. Jim Hill was still active in his position as a sales executive, and Sandy Sims was an artist of international repute. Doc Reames maintained a thriving practice in Whittier, California, for decades before retiring to Laguna Niguel, and Frank Walton's extensive public service career has been duly noted. It seemed as if only one of Black Sheep truly lived up to the squadron's euphemistic nickname, and that, of course, was Chris.

The group would get together for carefully planned lunches and dinners at some of New Orleans' finest eateries during the days that followed, but often the best times were the least formal. Every morning Chris and I would hike down to the waterfront, along with various members of the Black

Enjoying an al fresco breakfast at the Café Du Monde during the Black Sheep's fifty year reunion in May 1993: (L to R) Bruce Matheson, Dotty Bolt, Chris, John Bolt, Jim Hill, Muriel Hill, Bob McClurg, Julie McClurg   *Photo by author*

Sheep family, and enjoy the world famous *beignets* served at the Café Du Monde. There we'd invariably run across others from our group, and the warmth and camaraderie that ensued invigorated us for the rest of the day.

Except for one trolley trip to view the antebellum mansions of the city, Chris and I spent most of our time, day and night, hiking around the French Quarter or the waterfront. We made the more formal festivities of the first and last nights. Chris always dressed in black during our stay in the Crescent City, even the western-style hat he wore was black leather. Once I jokingly asked him if he was Paladin, the stylish hero portrayed by Richard Boone in the old TV series *Have Gun, Will Travel.*

Chris answered that no, he was "Chris." Then, failing to get a rise out of me, he added, "You saw *The Magnificent Seven,* didn't you? Remember the name of the Yul Brynner character?" That's when I figured it out: by wearing black, Chris was just being "Chris."

New Orleans was full of action—obviously Chris's kind of town. He told me he'd been there on several occasions, but his fondest remembrance was of his first trip. It happened shortly after World War II began in Europe when he and two friends hitchhiked to New Orleans in hope of gaining passage aboard a merchant ship heading for England. Incredibly, the three young men believed they could enlist in the RAF and immediately start training to become fighter pilots. As it turned out, the Neutrality Law in effect at the time prevented them from following that pipe dream, and Chris and his buddies were soon on their way back to Chicago.

Nearby Bourbon Street really started cooking, musically, after the sun went down, but several of the Black Sheep preferred the frenetic ambience and uncooked delicacies of the Acme Oyster Bar. The rather unsavory looking little denizens of the half-shell had no appeal to me, but several of the guys, especially Fred Losch and Al Marker, couldn't seem to get enough of them. While I contented myself with landlocked treats such as po' boy sandwiches, Fred and Al and others would hold contests to see who could swallow the greatest number of the slimy shell-dwellers. Apparently, a few beers helped make the passage from mouth to stomach a little easier.

Thanks to the event's organizers, the reunion received plenty of attention in the local media. In a rather controversial article in the *Times-Picayune,* one of the pilots was quoted as saying something to the effect that Pappy Boyington "wasn't really a great fighter pilot, just persistent." The others were quick to defend their late squadron leader, of course, and the offending party claimed he'd been misquoted.

Another piece on Frank Walton from the same newspaper—this by a local society columnist—was so wildly inaccurate it brought huge guffaws from everyone in our party. The story claimed Walton's book, published in 1986, "inspired" the Black Sheep Squadron TV series of the late seventies. She also credited Frank with being a "two-time Olympic-winning swimmer" and "once the stand-in for ... Tyrone Power." Frank had, in fact, been a member of the 1948 U.S. Water Polo Team that didn't win a medal, but the idea of the rangy, red-headed Irishman standing in for the swarthy, smallish Power boggles the mind. Later, Chris and I, along with some of the others, discussed who the likely source for the columnist's misinformation might be. We never found out, but my money is still on the pixieish Bob McClurg.

The only low point of the trip happened on the third evening. Several of us were walking to a group dinner at a well-known Italian restaurant when Long Tom Emrich slipped off a curb, twisting his ankle and falling in a heap. Chris was the first to reach his stricken comrade—a good-sized fellow—and, with no apparent strain, gently lifted him to his feet. Fred Losch arrived to assist Chris seconds later, and helped Emrich back to the hotel. Tom's pants had been ripped in the fall and were ruined, but he and Fred caught a cab and made it to the restaurant in time for dinner with the rest of us. The next day we learned that Tom had broken his ankle in the spill.

Our final night in New Orleans brought the golden reunion to a grand and fitting climax. Some of our group planned to take a riverboat cruise up the Mississippi over the next few days, but for the others—including Chris and me—it was the last hurrah before going home. A chartered bus carried everyone to the sprawling suburban estate of Hank Bourgeois' cousin, Joanne Rizal and her husband Rene. We were greeted warmly as we entered the home by several of the Rizal women—all of them seemingly young, tall, and gorgeous.

The backyard and patio where most of the socializing took place was surrounded by lovely tropical flora and had tables full of incredibly tasty Cajun food. Some of us danced to the wonderful tunes of the 1940s that were performed and sung by a talented young musical duo, while many of the younger Rizal family members and friends listened attentively to the reminiscences of the Black Sheep. They must have especially enjoyed Bill Case's account of his last mission with the squadron. The diminutive Case had been unable to adjust his pilot seat upward to an optimum level that would afford both passable vision and full protection from his armored seat back. Later, however, he was happy for that slight inconvenience when a bullet from an attacking Zero passed through the rear of his cockpit and barely grazed the top of his helmet. Bill let everyone know he "got religion" after that experience.

It was a joyful evening, yet one could detect a tiny underlying note of sadness. As Bruce Matheson told me, "This is probably the last time all of us will be together." Just before the time came to get on the bus and return to the hotel, the musicians played the Black Sheep's nostalgic trademark theme, "The Whiffenpoof Song," made famous by the Yale Glee Club with melancholy lyrics borrowed from a Kipling poem written more than a century before. Everyone who knew the words of that timeless number sang along. I don't think there was a dry eye in the house when it was over, not even among the many guests who, like myself, hadn't yet been born when the Black Sheep Squadron was the scourge of the Solomons. The bus trip back was anything but subdued, however, because Flo Olander led everybody in a singalong. The guys even managed renditions of a few of the less bawdy tunes they'd sung a half century before during long, balmy evenings in the South Pacific, far from home and family. It occurred to me that—except in church—people seldom sing together anymore. Perhaps, we're all missing something.

∽

After flying back to Chicago with Chris, I spent the next two nights in Mundelein before heading home. Joan was in a local hospital with a "mystery" ailment, so her bed was available. Later, she would undergo chemotherapy for several weeks. The reason one would suffer that procedure for an unspecified condition escapes me, but apparently Joan requested it and the doctors approved. In the long run the benefits proved, at best, minimal. Every time I called Chris before and since that visit, Joan would pick up the phone and her reply to my friendly greeting, "Hi, Joan. How are you?" was invariably, "Not so good . . ." and she would briefly describe her current affliction before calling Chris to the phone. That she had lasted five years after our first meeting seemed miraculous, and that Chris willingly stayed with her when he could have easily moved into one of Zona's many spare bedrooms was a testimony to his loyalty.

In the summer of 1993 I accomplished something I'd never quite managed before: I bought my first home. My income from work never amounted to much, but over the years I'd maintained a minimalist lifestyle and managed to save enough for a down payment that was enough to qualify me for a VA loan. I could have purchased earlier had I been willing to set up residence in a less desirable Orange County community, but I was determined to remain in Huntington Beach, my hometown since 1973. The two-bedroom, two-story townhome was far from new, but is located in a quiet, low-density complex with well-kept grounds. Soon after escrow closed I called Chris and invited him to visit any time, assuring him my new digs were far less cramped than the little apartment where he stayed for three days in 1989.

Chapter 19

Passages

⎯

On November 20, 1993, six months after the reunion he described as, "the very best ever," Frank Walton died. His cancer returned with a vengeance, and his final illness was a short one. A few days later in a simple, tasteful service, Virginia scattered Frank's ashes in the Pacific Ocean, not far from where he made his daily swims. As Bruce Matheson, his best friend, wrote in a letter to the other Black Sheep: "Frank would have liked it because it was short, it was on time, there wasn't an inordinate amount of BS, and all of us knew that this was exactly the way he wanted to be sent off." The *Los Angeles Times* published an impressive obituary article about its city's former Deputy Chief of Police, and I sent copies to Chris and to Virginia Walton.

Frank Walton reminded me a lot of Dad: he was a true everyday hero, a man who always took the "high road." And—perhaps because he was so much like Bill Reed—I found him a little intimidating, at least the first time we met. I have a feeling most of the Black Sheep probably had the same reaction to Frank back during their halcyon days in the Solomons. He may have been "one of the boys," but he was always the older, more mature brother. If Pappy Boyington was the heart of the Black Sheep Squadron, Frank Walton was its soul. A letter Chris sent to Frank prior to major surgery in the summer of 1988 eloquently describes how much he and all his comrades thought of their intelligence officer, and serves as a most fitting tribute:

Dear Frank,

Was just informed via the A.M. mail that you're getting the old fuselage repaired. Will expect you back around the Ready Tent as soon as you're mended. We all need you there, and the legend you've done so much to create and maintain needs you there. Valhalla and the Valkyries can wait. Had ours been an age of poetry you might have been the Taliesen, Welsh bard of Arthurian fame.

Sure, without you there still would have been a Black Sheep squadron, but you lifted it above its context, gave it a mythic dimension, a constellation among the archetypes. Yet the legend is also organic, connected with the Earth, living and growing beyond its roots, beyond the generation (like a Banyan tree), reaching out, drawing vitality from wherever it finds new places to take root in the imaginations of so many that were then yet unborn. You have helped so much to give them something to identify with, and to recreate in their minds and hearts where it will remain forever young.

Certainly, the content you had presented to you was a great source of inspiration—as those of us who served earlier and later with other squadrons can and do affirm—but inspiration too often finds no response, no readiness. Falling onto fallow minds and hearts that failed to absorb it, what had been potent content soon loses any link it had with the living imagination which is a springboard to that higher reality, one of greater wholes, outside of time.

You saw or felt, consciously or intuitively, in that content something that must not be lost to the episodic, to the May Fly transience of particulars, to the deserts of record and statistic where the human heart dries up and petrifies because there is no Garden of Allah, no oasis where springs of human feeling connect us with the Eternal and with the Earth and with one another. You gave it added life, added power, and a form that enabled it to move, or be moved, thru time and beyond: into the imagination.

Thus, Frank, you are an artist in that you have lifted something temporal a little closer to the Eternal and yet have kept its connection with the living Earth.

We have all—living and dead—been fortunate to have shared those few brief months in a place apart, a strange primordial world that only grows stranger, more enigmatic in the memory as the years stretch away from it. At times it is as if I am remembering a marvelous story told to me as a child, the events of which have been lifted away from the Earth and given a place in that realm where myths are real. But then again I know that we all have a very real Earth connection with that time, that place and one another. And that connection has been kept strong, alive and warm because you have so faithfully tended it.

We have all been fortunate to know you and to have you as the keeper of our flame.

Chris and I made plans to get together again in August 1994 after a Reed family reunion in Branson, Missouri. Jim and Muriel Hill kindly provided my sleeping accommodations during the three nights I spent in Chicago, as Zona was away visiting one of her daughters. The highlight for Chris and me came on my last full day when we drove north across the Wisconsin state line to attend the annual Bristol Renaissance Faire. Chris obviously enjoyed the Elizabethan-style pageantry and colorful jousting tournaments as well as the various street performers and artsy-craftsy shops. He mingled with different artists at their booths and mini-galleries, and—although no purchases were ever made—they all seemed to enjoy chatting with someone who understood and appreciated their works. As usual, by day's end I was the one worse for wear from all the walking around and the heat and humidity. I had long since ceased being amazed by Chris's fitness and stamina. At seventy-seven, he showed no signs of slowing down.

I felt pretty fortunate as 1995 began. Life was good, I was healthy and my home was in good repair. Unlike most people of middle age, I was secure in the knowledge that both my parents were alive and well and ready to help if I needed it. My greatest treasure, of course, was my girlfriend. I felt lucky that such a beautiful, loving woman would stick with me through thick and thin for so many years. I saw her almost every day, and when we weren't actually together we kept the phone lines buzzing.

And then, of course, there was Chris. He had come to mean a lot to me during the past seven years. Whatever shortcomings or character flaws he may have had simply didn't exist anymore, as far as I was concerned. Although I had no desire to emulate Chris, especially in the humble lifestyle of his twilight years, he had become—in some undefinable way—my mentor. We had long telephone conversations every month or so, and never seemed to run out of topics of mutual interest. Despite his intellectuality, the discussions were seldom of an esoteric nature. Television, for example, was a frequent subject. Chris watched the Chicago public broadcasting channels often, but he was not a PBS snob by any stretch of the imagination. Most of the situation comedies on commercial TV turned him off, but he was a big fan of some of the more quirky and character-driven dramas and adventure series. Among his favorites were *Wise Guy, Twin Peaks, Highlander,* and *The X-Files.* Chris was also very fond of *Northern Exposure,* and I sometimes kidded him about his being the likely inspiration for one of the main players in that show. The character was an easy-going small town radio personality who had served time in prison for car theft. He could quote famous poets and existential philosophers at the drop of a hat, yet never sounded pretentious. That this fictitious individual was named "Chris" seemed like more than mere coincidence to me.

With everything going so well in my life for so long, the pendulum was due to swing the other way, and it did. In March I parted company with my employer. Eight years is a long time to spend, even part-time, on a job you don't like. The day finally came when I was asked to sign a corrective because of a minor disagreement between myself and a veteran full-time salesman. I responded to my manager's request with four words: "Not in this lifetime," and walked out.

Aside from the reduction in income, being unemployed wasn't all that traumatic in the beginning. The first thing I learned as I began to explore the job market in the fields of journalism and advertising was that one needed a network, something I completely lacked. My second discovery was that potential employers weren't exactly scouting the hinterland for middle-aged guys sans hefty/impressive portfolios.

Then more bad news filtered my way. My mother suffered from clinical depression, but medication had kept the condition in check until recently. When a pharmacist told her the stuff she was taking was about to be discontinued, she cut back on her daily dosage, apparently, to make her supply last as long as possible. She learned, too late, the actual drug was still available, just under a different name. When she got back on the proper medication schedule, it no longer worked. Mom's condition was really tough on Dad, too. He waited on her hand and foot, attending to her every need, but despite all his efforts, there was little improvement.

The year's sole high spot came that summer, when my old Navy buddy Mike Wheat called from Oklahoma to let me know that several of our old PAO gang were getting together at Alameda Naval Air Station for an open house aboard *Hornet.* It was quite a surprise. Our former ship had been mothballed at Bremerton, Washington in 1970, and I'd half expected to learn she had been sold for scrap long ago; but according to Wheat, the city of Alameda had gotten together with the commanding officer of the Naval Air Station there to save *Hornet* and make her an historical-showcase ship and museum for the public to tour in the years to come.

So I traveled to Northern California on a bright Sunday in July and walked up a gangplank onto the quarterdeck of a ship I thought I'd never set foot on again. After a brief search, I found my old shipmates: Wheat, Gary Froseth, Jim Missett, our boss Tim Wilson, and even Tim's PAO predecessor, Tim Jacobs. Wheat and Missett brought their wives along, and everyone appeared to have weathered the past twenty-five extremely well. Wilson was the biggest surprise of all. It wasn't that he'd become a very successful Marin County land developer—we all could have predicted a bright financial future for him. What amazed us was that he appeared not to have aged a day in twenty-five years. He could have put on his old Lt. (jg) uniform, and no one would have been the wiser. I theorized that Tim probably either traded his soul to the devil for eternal youth, or there was a portrait hidden away in his attic of a salty old naval officer aging day by day.

It was a treat to get together with the guys again, but I couldn't help reflecting on the difference between our little gathering and the Black Sheep reunions I'd attended. We took each other's addresses and phone numbers, but nobody seriously discussed the possibility of trying to get all the fellows who had served in PAO together again at some future date and place. Perhaps it was because we served at a different time under different circumstances in a non-combative role—I don't know. What is for certain, we never experienced the level of camaraderie and esprit de corps so evident in the men of VMF 214.

∞

By October, my personal ship was sinking, and there wasn't a life preserver in sight. I was fifty years old, and jobless with no prospects. My unemployment insurance ran out, and I was living on ever-dwindling savings. It also disturbed me that, for the first time since 1988, I wouldn't be seeing Chris. Due to my present circumstances I really couldn't afford to fly back to Chicago, although I was anxious to visit him at the new apartment in Crystal Lake he and Joan moved into earlier in the year. A phone conversation with him in the latter part of the month cheered me up considerably—as our talks always did—and he even suggested that he'd try to get out to see me during the coming winter. I told Chris he'd be welcome any time, and I sincerely hoped he could make the trip.

I received news through the Black Sheep grapevine in mid-November that two of the pilots, John Begert and Bill Case, had recently passed away. I never met Begert, but did converse with Case and will never forget the story of his incredible last mission with the squadron. Bill sincerely believed that the fact he escaped with his life was a miracle, and he considered every day that followed a bonus. I guess one can't complain about being given fifty-two years worth of bonus days. Later, I learned that big, loveable Don Fisher had died of cancer around the same time as Case. I'd really enjoyed the times with Don and his wife Betty at the two reunions I attended. He was an ace during the war and continued to set similarly high standards throughout a life of public service.

Chris and I discussed the passing of his wartime comrades during a long Thanksgiving phone call. Despite the sad news, our conversation was generally upbeat, as usual, although I couldn't help notice a slight weakness in his usually hearty voice. When I asked if he'd picked up a cold or a case of the flu, Chris answered with a statement to the effect of "there's always something going around." What I most remember about the call was that he told me he was going to try and "dig up" some of the poems and stories he wrote in prison and send them out to me. Many times I'd asked him to show me his writings, but he always replied that he'd squirreled them away long ago, and wasn't certain where. Based upon the literary virtuosity I'd seen in his letters, I really looked forward to reading those compositions.

∞

On Saturday, December 23, I caught a plane out of John Wayne Airport for the annual Christmas pilgrimage to my parents' home. Anne and her family remained as always in Massachusetts and Ed couldn't get the time off from his job in Anchorage, but my sisters Diana, Nancy, and Barbie were there, along with Barbie's precocious eleven-year-old, Paige. Mom still hadn't found a cure for what was ailing her, but seemed in slightly better spirits than when we last talked. The effect her illness had on Dad was evident. Now seventy-five, he seemed much less energetic than usual, and was starting to show his age.

My parents must have sensed my career was stalled at a crossroads, because their gift was a Macintosh computer and printer. I couldn't thank them enough. Diana, the most successful and generous of my siblings even offered me a bonus gift: frequent flyer coupons good for a round trip almost anywhere in the U.S. She said her company was about to transfer her from Sacramento to Harrisburg, Pennsylvania, so she had no use for them. I was happy to accept her kind offer, figuring that if I didn't use the coupons myself, I'd send them to Chris, so he could fly out to see me. Before my return flight the following afternoon, Dad and I took my new computer system to the local UPS office and arranged to have it sent to my home.

As I entered my house in the late afternoon of Tuesday, December 26, I noticed that my answering machine was blinking with a single message. It was Chris. "Hello, Bob," his voice said, seeming slightly strained as in our November chat. "It's Chris calling to say, 'Merry Christmas and what follows.' So, I guess I'll talk to you later. Good-bye." The call had been made the previous afternoon. I thought about getting back to Chris right away, but decided to wait a few days until January 1, so I could wish him a "Happy New Year."

The next day, my girlfriend and I picked up a computer work station—her gift to me—at a local department store and somehow managed to get the heavy kit home in my little hatchback. I could see putting it together was going to be a task of staggering proportions.

My new Mac arrived the morning of the 28th. The boxes appeared none the worse for wear, but I decided to leave them unopened until the work station was completely assembled. That afternoon, as my girlfriend and I were enjoying a quiet conversation, my phone rang. "I wonder who that can be?" I quipped. "Maybe it's somebody about a job."

No such luck; I picked up the phone and was completely surprised to hear the voice of Zona. "Bob," she said, "I have some news . . . and it's not good." She paused for a second or so. "Chris died."

I felt as if I'd been shot in the heart, but managed to ask for the details. The story Zona told me was that Chris had checked himself into the Chicago V.A. Hospital earlier that month complaining about pain in the lower abdomen. The doctors discovered another colon tumor—the problem actually surfaced several months earlier, but testing was delayed again and again due the sort of snafu one becomes accustomed to when dealing with a bureaucracy. Chris spent about two weeks in the hospital, but was released long enough to enjoy Christmas at home before returning on the afternoon of the twenty-sixth. His surgery, scheduled for the next morning, should have taken only four hours or so, but scar tissue from previous operations complicated matters. Then, things got even worse when the doctors found a second tumor. They decided to go ahead and remove it, as well, but even a fit seventy-eight-year-old body can take only so much. After twelve hours on the operating table, according to Zona, Chris's heart simply stopped. He couldn't be resuscitated.

I had to get off the phone while I was still in control of my emotions, so I told Zona I'd call later to discuss funeral details. My girlfriend, who hadn't paid much attention to the conversation, could see I was shaken and asked what was wrong. "Chris is dead," I told her in a voice so weak she had to ask me to repeat myself. She'd met Chris only once, but knew how close we were. "He was a little eccentric," she said, "but really a nice guy." It is impossible, of course, to describe this most complex of individuals in one short sentence, but my petite companion came about as close as anyone could.

Zona and I talked several times in the days that followed. Chris obviously had fully expected not only to survive the surgery, but to continue life as before. He left no will or any instructions regarding funeral arrangements. In a call to a distraught Joan, Zona ascertained that Chris once indicated he wanted to be cremated because, "that's the cheapest way." After some discussion we decided to carry out his wishes, although Zona was at a loss as to what to do with the ashes. My suggestion that they be interred in Arlington National Cemetery met with her enthusiastic approval, but that would turn out to be a complicated process.

Chris's sister was up to the task, however, and despite two government shutdowns—one due to budget problems, one to bad weather—and the usual bureaucratic red tape, eventually all the necessary official documents were in order—or so we thought—and a memorial service was scheduled for January 13, 1996.

Chapter 20

Letters

—

The first call I made after learning of Chris's untimely demise was to Jim and Muriel Hill. I was under the impression that Zona had already informed them of the bad news, but I was wrong. The Hills were stunned when I told them. Jim said he'd had a long phone conversation with Chris on December 26, and Chris had filled him in on his imminent surgery, but played down the seriousness of the procedure. Before getting off the phone I told Jim I'd let him know as soon as funeral arrangements were finalized, and he invited me to stay at his home should I attend the services. He also promised to pass along the information about Chris's death to the other Black Sheep.

Within days, letters and cards of condolence began appearing in my mailbox. I've reproduced some in excerpted form.

From Ed Olander:

(Bob—to let you know the Black Sheep survivors have been notified. Flo and I share your grief.)

Dear Sheep:

He is the only man I can recall who took his bar bells to war with him. I can close my eyes now and see him working out with them in that coconut grove we called home on Espiritu Santo. Of course, his costume was those ever-present blue and white-striped brief swim trunks.

Chris Magee died yesterday in suburban Chicago after ten hours on an operating table. Jim Hill, who called to report Chris' demise, said he had been feeling poorly for several weeks but his death was a shock to those who saw him frequently.

Chris lived his seventy eight years on life's cutting edge, and he was happy there. Would that one of us had the talent to write a book or a movie script of Chris' experiences. Either could be a classic message found in Robert Frost's The Road Not Taken:

... Long I stood and looked down one to where it bent in the undergrowth, then took the other as just as fair but having, perhaps, the better claim for being grassy and wanting wear ... and that has made all the difference.

Our ranks are getting thinner (now 23). We will sorely miss our friend and comrade Chris ...

From Bob McClurg:

Dear Bob,

Julie and I are really so sorry to learn of your dad's passing. We extend our deep sympathy to you and your family.

With Chris, Moe Fisher, Bill Case and Begert heading up to fly high cover for us remaining Sheep, you can bet we'll be protected well.

It was so nice we all could spend that time together on that reunion. I sure am very happy Julie could meet your dad!

Chris was like a big brother to me. Between "Pappy" and Chris, they brought me back from the Pacific.

I have many fond memories flying with Chris in our division of four. Some day I will get some of those missions written for all to read ....

From Bill and Carolyn Heier:

Dear Bob,

Bill and I have just learned of your father's passing. We extend our deepest sympathy to you and other members of your family. His life was such a colorful one; he certainly overcame many adversities. We are glad we had the opportunity to know him, even though the time was short. I'm sure your memories will sustain you ....

From Fred Losch:

1/8/96

Dear Bob,

Was shocked and saddened to hear of Chris' demise. He was one hell of a guy—in a class by himself . . . .

From Bruce Matheson:

January 3, 1996

Dear Bob:

Ed Olander's note to all the Sheep provided me with your address so I thought I'd drop you a line and offer my deepest sympathy regarding the passing of your dad.

Although he and I were both products of the South Side of Chicago (that's the "good" side, of course) we didn't meet until WWII. My first recollection of your dad was one Saturday afternoon in a hotel in Jacksonville, Florida. He evidently had been fairly newly commissioned. In those days all of the young airplane drivers (cadets as well as newly-commissioned types) hung out in hotel ballrooms—which featured fairly large swing bands and (more importantly) lots of the local fair sex.

Noticed your dad on the dance floor clad in our "work" uniform—sort of cotton khaki. Didn't pay all that much attention until I saw him sometime later—this time clad in his "work green" uniform. Again didn't give that too much thought, since I figured he either had spilled or was too cold or whatever. But I was really intrigued later on when the same person reappeared on the dance floor—this time in Marine Corps dress blues! Well, you know the rest of the story; he made one final transformation a bit later into what I always considered one of our nicest uniforms—whites. I was still a cadet at the time but I told that story to any and all who would listen; not dreaming that I would end up in the same squadron six months later. Evidently your dad had just taken delivery of his full set of uniforms (which all of us had to buy) and figured he'd might as well try them on in public, as it were. Must say it was a colorful performance!

Having flown a considerable amount in the RCAF, Chris was well-qualified to make his move from a wingman (like the rest of us new second lieutenants) to a section leader. And for quite a while he was Pappy Boyington's section leader.

This proved to be a very productive assignment; as I recall Chris shot down a lot of jap planes while so operating. He was the second high scorer after Boyington, which I'm sure you were aware of.

Since I stayed on in the regular Marine Corps after the war, and didn't get back to Chicago except very infrequently in the years of marriage and children and so forth, Chris pretty well dropped out of the loop as far as I was concerned. Therefore, it was particularly wonderful when (through Jim Hill) we were able to get him out here to Hawaii for our 1989 cruise around the islands . . . . Never will forget the entrance he made (in a Waikiki suite) with a huge planter's straw hat. Came to find out, of course, that his erstwhile dark curly hair had departed some years before!

. . . It was so wonderful that he established contact with you after a very long separation. You were deprived of knowing him for much of your life, of course, but in your remaining years (of which I hope there will be many happy, healthy ones) you can take comfort in the fact that your dad was a hero in the true sense of the word.

We have a tendency these days to apply that term to just about anyone who served during Viet Nam; that differentiates them from our draft-sensitive President. Having flown combat missions in the three wars of my generation, I feel fully qualified to separate the heroes from the herd—and your dad is very definitely a bona fide hero. Lots of us were shot at and hit; and lots of us shot down a jap or two, but your dad was tough, aggressive, and extremely capable and the japs in our theater paid a heavy price for having to face him and Pappy Boyington.

Like Pappy, your dad had some downer years after WWII; hard to tell if the war had caused it or if it just would have happened on its own. At any rate, we don't dwell on the bad years; we glory in the good ones and I'm sure that your dad has told you that the 1943–4 period was the very acme of his life. I think that all of us in the Sheep feel the same way.

As you know, we've lost three of our Black Sheep aces in the past three months: Don Fisher, Bill Case and now your dad. Guess we shouldn't be surprised since all of us are well beyond our Biblical "threescore and ten." But it's still tough to lose a comrade—and that is what we've lost in Chris Magee. All of us shared a challenging experience, and the finest thing I can say about him is that which we reserve for those who rate it—He was a good Marine . . . .

Chapter 21

In (Selected) Memoriam

⌣

T he Chicago area weather was on its best behavior that Saturday morning, January 13, 1996, when family and friends
gathered to bid Chris Magee farewell. Later, we learned that
a series of inexplicable bureaucratic foul-ups delayed the actual burial
at Arlington until May.

The frequent flyer coupons given me by my sister Diana had to be used
sooner than expected, so I flew into Midway Airport the previous evening
and stayed overnight in Skokie with Jim and Muriel. The services were held
at St. Joseph's Catholic Church in Libertyville. Zona clearly had gone out
of her way to give Chris a grand, but dignified send off. His urn was en-
graved with the words "Black Sheep Squadron" and there were numerous
floral arrangements, including one sent by the Black Sheep as a group and
another from Fred and Jean Losch.

All Zona's children were in attendance. I'd already met Kathy Lunardi—
who flew in from California—and Sue and her family, but it was the first
time I met her son Bill and youngest daughter Betty Samelson, a Colorado
Springs resident. Conspicuous by her absence was Joan—she was too ill. I
really wasn't surprised and wondered how Joan would manage without
Chris. According to Zona she was less ambulatory than ever, and he'd been
doing all the shopping, cooking, and laundering for the past several months.
Helen Magee couldn't make it either. Even had she been able to find a ride,
her spinal condition would have made the one-hour car trip excruciating.

Of all Chris's friends who were there, only two names besides the Hills were familiar. Norm Pritchard, a Lake Forest resident whom Zona had mentioned, was a slim, intellectual fellow Chris befriended many years before at one of his discussion groups. Ed Smart was a different breed of cat altogether. Chris had often mentioned his good buddy Smart, who turned out to be a wiry guy of above average height with a full head of reddish-gray hair. His face had a slightly grizzled look, and there was a twinkle in his eye that reminded me of Chris. I didn't get a chance to talk with Ed before the service, but looked forward to the opportunity.

At the time, I didn't mind not being asked to deliver a eulogy. I was given a place with the family in the first pew and asked—along with Jim Hill and Kathy—to present one of the "gifts" at the altar. It turned out to be a fairly simple procedure that even non-Catholics like Jim and me could figure out. My "gift" was what appeared to be a decanter of olive oil, something that, I'm sure, has symbolic significance, but I couldn't help musing about how it would be used in the next world.

As part of the service, Norm read Chris's poem that appeared in *Once They Were Eagles*. Ed was the next speaker, and he delivered a fanciful tale about how Eddie Rickenbacker shot down Germany's greatest ace, Baron von Richthofen, to set the American standard of twenty-six aerial victories in the First World War; then Pappy Boyington came along in WWII and broke the record with the able assistance of his wingman, Chris Magee. Ed closed with the poignant comment, "Chris was my wingman." The story was almost completely bogus, of course. Rickenbacker never faced the "Red Baron," and Chris was not Boyington's wingman, a role he turned down. Still, I appreciated the story as a leavening moment in what could otherwise have been a rather somber ceremony.

Betty gave the only true eulogy, briefly talking about her uncle's lifelong search for adventure and knowledge, but she became so emotional she had to hurry through her speech to avoid breaking down completely. I concluded she must have spent time with Chris recently, because she certainly seemed to know the basics of what he was really about.

Zona had hand-picked the priest, and I doubt she could have made a better choice. He was a former Navy chaplain who had been assigned to the Marine Corps during both the Korean and Vietnam wars, and he clearly understood what heroism in battle was all about. He'd never met the deceased—I doubt Chris spent much time in church over the past half century or so—and it seems highly likely the good father had been instructed by Zona regarding what to say. The resulting sermon he delivered was full of platitudes about Chris's remarkable war record and patriotism, tempered by numerous carefully worded references to man's imperfection and God's forgiveness of his foibles. With the exception of his volunteer stint in Israel, nothing about the life Chris led after the war was mentioned. It was as if he'd been in a coma since the fall of 1948, and finally expired in the last week of 1995. The ancient Greek sage Solon's twenty-six century-old admonition to "speak no ill of the dead" was followed to the letter.

When the service ended, I was wishing that Zona would have asked me to deliver a eulogy. Most of the people in attendance hadn't known Chris during his final years, and who besides myself was better qualified to tell them how this extraordinary man had enriched the lives of those of us fortunate enough to share his friendship?

Zona held a very nice buffet reception at her place after the service. It was there I was introduced to a tall, dignified gentleman named Godfrey Stake and his charming wife Mary. Stake grew up with Chris in the same South Side neighborhood and had continued to see him socially for some time after the war. I was touched when he recalled that he held me in his arms when I was a baby. Godfrey hadn't talked to Zona in decades. He'd found out about Chris's death in the newspaper and called the funeral home mentioned in the article to get the information about the arrangements.

This news made me feel pretty good. A week or so before, I'd sent a press release to the *Sun-Times*—a paper that printed numerous articles about Chris during the war—announcing his death. My story was headlined: "Chris Magee, Black Sheep Ace." Later, a reporter called to ask for additional information, mostly about his prison sentence. I made no mention of Chris's criminal past in my piece, but like any good reporter, this guy did some digging. Obviously there are few fans of Solon among the fourth estate, for the headline that appeared on the printed article read: "Chris Magee, War Hero, Convict." The realization that I was responsible for the story in the first place was a cause for regret until I talked with Godfrey.

During a conversation with Zona and Norm, Zona mentioned Joan told her that Chris kept almost none of his possessions in her apartment. Nearly all his worldly goods were apparently to be found in a Mundelein storage facility, and only Zona had access to the entry code and the lock's combination. Norm and I volunteered to go check the place out, but Zona seemed less than enthusiastic about the idea, mentioning something about the possible interest of the state in what could have been a probate matter.

Since Zona was the sort of person who believed in always doing the right thing, I decided not to persist.

Chatting with Kathy and Betty, I learned that the previous evening at Zona's turned out to be quite memorable thanks to Ed Smart, who was an overnight guest. Ed regaled the family with wonderful stories about the many adventures he and Chris shared during their lifelong friendship. Because Zona told me there would be no wake, I went straight from the airport to Jim Hill's place. Now I wished I'd done things differently.

It wasn't long, though, before I located Ed in the basement family room. We'd been introduced earlier, but because of my different surname he didn't realize I was Chris's son; though once he was aware, we connected comfortably. Ed told me he'd known Chris since they were toddlers and considered him his brother. It soon became apparent why Ed and Chris were so close over the years: they seemed cut from the same cloth. The major difference between them was that, while both were seekers of adventure and knowledge, Ed used some of that knowledge to accumulate wealth. And he'd done a good job. He was quite the entrepreneur—mining engineer, recording studio owner, and licensed yacht captain among other things. On the business card he gave me he was listed as president of Institute for Mesoamerican Studies. No less than four city addresses were on his card: Aspen, Colorado; Bluff, Utah; Tucson, Arizona; and La Paz, Baja California. He penciled in two more, both in Grand Junction, Colorado, before handing it to me.

Ed was also completely unaware of the illness that led to Chris's demise. We agreed that he, no doubt, went into surgery without really considering the possibility he might not survive it. "Dying in a hospital wasn't the way Chris would have wanted to go," Ed told me. "If he thought the end was near he would have gone off somewhere by himself without telling anybody. That's the kind of guy he was."

I spent most of the rest of that afternoon in conversation with this truly colorful character, and when he mentioned that he needed to call a cab for the long trip to a downtown Chicago hotel, I quickly offered to take him. Once there, Ed asked me to join him for drinks in the lounge. There we toasted the memory of the man who had meant so much to both of us, then he invited me to dinner in the hotel's restaurant. Over a fine, rather pricey meal, Ed told some of the stories Zona's kids probably listened to the night before—of daredevil boyhood stunts and thrilling postwar escapades running illegal liquor into still dry Kansas, with Chris at the wheel of his big Lincoln Zephyr. Another adventure recalled was an expedition he and Chris joined to seek a herd of miniature horses in the Grand Canyon. They didn't find their quarry but were introduced to a strange new type of aircraft called a helicopter. Ed's memory for details was generally quite good, even if the time frame of the events was sometimes foggy. One subject he mentioned, but seemed rather circumspect about, was their involvement in covert revolutionary activities in Latin America. His only clear recollection was that, as a way to avoid suspicion when traveling south of the border, he and Chris used student visas. Ed also related some of the good times he spent with his close buddy and sometime business partner, movie legend "Duke" Wayne.

In the years I knew Chris, we never discussed the bank robberies. Ed, however, was quite candid about the subject. It seems as if he had been suspected of being an accomplice, or possibly a getaway driver for Chris until the police learned he was at his home in Colorado during the time of the holdups. According to Ed, Chris phoned him a few days before each incident to make certain he wasn't planning to be in Chicago. He never said why he was calling, but Ed concluded much later that his buddy simply wanted to protect him and his young family from embarrassing police scrutiny in the event of his own arrest.

Ed's lean, grizzled face lit up when he talked about the wild times he and his buddy C.L. enjoyed in postwar Chicago. He reminisced fondly about friendships with such people as Nelson Algren, acclaimed author of *The Man with the Golden Arm* and *Walk on the Wild Side*, among other notable works. His voice took on a different tone, however, when he brought up the name of one Blackie Lucas. "I never liked Blackie," he told me, "and I never understood why C.L. did." Ed went on to say that Lucas was a talented heavyweight prize fighter whose virtuosity did not extend beyond the ring. "He was a lowlife from the wrong side of the tracks—very crude." That Chris had done some boxing—on the amateur and collegiate level— seemed the only common ground the two shared. As a teenager, Lucas had idolized the older Magee, though, and after the war ended, they were frequently seen together at downtown watering holes.

Blackie met an untimely end one night following the robbery of a home belonging to a local Chinese Tong chieftain. According to Ed, Blackie and another man tied up their victim, then began searching the house for jewelry and other valuables. Unknown to both of them, however, the gangster managed to free himself from the bonds and grab a loaded rifle. As the two robbers left the house with their loot and started across the lawn, their victim began firing at them from a second story window. One of the bullets mortally wounded Lucas. His partner in crime got away, but not before risking his own life to drag the 200-pound-plus boxer out of the line of fire. It wasn't until he'd ascertained that Blackie was dead that the other man finally left the scene.

The Chicago police investigated, and—noting the heel marks made by Blackie's partner when he was dragged across the lawn—concluded that the second robber was obviously a powerful man. He was never caught, however. It's doubtful the force wasted many man-hours on the search. The robbery victim was a known underworld figure and a Chinese one at that.

While he'd never questioned his buddy about the incident, Ed admitted to me that he was pretty sure Chris was Blackie's cohort that night.

Ed also had very strong opinions about Chris's younger brother. He told me that Bud—two years his junior—had been a likeable kid, but turned mean after he returned from the war and joined the police force. At Ed's wedding to Myrtle—one of the younger Magee's many former girlfriends—Bud took Ed aside and said something to the order of, "If I ever hear you're not treating her right, I'll kill you," and there wasn't even a hint of humor in his voice. The outspoken Ed accused Bud and other family members of ostracizing Chris completely when he was sent to prison, never visiting or writing to him during his entire term. He also made reference to family matriarch Marie Magee as not being an especially warm individual. I had heard, and would continue to hear similar opinions of Bud and Marie expressed by Zona's children and others. However, Zona herself was never critical of anyone in her family, as evidenced at the memorial service by the priest's avoidance of Chris's well-chronicled misdeeds.

Before I drove back to the Hill's place that night, Ed placed a long distance call to a lady named Jean Scott in Northern California. He described Jean as a mutual friend with whom both he and Chris had probably been in love at one time or another. Jean sounded genial and charming over the phone and expressed her regrets that she couldn't attend the service due to her fear of flying. She also invited me to come visit her Marin County home, and I promised I would if I were ever in that area.

The evening with Ed was the first truly good time for me since I learned of Chris's death. The only thing that could have made it more enjoyable would have been if Chris were there. In a sense, perhaps, he was. I left Chicago the next day with the feeling that though I had lost someone very dear to me, I'd made—in Ed Smart—a fascinating new friend who would help ease the loss and keep my precious memories of Chris ever green.

Chapter 22

Magee's Closet

I n mid-February Zona telephoned to inform me her legal counsel
had concluded that everything Chris kept in his rented storage
room belonged to my sister and me. When I called Anne with the
news she told me I could have it all, unless—she jokingly added—I
happened to discover a large sum of cash among his worldly goods.
Nightly TV weather reports from the Midwest made it abundantly
clear that a trip to Chicago in February was ill advised, so I sent a
check for two months space rent to the storage facility's operators and
made airline reservations for early spring.

I flew into O'Hare on Saturday, March 30, bringing along an additional
extra-large suitcase loaned to me by my girlfriend. At the car rental agency,
I learned there were no more economy models available and was given a
minivan instead. Although the bigger vehicle required more of an expenditure
for gasoline, it did prove useful in other respects. The only good thing
about being unemployed was that I could set my own schedule. Among
countless negatives is a need for frugality that would make Ebeneezer
Scrooge cringe. Between the storage charges, airline tickets, and car rental, I
was stretched to the limit. Fortunately, Zona was kind enough to allow me
to stay over at her home. Lord knows, I didn't do her any favors on this trip.

It took me awhile that cool Sunday morning to find Chris's storage
room in the hallway of one of the many buildings on the lot and even

longer to get the combination of the lock correct. I'd been forewarned by Zona but was still amazed at the accumulation of pasteboard boxes and other paraphernalia that had literally been stuffed into what amounted to a six-foot wide by five-foot deep by eight-foot high closet. I spent at least an hour removing everything, and five or six more hours sorting through the contents of the boxes, many of which, fortunately, were labeled. Mostly what I found were books, books, and more books: books on literature, art, philosophy, the occult, and a myriad of other subjects. One carton contained nothing but books written by Rudolf Steiner, founder of the school of thought called Anthroposophy, a subject Chris had discussed with me on occasion. I couldn't help noticing that many of the texts were once library books, only a few of which contained any indication inside the cover that they'd been sold or given away. None of these particular volumes had publishing dates later than the mid-1950s, though.

Of course there were other things besides books to be found. Inside two large boxes were Chris's summer and winter wardrobes, including a collection of wide-brimmed hats. A few household items were squirreled away in others. My main reason for coming was the hope of finding the writings Chris had promised to send me in November—I wasn't disappointed. Some of the cartons held large manila envelopes containing poetry, short stories, essays, and even correspondence—most sent to him by others, but also a few of his own letters that he'd made copies of. These I placed in the "keep" file. There were also hundreds of pages and scraps of paper containing notes from books, lectures, and educational television shows. I chose to leave these behind. Chris's handwriting was so small as to be virtually unintelligible, and there seemed little reason to hang on to them. A number of audio cassettes, mostly tapes of PBS TV programs, met a similar fate.

Other envelopes full of old photos of family and friends—some captioned on the back, some not—and many more from the Black Sheep days and his Israeli experience were, of course, keepers. Unfortunately, the only recent shots were some I sent him. There were literally no pictures of Chris during the period from the mid-1950s to the mid-1980s. Among the greatest treasures—at least to me—were his pilot's logs from the Marine Corps and the RCAF and five separate issues of *New Era*, the magazine he wrote for and eventually served as editor-in-chief while in Leavenworth. In reading the publications later I was astounded by the quality of the magazine as a whole and by the prose and poetry created by the inmates in particular.

Possibly the best surprise of all came in the form of a flat cardboard box about eight inches long and four inches wide. Inside was a cloth covered metal case that opened to reveal a campaign ribbon and lapel pin, and the item they both represented—a Navy Cross. This find turned out to have a manufacture date of 1985. The box also contained a copy of the original citation.

```
THE SECRETARY OF THE NAVY
WASHINGTON

The President of the United States takes pleasure in
presenting the NAVY CROSS to
FIRST LIEUTENANT CHRISTOPHER L. MAGEE
UNITED STATES MARINE CORPS RESERVE
for service as set forth in the following
CITATION:
For extraordinary heroism as a pilot of a fighter plane
attached to Marine Fighting Squadron Two Fourteen oper-
ating against enemy Japanese forces in the Solomon Is-
lands area from September 12 to October 22, 1943. Dis-
playing superb flying ability and fearless intrepidity,
First Lieutenant Magee participated in numerous strike
escorts, task force covers, fighter sweeps, strafing mis-
sions, and patrols. As member of a division of four
planes acting as task force cover on September 18, he
daringly maneuvered his craft against thirty enemy dive
bombers with fighter escorts and, pressing home his at-
tack with skill and determination, destroyed two dive
bombers and probably a third. During two subsequent
fighter sweeps over Kahill [sic] Airdrome on October 17-18,
he valiantly engaged superior numbers of Japanese fight-
ers which attempted to intercept our forces and suc-
ceeded in shooting down five Zeroes. The following day,
volunteering to strafe Kara Airfield, Bougainville Is-
land, he dived with another plane through intense anti-
aircraft fire to a 40-foot level in a strafing run, leav-
ing eight enemy aircraft blazing. First Lieutenant
Magee's brilliant airmanship and indomitable fighting
spirit contributed to the success of many vital mis-
sions and were in keeping with the highest traditions
of the United States Naval Service.

                         For the President,

                         /S/JAMES FORRESTAL
                         Secretary of the Navy
```

Chris said he'd loaned his medal to a neighbor kid after the war and never saw it again. The loss didn't seem to bother him, or so he would have everyone believe. That he apparently took the trouble to order a duplicate after some thirty years, however, mystified me. It just didn't sound like something he would do.

By the time I'd moved everything I considered worth taking into the van and returned the rest of Chris's stuff to the closet, my fifty-year-old back was killing me. I felt completely bushed.

That night Zona helped me sift through the items I had chosen to bring back, and we managed to reduce their numbers by about one-quarter. I had only so much room in my luggage, and my financial situation made it ill-advised to consider shipping anything home. Zona had mentioned at the memorial service in January that she wanted the Navy Cross if it turned up, but when I placed it in front of her with the comment, "There you are," and quickly added, "It's not the original, just a reissue," she picked the medal up and looked at it, then placed it back in the pile. Had she told me she wanted to keep it, I would have felt duty-bound to let her have it, but she didn't.

I told Zona about other items still in the closet, including a couple of brand new corn poppers Chris had apparently purchased as potential gifts, a nice director's chair, and a metal detector; then advised her that she and Sue's family were welcome to take whatever they wanted. Zona didn't appear interested, however. She thought we should arrange for some charitable organization to go out and remove whatever was left. I assured her the owners of the storage buildings had contingency plans for this sort of situation, and would dispose of the leftovers in an efficient—and likely profitable—manner, once I advised them no more rent payments were forthcoming.

Monday night, my last of the trip, was spent at Helen Magee's home. For once the guest came bearing gifts—a small tent for her grandchildren, the director's chair for son Mike, and a corn popper for her—all compliments of her late brother-in-law. I kept the metal detector, which miraculously fitted easily into my big suitcase. I also took Chris's well-worn black leather cowboy hat and the matching backpack that contained it, both of which he'd stowed in a closet at Zona's before leaving for his final stay at the hospital. That slightly battered piece of headgear hangs in my home alongside other items of memorabilia from his stash: the Navy Cross and its citation; a few faded photographs of real-life war heroes with the wonderful winged chariots they flew; and an old, faded blue and white bandanna.

Chapter 23

To Sail Beyond the Sunset

—

In a radio address shortly after World War II began in Europe, Winston Churchill, frustrated by his inability to forecast the actions of Soviet Russia, described that nation as "a riddle wrapped in a mystery inside an enigma." That is, perhaps, also an apt description of Chris Magee's life, especially during the dozen or so years that followed the war.

Undoubtedly the most baffling source of consternation among everyone who knew Chris was the motivation behind his bank robberies. Even Joan Allen—the person closest to him over the last forty years of his life—didn't have a clue, although after his death she said that to the best of her knowledge he wasn't hard up for money at that time.

In an extensive, in-depth interview during the summer of 1988, Chris revealed to Neal Gendler of the *Minneapolis Star-Tribune* that he did the crimes because of "certain obligations," but wouldn't elaborate beyond that.

Ed Smart indicated that his buddy was betting on the horses quite heavily back in the 1950s, and may have found himself so deeply in debt with bookies or loan sharks that he was forced to take drastic steps. The horse playing was brought up at the trial in April 1958, but Chris stated at that time he was involved in gambling as a means to finance a trip to Europe, where he planned to study the trade fair system. He also claimed the betting netted him a $3,000 profit the previous year.

The most intriguing explanation of all, however, was offered by one of the Black Sheep, Denmark Groover, in a late 1996 phone conversation. During the squadron's 1989 Hawaiian cruise, the multi-term Georgia state senator had an opportunity to speak with Chris in private. Groover, who is regarded as one of the best trial lawyers in the South, utilized his genial eloquence to draw out information Chris hadn't told anyone else, as far as I know. His story revealed Chris needed about $50,000 in order to purchase an airplane, presumably a DC-3, and start a legitimate cargo service in Central America. With his spotty employment record and lack of property, no bank would loan him the money, so he took rather extraordinary measures to get his hands on it.

That the story has a ring of truth to it can't be denied. Chris made numerous trips to Latin America during the postwar period, and no doubt had his eyes open for a potentially profitable way to do business in that region that would allow him to fly again. One has to speculate that such a private venture in the 1950s would have had to operate under contract to the U.S. State Department. Still, the question lingers, why rob a bank? Did Chris exhaust every other possibility? Certainly a good friend like Smart could have been interested in a partnership, and probably would have fronted the money had he been approached.

During his heart-to-heart talk with Chris, Groover became curious as to why his old squadron mate was forced to spend such a lengthy time in prison before he was finally paroled. Throughout his long experience as a trial lawyer, Groover had seldom known of anyone having to serve more than five or six years for bank robbery when no parties were injured. Chris told him that he, too, had been befuddled by the parole board's rejections. It wasn't until his fifth annual hearing, when he decided to ask the interviewer why he was being turned down year after year, that he finally learned the reason. It seems there was a major foul-up in the record-keeping, and Chris had inexplicably been credited with additional holdups he not only had not committed, but never even been accused of. Once the mistake was corrected, he was quickly released—about three years later than his crimes probably merited.

Chris never mentioned the name of the stool pigeon who informed the police about the Cicero robberies, but a four-page set of legal papers I found among his personal effects certainly provided food for thought. The document is a transcription of a federal district court proceeding that took place on December 11, 1958. In it, an appointed attorney representing an individual named John Hawley requests a sentence reduction for his client because the man was not the "moving principal" in "an armed robbery of a federally-insured savings and loan association in 1956." The U.S. attorney did not oppose the request, and the judge ordered Hawley's sentence be reduced to five years, with eligibility for parole after just one year. The document mentions that Hawley had "been brought here from the medical center in Lexington, Kentucky, where he is under treatment for narcotics addiction." This was the first I'd heard about Chris having a partner in any of the holdups. What was Hawley's actual role in the crime? Was he the informer? If not, then, did he talk about the robbery to the person who became the informer? If I had an opportunity now to interview Chris about the whole sordid affair, I'd probably ask him, "Why would you use a drug addict for an accomplice, anyway?" Of course, I can't dismiss the possibility that Hawley pulled off the 1956 holdup on his own after hearing about Chris's successful heist of the previous year.

Perhaps the most serious repercussion of the conviction and prison sentence Chris received was his apparent eviction from his family. Only Bud Magee attended the trial, and he made himself incommunicado with Chris once he was given power of attorney over his brother's finances. I'm not certain whether Chris ever spoke with Bud again after that, nor do I have any idea what happened to any money Chris may have had—rightfully earned or ill gotten. We never discussed such matters. At the time of the trial, the reportedly senile Fred Magee, Sr. probably had little cognizance about what was happening, and the bad news about her son may well have contributed to the strokes Marie Magee suffered. Zona, as previously mentioned, was going through some extremely trying times during the late fifties and early sixties. Still, I'll never understand why no one in the family ever visited Chris in prison, and why only Helen—his kindhearted former sister-in-law— seems to have cared enough to correspond with him after he was sent to Leavenworth.

Unquestionably, the years in prison changed Chris Magee's life for the better. The numerous college courses he completed and the body of literary work he produced attest to this, but perhaps most important of all was the spiritual growth he experienced while inside. The forty-nine-year-old man who emerged from behind the walls of J. Edgar Hoover's Leavenworth resort late in 1966 was a far cry from the rather self-indulgent adventurer convicted of bank robbery in the spring of 1958. The new inward direction of his life was apparent long before his release, as evidenced by these excerpts from Chris's letter to Bill Lichtman, dated September 2, 1963:

. . . We are all of us raised in a schizoid milieu. When we are young, we hear and read about the kinds of values and aspirations that geniuses of the spirit have found pertain to man's higher nature. We feel guilty of our omissions and commissions that violate these precepts. Then one day we awaken to the way human nature really functions, to the animal in man that dominates his nature, even though there is that within him which cannot abide this thralldom. Far, far too often he goes from his unconscious childhood beliefs into disillusionment and its loneliness. To appease this, he joins into the human-animal world thinking that there he will find a substitute for what he has lost. He doesn't. It isn't there. The lone direction is the one from which he descended. However, he had to descend because to follow in ignorance is not man's lot. He must enter the world and through his interactions with it, through his Calvary of pain and suffering, gain a consciousness that will guide him to the higher instincts, those that will in time bring him to a realization of his humanness . . . .

How infinitely capable of deluding himself is man! Yet the sacred literatures of the world tell him again and again of these things. . . More and more western man is driven to an existential viewpoint, an intellectual viewpoint of the great world. Even the great churches of the West, including the Catholic, have had to seek new alignments, have been forced to come farther into the world than their old spiritual attachments allowed. This, I believe, is good because there was formerly too strong a tendency to reject the world as evil. You can't accomplish redemption by rejecting that which you are meant to redeem. On the other hand, neither can you redeem it until you have moved farther up the scale of being, beyond its ability to dominate you . . . .

However, atheistic Existentialism as propagated by Camus, Sartre, de Beauvoir and others is a warning of the sort of cul de sac into which a rejection of the other side of man's nature may pitch one. Such distortions of a human soul are far from uncommon in our time, especially when our educational techniques are so acutely tilted in the direction of intellect that the spiritual development gets no formal recognition at all.

We see the results, of course; but we do not comprehend the reasons. We seek solutions in the existential alone rather than in a combination that includes it with the spiritual. We are in trouble! . . . .

We are all on the same path and we can help out one another; but, especially in ages like ours, it is far wiser to seek a higher involvement, the highest

we are capable of conceiving—and never relinquishing its priority. Every-
thing must keep its proper place below this. Otherwise we come into conflict
with the demands of our higher nature which commands we become that of
which we are yet but the embryo: a being both of the world and above it,
whose transcendent nature makes him capable of work with the world, work
the nature of which is still beyond the grasp of his embryo consciousness.

At a Reed family reunion in Colorado Springs during the summer of 1996, I managed to escape for a couple hours to visit Zona's youngest daughter Betty and her husband Kirk Samelson in their lovely, rustic home near the U.S. Air Force Academy. It was there I learned that the multi-faceted Chris had still another side hitherto unfamiliar to me. My previous assumption that Betty—who delivered a tearful eulogy at Chris's memorial service—had recently spent time with her uncle was wrong. Except for his brief appearance at her sister Kathy's 1967 nursing school graduation, she hadn't seen or talked with him since she was a first grader in 1957. Her emotions at the service came from rekindled memories of a man she described as "my favorite relative."

"We loved it when Uncle C.L. came to visit," she said. "He would toss me way up in the air and catch me. He even did handsprings to entertain us." Betty added that she couldn't understand why her uncle suddenly stopped coming. She didn't learn he'd been in prison until after his release. Chris had gone from number one on the family's popularity chart to a non-person overnight.

The Musser children all seemed to love their Uncle C.L., but Uncle Bud was a different matter entirely. He may have been one of Chicago's Finest, but that opinion certainly wasn't shared in Mundelein. "He was really mean," Betty said. "We were all afraid of him." She recalled a family visit to Bud's West Side home in the early sixties when he literally threw her mother out of the house. According to Betty, Bud and Zona had suppos-edly been discussing the cost of Marie Magee's nursing care, and he'd be-come agitated when Zona suggested he help share the financial burden. Older sister Kathy Lunardi later confirmed the incident, although she was uncertain of the exact cause of the argument. Brother and sister apparently reconciled at a later date, but it didn't change the way the Musser kids felt about Bud. Regardless, I never heard either Zona or Chris make a deroga-tory comment about Bud or any other family member.

A month or so earlier, I'd talked with someone who had a similar im-pression of Chris and a vastly different one of his younger brother. The person expressing fondness for both Magees was Jean Scott. I stopped to see Jean in her Marin County home after a visit to my parent's place, about three hours away. She was every bit as beautiful as Ed Smart had described her—far too trim and youthful to be almost seventy-two, as she claimed.

I spent most of the afternoon and part of the evening engaged in lively conversation with Jean, who prepared a tasty dinner that featured salmon fillets barbecued on her outdoor grill. She told me that she had fully expected to marry Bud Magee until she saw his handsome older brother resplendent in a Marine officer's uniform at Zona's wedding. Jean couldn't make up her mind which Magee she preferred, as both were well-spoken, fun to be around and quite gentlemanly. She never saw Bud again after her move to California, and didn't hear from Chris for many years following a brief period shortly after the end of World War II, when she and her husband temporarily moved back to Chicago. They'd re-established contact in the eighties, thanks to Ed Smart, and talked occasionally on the telephone. Jean's marriage to Mr. McKee ended in divorce, as did three subsequent trips to the altar. She now shared her home with "Holly," a Yorkshire Terrier. Her previous canine pal had been named "Magee." I couldn't help speculating about what might have been had Jean and Chris crossed paths again, say, in the early or mid-1950s.

Of all the items that turned up while I was going through Chris's worldly possessions, the most delightfully unexpected was the Navy Cross. I couldn't help but wonder why he'd left it buried deep in a cardboard box after seemingly going to the trouble of re-ordering a replacement sometime after 1985 (the date of manufacture inside the medal's container). The mystery was solved in a phone conversation with Leon Frankel, a gentleman who flew with Chris as an Israeli Air Force fighter pilot in 1948, and became a good friend during and after the 1986 reunion of the 101 Squadron in Tel Aviv. Chris was a guest in Leon's Minneapolis home in the summer of 1988 when Frankel showed him his own Navy Cross on display, then inquired as to where Chris kept his. When Chris told him the medal had been lost shortly after the end of World War II, the discussion ended. Unbeknownst to Chris, however, Leon was soon formulating a plan. With the help of another friend, retired Rear Admiral James Flatley, he managed to get Chris's Navy Cross and its accompanying certificate reissued. Leon even planned to hold an award ceremony to surprise Chris, but when they were unable to get together right away he decided to mail the medal to the Mundelein address.

I have no doubt Chris was touched by his friend's gesture, but I'm not in the least surprised that the Navy Cross ended up in the bottom of a storage carton. Unlike the homes of other members of the Black Sheep or 101 Squadron I have visited, there was nothing on display in Chris's place—not even a photograph—to remind a visitor of his glorious wartime exploits.

Chris had an extraordinary life, but—although tidbits will no doubt surface from time to time—much of it will remain a mystery. Many times I gently suggested he pen his autobiography and he'd invariably smile, then with a mischievous twinkle in his eye say something like "I'd have to write it as fiction; nobody'd believe it was true."

Of particular fascination to me were his postwar activities in Latin America (1946–57), something to which he never made more than vague reference but Ed Smart has assured me were quite extensive. Smart recalled one time when Chris phoned him in Colorado to say he had a buyer who needed 2,000 military rifles and asked Ed if he knew where such a large quantity could be found. I've a feeling there may be an interesting file under Chris's name buried deep in a vault at CIA headquarters, but it's highly unlikely I'll ever see it. My attempts to gain access to his FBI records through the Freedom of Information – Privacy Acts proved fruitless when I was informed—after waiting for nearly a year—that they had been destroyed "in full compliance with the provisions of Title 44, Regulations, Chapter 12, Subchapter B, Part 1228."

It is easy to say in retrospect that I wish I'd asked more probing questions of Chris because there is so much about him I don't know and now never will. I doubt that I was afraid of what might be revealed. Every time he'd start to become evasive during a discussion of his past, I would respectfully and discreetly change the subject. During the all-too-rare occasions we spent together, I think he cared very much that I maintain a positive impression of him. He really didn't have anything to worry about. There was an unspoken, unconditional acceptance of each other from the very beginning of our friendship. I had far too much love and respect for him to let any long past transgressions matter even a little.

The Chris Magee I knew in his twilight years had almost nothing in the way of material wealth, yet he never bemoaned his financial condition. He may have had to get by on a small monthly Social Security stipend, but that didn't keep him from picking up the tab—or at least trying to— whenever the occasion presented itself. I remember well the last time we dined out with Jim and Muriel Hill. The four of us had just completed an excellent meal at one of Jim's favorite eateries when Chris excused himself, apparently to visit the rest room. Once he was out of earshot, Jim and I began a good-natured argument about who was going to pay. Jim—a gentleman of boundless generosity—had never allowed me to spend a cent of my money, but this time I was determined. The discussion continued after Chris returned. He sat quietly as our waiter finally approached us, and Jim and I both waved our credit cards to get the man's attention. The waiter just smiled, and placed a receipt on the table in front of Chris. "Your friend has already taken care of the check," he informed us, then walked away.

Chris lived life on his own terms without seeking either the approval or disapproval of the general public. He treated others kindly and fairly, and didn't pass judgment; nor did he worry about how most people judged him. As a result, he was respected and admired by nearly all who crossed his path. Referring to Chris in *Once They Were Eagles*, Frank Walton wrote: "The world has a desperate need for free spirits, even those who suffer occasional aberrations."

Ed Smart once told me that the two greatest friends he ever had were Chris Magee and John Wayne. To be put in such company, I have to believe that the Duke was one helluva guy.

Epilogue

The Dream

Who among us after the loss of a loved one hasn't hoped that somehow the dearly departed would manage to make contact from the other side with assurances that all was well? Anyone who devoted as much time to occult studies and the teachings of Rudolf Steiner as Chris did certainly considered such communication possible. I've always been somewhat skeptical about that sort of stuff, but my many conversations with Chris taught me to at least keep an open mind. To borrow the familiar lines from Hamlet, "There are more things in heaven and earth, Horatio, than are dreamt of in your philosophy." Plus, I reasoned, his spirit was so indomitable that if anyone could do it, Chris could.

He'd been dead more than a year when the dream came to me. With nearly all my dreams, I can never remember more than a few, if any, details the following day. Most of the images from this one, however, remain vivid.

It is a bright spring morning, and the two of us are walking near a large body of water: Lake Michigan, the Pacific, or perhaps the Caribbean. It could even be the Mississippi, alongside which I fondly remember strolling with Chris during our stay in New Orleans. We pass by some boats, but I don't notice any other people.

Chris looks pretty much the same as I remember him, only he seems somehow younger. His gait is, as always, long-striding and very military. He wears familiar garb: slacks, long-sleeved blue shirt, and a planter's hat, of course. As we proceed along the shoreline, we carry on a casual conversation. I do most of the talking, telling him, among other things, how much I've missed him and that I wish we'd had more time to spend together. I wonder, of course, about how he managed his resurrection, but feel it prudent not to ask.

After a while we turn away from the water's edge and begin to walk uphill. It is then I notice that although there are two of us, only one shadow, mine, follows along. It occurs to me that his presence is spiritual, not physical. We stop, and face each other. He appears to be fading away now, and I sense his visit to the mortal plane is almost over. "Do you have to go back?" I ask him.

"Yes," he says, his blue eyes twinkling, "but don't worry about me. I'm doing fine."

"Will I see you again?"

"Of course," the kindest voice I'll ever hear answers. Then, he smiles at me warmly, revealing a full set of sparkling white teeth.

Tears fill my eyes and blur my vision. When I blink them away he is gone.

Keep Moving!

The following allegorical short story tells about the struggles of an individual in a mythical society that demands conformity. It was written in Leavenworth Federal Penitentiary and first published in the autumn 1962 issue of *New Era*.

Keep Moving!

by Chris Magee

"Sir, have you ever looked in your bag?"

The old man gazed absently at the hand that touched his arm so lightly. It was a young hand; and when he turned his head, he saw on the face of the young man an expression of respect. Nevertheless, he felt anger flame in his head and along his veins. Then the past burst through with its tidal wave of memories, and the burning was gone.

Have you ever looked in your bag? How long had it been since he had heard that question. The old man came floating to the surface of the flood and saw all about him the flotsam of the past: some of it still bright, some dull and vague, so vague. Yes, it had been a very long time ago. He had been young and strong then too; like this fellow. But as the vision, with insistent demanding, fought for sharper edges, he saw all of it as if it had happened to someone else; as if he, himself, had always been as he was now ....

There were long lines of people climbing a steep hill that went on and on; people of all ages whose faces, because of some peculiarity of the light, were not very distinct. All were carrying bags: some small, some very large; so large their bearers bent almost double beneath them. Among them was a young man who carried a fair sized bag; but there was a lightness in his step, and he walked as if he were unaware of his burden. By his side was a man who was somewhat older. As they walked they talked, and their talk was unmemorable.

They came to one who stood several yards from the road, a man who laughed and called out to them as they passed, "What's in the bag, friend, what's in the bag?" The young man thought this was a very strange question, and he turned to his companion. At that moment there was the sound of hooves scrambling among loose stones, and a great black stallion bounded from behind an outcropping of jagged gray rock. He snorted with pain and anger as his rider cruelly jerked the reins and drove him at a gallop along the line of travelers. The horseman was sheathed in a single piece of black material that covered completely his giant frame. On his head was a full steel helmet of ebon gloss; its visor was closed.

The laughing man who had spoken of bags laughed no more, nor did he speak. With amazement the young traveler saw that he was now doing handsprings and rolling in the dust. As a final feat he stood on his head and clapped his feet together. The horseman had come to a halt close to this man and sat watching his strange antics. When these had ended, he lifted his visor a trifle and spat upon the fellow.

"Keep moving," he said to the lines of people who had stopped to watch. "Keep moving." Then he rode away.

The two travelers walked on. For a time they did not speak, then the young man said, "Who was that?"

His companion shrugged, "A madman."

"But he asked me what was in my bag. Why did he do that?"

"Who knows a madman's reasons? Damn it, why did we have to meet with him. I'd forgotten about my bag."

"I too. It seemed so light but now it has become heavier," said the young man. He walked in thought for some distance before he spoke again. "No one ever asked me that until now," he said. "In fact, I've never asked myself."

"Asked yourself what?" said the other.

"What's in my bag."

"Have you had yours long?"

"That's a strange thing too. I've just begun to think about it, but it seems I've had it as long as I can remember. My first day in school: it was such a little bag. But after that somebody was always putting things into it. By graduation it had become quite large. I wonder why I haven't thought of it before."

"What's the use?"

"But wouldn't you like to know what's in your bag?"

"Why are you asking me these questions? Just carry your bag like everyone else and shut up." His voice was angry and he looked away.

The young traveler was quiet in thought until a man swung past them on crutches and turned off toward a grove of trees from which there came a singing of birds and the sound of water falling in the distance. He appeared to have been beaten recently, for there was a patch on his head and his face was badly discolored. But he had no bag.

"Who was he?"

"Another madman," was the sullen reply.

The young fellow stopped and upon his face were signs of strong inner conflict. Abruptly they were gone. "The hell with it," he said, I think I'll go with him." With that he dropped his bag to the ground and stepped out of line. Immediately five or six of the nearest wayfarers leaped upon him kicking and punching.

His companion was one of them.

Suddenly the rider and his black steed were among them. Savagely he struck about him with a flail until all were back in line carrying their bags. The young man was badly bruised. He walked alone now and the others gave him only dark looks and muttered curses.

Sometime later, when they had apparently forgotten him, he let his pace lag until he fell behind and came among others who did not know him and his deed. At times the hill got very steep and rough, but he noticed that no one put down his bag. Once he asked an old man who was stooped beneath the weight of a great bag if he might help him carry it. But the man only looked at him suspiciously and shook his head. Almost desperately the young fellow cried out, "Why not? What have you got that's so precious?" The old man only clutched his bag tighter and shook his head. A dark-clad horseman rode past and shouted at them, "Keep moving."

Later he fell in with another traveler who seemed quite jovial, who laughed and talked of light things. The young man thought him an excellent companion, and he resolved to say nothing more of the bags. Presently they came to a small station house, one of many check points along the path. Here two men clad darkly from crown to foot came to him. One opened his bag, the other thrust something into it. Such occurrences had happened many times before, and he had thought nothing of it. Now, however, it was different. Curiosity stirred him.

"What was it?" he asked one of the guards.

"Keep moving," the man jerked his thumb.

"But . . . ?"

"Keep moving."

He caught up with his jolly companion, but for some reason the bag seemed heavier now. For a while he listened absently to one bright sally after another. Then, as if he had made a decision, he spoke, "You know, I don't think I'll let them put anything in my bag again."

His friend had started to laugh but stopped abruptly, his mouth half open, and stared. Then his face flushed; and when he spoke, his voice was vibrant with indignation. "Why shouldn't you let them put something into your bag? They put things into my bag, don't they? And into everybody else's too. What makes you so special; you're one of us aren't you?"

The young man saw that he had made a mistake again. He said nothing to break the gloom that had come about them, and after a time he dropped farther to the rear of his line.

He talked to many other men who were on the journey, but now he was more careful to sound out their temperaments before he would query them. Especially after he asked an old, richly adorned gentleman what he had in his huge bag. The old fellow replied angrily, "Why did you ask about my bag? I'd forgotten it." And he had been delivered a sharp kick in the shin. Several days later this man had fallen in the dust and died. The others had dug a deep hole in the ground and were about to bury him and his bag—he clung so tightly to it—when one of the horsemen galloped up, snatched the bag roughly from him, and rode away.

Now many questions began to come to his thoughts that had never been there before, and they troubled him deeply. So many blows and curses did he get from the others when he tried to speak with them of these things that he finally ceased. But the questions did not stop. He grew moody and at times found he was talking to himself aloud. Others noticed this too and began to glance at one another with knowing in their eyes.

One day a very powerful thought came to him. So demanding was it that he forgot his caution and asked his companion of the moment if he had ever put anything of his own in his bag. The fellow did have many things he had evidently picked up at random hanging from his belt and protruding awkwardly from his pockets. But these often fell away and were lost. The man replied kindly, for he had been warned that the sanity of this traveler who asked questions was under suspicion. "No," he said, "we are not allowed to do that. Of course, there have been those who did sneak things into their bags when others were not looking; but they were found out."

"What happened to them?"asked the young man.

"I don't know. They were taken away somewhere by someone. I don't remember by whom."

"But why aren't we allowed to put anything of our own into our bags?"

"Why? Why just because we're not. Everyone knows that. Is there something wrong? You look as if you didn't feel well."

A horseman went by swinging his flail and the discussion faded away. After he had passed, the man spoke to him again.

"Do you see that building just ahead?"

He nodded. A low structure stood close to the roadside, but due to a trick of light, no doubt, it gave the illusion of being indistinct, as if it were much farther off than it was.

"Look in the window as we pass and tell me what you see."

When they came abreast a barred window the young man glanced in, then stopped and stared until the other pulled on his sleeve. After they had moved on, the stranger gave him a look of inquiry. "What did you see?"

"I saw a man with a large bald head and the face of a wise old soldier who had known many kinds of battle. He was speaking with a number of other men who appeared unashamed of the tears that were flowing down their faces. Then another entered the room carrying a cup. He gave it to the old man who, after a few words with his friends, drank its contents, lay back on the pallet with his face to the wall and covered his head with a blanket. It was very strange."

"Yes, he was a strange man. He was one of those who wanted to know what was in his bag. They say he emptied it out and threw away the things he didn't want and put in other things that he had found along the way. Nor was that all, for he went about encouraging others to do the same. He was very bold, but eventually they found out about it."

"They?"

"Yes, they," he waved his hand vaguely. "Several came to give evidence against him and he was taken away."

For some days the man pondered this story. He became more and more confused, talked more and more to himself aloud, and even took to waving his hands in the air and tossing his head as if in argument. The others now openly cast significant glances at one another. Soon several of them came to him kindly, took him by the arms and led him away.

It was a large, airy room with chromium walls, soft indirect lighting, and soothing music. A man who wore thick glasses came every day to speak with him about his childhood, his mother and father—especially his mother—and girls. He was very interested in girls. There came a time when other people came to speak with him. He was told that they were his father and mother, his sisters and brothers, aunts, uncles, and friends—so many friends. They were very familiar with him, and friendly.

But they were strangers.

He felt that he should know them very well, that he must know them. And he laughed and talked and pretended. But they were strangers who told him how sick he had been. They told him that now he was getting well, going to be good as ever.

Like he used to be.

One day the man with the thick glasses came with a thick smile and told him he had made a marvelous recovery, a fine readjustment, and he was able to go away. He went but he was not alone now, talking to strangers on the road. There was a woman, and she walked with him, it seemed, for a very long time. It was then that his bag began to get very heavy. At every check point she would plead with the men to put some-thing extra into their bags, and the men would do so.

At first he protested, but she was so pleased when they were given more than their share. If he said anything cross about it, she would put her face against his and her body against his, until finally he let her have her way and said no more about it. There were times, too, when he believed she stole things from the bags of others while they slept during the night and put them into his bag. But he was never certain. Now and then she had accused him of tampering with her bag, of hiding his personal things in it to annoy her. There was always too much to argue about. Somewhere along the road she had disappeared, and he had never seen her again. He wondered for awhile, then forgot about it . . ..

The old man was still remembering, and it seemed to him so very long ago when that young fellow had stopped wondering, had stopped asking. His bag had grown heavier and heavier until now he was bent almost double beneath its weight.

The waters receded, carrying the flotsam back to the dark sea. And the remembered was forgotten.

The young traveler was touching his arm, speaking again. "Sir, I asked if you had ever looked into your bag?" He muttered angrily and shook his head. What right did this fellow with the fresh young face have to come asking these questions, reminding him of a bag that he had forgotten about so long ago? He turned and shuffled away.

Hooves were striking the ground, and he heard the impersonal, imperious voice: "Keep moving, keep moving."

Bibliography

Aloni, Shlomo. Year of the Mule, *Air Enthusiast Magazine*, Spring 1995.

Boyington, Gregory "Pappy." *Baa Baa Black Sheep*. G.P. Putnam's Sons, New York, 1958.

Earley, Pete. *The Hot House: Life Inside Leavenworth Prison*. New York, Bantam Books, 1992.

Gamble, Bruce. Unedited transcript of 1993 interview with Chris Magee.

Gendler, Neal. "Wings For Zion," an unpublished manuscript.

Magee, C.L. Pilot's logbooks (USAAF, RCAF, USMC) 1941–45.

Sherrod, Robert. *History of Marine Corps Aviation in World War II*. The Nautical And Aviation Publishing Co., Baltimore, 1987.

Swing, Julian. "God's Little Air Force," an unpublished manuscript.

Tuchman, Maurice, et al. *The Spiritual in Art: Abstract Painting 1890–1985*. New York, Abbeville Press, 1986.

Walton, Frank E. *Once They Were Eagles: The Men of the Black Sheep Squadron*. The University Press of Kentucky, 1986.

Index

New From

Hellgate Press

Of War Birds and Warriors

Pilots, Man Your Planes!
A History of Naval Aviation
by Wilbur H. Morrison   ISBN: 1-55571-466-8
474 pages, Hardcover: $33.95

An account of naval aviation from Kitty Hawk to the Gulf War, *Pilots, Man Your Planes!* tells the story of naval air growth from a time when planes were launched from battleships to the major strategic element of naval warfare it is today. This book is filled with rare photographs, detailed maps, and accurate accounts that can be found nowhere else. Ideal for anyone interested in aviation.

A Dying Breed
The Courage of the Mighty Eighth Air Force
by Neal B. Dillon   ISBN: 1-55571-529-X
342 pages, Paperback: $15.95

"Neal Dillon is a brilliant writer who puts you into that sturdy B-17 at 28,000 feet and takes you where the flak is intense and seventy-five Luftwaffe fighter aircraft are attacking from all directions. Even before you finish reading, you will be recommending it to your friends and family."

– Major General Perry M. Smith, USAF, retired
Author, *A Hero Among Heroes* and *Rules and Tools for Leaders*

Birds From Hell
History of the B-29
by Wilbur Morrison   ISBN 1-55571-550-8
400 pages, Paperback, $34.95

Birds from Hell presents the facts about Japan's defeat in 1945, and the role that the B-29 Superfortress played in that defeat. *Birds from Hell* is a fascinating history of the legendary B-29—and the air war against Japan—told by a man who was a part of that history from the day the first one rolled off the assembly line.

Some Other WWII Titles from Hellgate Press

Green Hell

The Battle for Guadalcanal

by William J. Owens   ISBN: 1-55571-498-6
                    284 pages, Paperback: $18.95

This is the story of the men who fought for a poor insignificant island in a faraway corner of the South Pacific during WWII. The real battle, it is said, was of man against jungle. *Green Hell* is the account of land, sea, and air action covering the entire six-month battle that was the turning point of the Pacific War.

Survival

Diary of an American POW in World War II

by Samuel G. Higgins   ISBN: 1-55571-514-1
                    228 pages, Paperback: $14.95

A patriotic southerner joined the army and was captured in one of the most intense battles of WWII. During his three months in the infamous Stalag IXB, he secretly made notes in the margins of his Bible. Fifty years later, those entries triggered recollections of the outrage he felt, the squalid living conditions, the treatment of the Jewish prisoners, and the starvation and death that surrounded him. It is a testament to what the human spirit can endure.

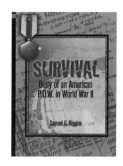

Through My Eyes

91st Infantry Division, Italian Campaign, 1942-1945

by Leon Weckstein   ISBN: 1-55571-497-8
                    208 pages, Paperback: $14.95

Through My Eyes is the true account of an Average Joe's infantry days before, during, and shortly after the furiously fought battle for Italy. The author's front row seat allows him to report the shocking account of casualties and the rest-time shenanigans during the six weeks of the occupation of the city of Trieste. He also recounts his personal roll in saving the historic Leaning Tower of Pisa.

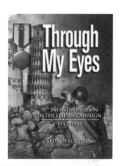